THE
BOND
KING

THE
BOND
KING

HOW ONE MAN MADE
a MARKET, BUILT an EMPIRE,
and LOST IT ALL

MARY CHILDS

FLATIRON
BOOKS
NEW YORK

www.flatironbooks.com

Designed by Steven Seighman

Library of Congress Cataloging-in-Publication Data

Names: Childs, Mary (Business journalist), author.
Title: The bond king : how one man made a market, built an empire, and
    lost it all / Mary Childs.
Description: First edition. | New York, NY : Flatiron Books, [2021] |
    Includes bibliographical references.
Identifiers: LCCN 2021026478 | ISBN 9781250120847 (hardcover) |
    ISBN 9781250120854 (ebook)
Subjects: LCSH: Gross, William H. (William Hunt), 1944– | Capitalists and
    financiers—United States—Biography. | Bonds—United States—History. |
    Investments—United States—History. | Finance—United States—History.
Classification: LCC HG172.G76 C45 2021 | DDC 332.6092 [B]—dc23
LC record available at https://lccn.loc.gov/2021026478

Our books may be purchased in bulk for promotional, educational, or business use. Please contact your local bookseller or the Macmillan Corporate and Premium Sales Department at 1-800-221-7945, extension 5442, or by email at MacmillanSpecialMarkets@macmillan.com.

First Edition: 2022

10 9 8 7 6 5 4 3 2 1

Contents

Introduction   1

1. The Housing Project   9
2. In the Beginning   24
3. The Turn   46
4. The Crisis   54
5. Constructive Paranoia   78
6. New Normal   95
7. Stinker   108
8. Edge   121
9. Grow or Die   143
10. Ratfucked   157
11. Taper Tantrum   172
12. Secretariat   193
13. Inside the Showdown   212
14. Stealing the Firm   229
15. Minutes   251
16. Bye-Bye to Those Days   272

Epilogue   298

AUTHOR'S NOTE   305
ACKNOWLEDGMENTS   311
NOTES   315

Introduction

In November 2013, I made a big, dumb mistake. I'd worked for weeks on this one story about one of the biggest money managers on the planet, Pacific Investment Management Company (aka Pimco), amassing a huge bet in the market I covered. I'd cajoled sources into telling me about the trade in the opaque credit-default swap market, I'd tabulated data, I'd compulsively fact-checked. I had run it by the Pimco communications guy so many times he seemed extremely tired of hearing from me. The night before it ran, I finished my last paranoid fact-check, and my editor queued up the story to be published overnight.

In the morning, I got a weird email from my colleague Cordell, full of exclamation marks yet seeming to apologize for something? Apparently Bill Gross, Pimco's legendary founder and star investor, had been on Bloomberg Radio and said something in my story was wrong. On the international radio. And he named me.

"I will take Mary to task in terms of her reporting," he'd said. "She needs to get her facts straight." He added that he'd speak with me "in a few minutes," after he hung up from the radio.

I thought I was going to vomit. I had botched a very basic and very important thing: the *performance* of Gross's biggest and most important fund. To investors, there is nothing more critical to get right. In the thirty-fourth paragraph, I'd written that the fund was down about 3 percent—I'd cited the fund's *price* return, not *total* return. An absolute rookie move that you will understand in about thirty pages.

On air, Gross had stated the fund's *actual* returns: "We're beating the market by a good seventy-five basis points."

So now I had to fix my big story. Mortified, I sat at my Bloomberg Terminal (the special machine on which all of Wall Street runs), frantically trying to replicate the numbers he'd said on air, that gain of 0.75 percent. Shouldn't be hard. But . . . I couldn't. I kept getting something different, the same answer over and over: that the fund had *lost* 1 percent. I tried different time horizons. I retyped the fund's name. I couldn't figure it out.

As promised, Gross called me after the radio interview. I did not vomit. I remember being surprised by how nice(-ish) he was about my mistake, perhaps because he'd already publicly excoriated me. After a little chatting, I told Bill that I was working on fixing my story—I kept trying to get the performance figures he'd said on air but couldn't. *What am I doing wrong?*

Yeah, well, he said with a little laugh. *You got to say your numbers, I got to say mine.*

That was our first interaction. Eight years ago. In the intervening years, we have chatted over hundreds of hours, about his firm, his career, his trades, his mistakes, his view of millennials, the nature of human connection, the meaning of a legacy. I have learned about his particular prides and insecurities, his relationship to numbers, and his relationship to the truth.

Few people in finance attracted as much sustained attention as Bill Gross, with his folksy Ohio humility and his catchphrases and his billions of dollars of personal wealth and trillions of dollars of other people's money that he invested, for them, through Pimco. He's been finance-famous for decades, beginning in the 1980s, when the sun had just risen on his empire.

Then, we were just a few years into an unprecedented boom in lending and borrowing. Money was pouring into any economically productive behavior, supercharging growth. The wild, free market was running tangly and overgrown, sprouting blue-chip industrial companies, revolutionary technologies, fringe start-ups. This great experiment helped fuel progress, creating affordable tools to improve life for billions of people.

Gross was at the forefront of all this. He was instrumental in creating and shaping the "bond market" that continues to fund corporations around the world; he inspired thousands of people who wanted to invest like him, trade like him, make money into more money like him.

Despite his best efforts, Gross's fame rarely spilled outside the world of finance. Largely because normal people don't like to talk about "bonds." People think they're too complicated, confusing. Instead, we like to talk about *stocks,* which are also claims on a company but are riskier, more whimsical. People think stocks are more fun, but, in my opinion, they are wrong. Stocks are dumb.

Stocks are the pieces of paper they let people like you and me buy—a tiny slice of ownership in a company, and if our company flourishes, you and I are richer by some degree. If it fails, we lose some or all of our money. That's the game we've all agreed to.

Above the heads of people like you and me sits a larger, much more interesting and more influential world: the bond market. Bonds are mostly bought by sophisticated, institutional investors—big kids. They generally don't come in small sizes; a normal trade is in the millions.

Despite their intimidating reputation, bonds and loans are not difficult to understand: everyone needs money, and sometimes that's a lump sum of money to buy a big thing or build a big thing. Issuing a bond is just transforming future payments into money upfront today. If you've ever bought a home or a car or Invisalign with financing, you're a bond issuer. Your lender makes their profit on your interest payments. Companies borrow money, and then they pay an interest rate on what they borrowed, just like you and me.

And, just like a mortgage, bonds and loans come in different structures and flavors. Some borrowings are backed by collateral—tangible stuff that can be sold, should the borrower be incapable of paying the money back, while others are just paper agreements backed by good faith and the court system.

Since the first corporate bond was issued nearly four hundred years ago, many nuances and complexities have developed, accelerating in the past half-century. New structures sprang up, new products. There's a new one blossoming as you read this. It's fun and exciting. It keeps you young.

Some people—like the ones you're about to meet—love this. Thrive on it. Know the different varietals and treasure their peculiarities, like lepidopterists pinning butterflies in their display cases.

King among these was Gross. He wandered into the nascent market by accident, but he was there at the dawn of that acceleration and helped invent new ways to make buying bonds profitable, extremely profitable. In his enthusiasm, he helped to punctuate, if not bring about, the end of this golden age.

In the financial crisis of 2008, when the bill for decades of corporate borrowing came due, instead of the borrowers paying, the government did. Companies, and financial institutions, were "bailed out" of their losses, by the government—to some extent, by people like you and me.

This was most pronounced in home mortgages. And none played this moment more masterfully than Bill Gross and Pimco. Until this point, the U.S. mortgage market had long been halfway socialist (though we'd never call it that). The government had always sort of promised it would step in and "guarantee" mortgages; Gross and Pimco, more than any other players, bullied the government into making that guarantee explicit. The government would make sure the end buyers of mortgage products, the investors, were "made whole" and did not lose money—the people safe on the island of finance. By extension, that included those who'd paid to invest their money into 401(k)s and mutual funds and hedge funds. But not those still paying their mortgages—*they* were now paying into a negative space, where they owed more than the house was worth.

In a society that professes to love those tangly, unfettered free markets, backing the mortgage market might have been an aberration—except that, in the years since, the government backing has grown, metastasized. Implicit and explicit, most parts of financial markets now feel secured by the full faith and credit of the U.S. government. Before, if lenders suddenly didn't want to lend, companies didn't get loans; now, ten years after the financial crisis broke the seal, the Federal Reserve steps in. "Creative destruction"—letting things fail, for the health of the ecosystem—now seems too destructive. What they still call *capitalism* has become a fun sandbox where someone always comes running if you get hurt.

In this book, a window into a crucible of money management in Southern California, you'll see them lay the groundwork for the system we have today.

The system Gross inherited in the 1970s wasn't perfect; it was built by men who only saw part of the world, so when they sought to describe that world in numbers—this profit, this year, this cost, this pace of amortization—they excluded a ton of things that would have made the game less fun or less profitable. Like discrimination, which contorts economic actors and makes pricing whack, or pricing the environment, which is how drinking water costs $0 but so does polluting it. Thanks to the power of compounding, those little flaws added up over time and became huge, while the arbitrary lines they drew around profits help compound money invested in these arbitrary markets. It, too, became huge.

That's the game that Gross stepped into in 1971. Over the next five decades he, and Pimco, helped to push it further; they were very good at playing, and they extracted billions of dollars from it—for their clients, and for themselves. At times, Gross knew they were taking too much. To make up for it, he gave away almost $1 billion, to charities and efforts and people he deemed worthy. But he continued to play the game.

Pimco's partners work still to preserve that game, so that they can continue to enjoy it without interruption or degradation. These systems helped to create tributaries of power and money that flow into our economy and our social landscape. They fund the political careers of people who help protect the tributaries. They lobby for housing policies to keep their neighborhoods from changing. They send their kids to the country's best colleges with legal and, in at least one notorious instance, illegal bribes.

When I started covering Pimco (and other asset managers) full-time as a "beat reporter" in the spring of 2014, I had written about corporate bonds for four years, so I could speak their language. I too worked in a pressure cooker where aggressively cc'd emails were preferred to normal conversation, so I already understood much of their culture.

My job meant that I wrote up their outlook for the U.S. economy, their interviews on television and radio, their white papers and lobbying attempts. I talked to anyone in the building whom the communications team would allow; anyone I messaged independently would immediately forward my note to the communications team, who would then mock or scold me for trying to talk to people out of turn. I would remind them it was my job to try; we would continue on.

That was in the interest of breaking news, of knowing what was going on right then. For this book, I had to go back in time. I talked to founding partners, the first clients and former clients, consultants who worked with the proto-Pimco in the 1970s, people who worked there until last week, people still there. I talked to wives and friends, competitors and enemies, one of Bill Gross's high school classmates, and one ventriloquist.

I listened to everyone who would talk to me. The story in this book is based on those interviews—hundreds of hours with over two hundred people with direct knowledge or experience of Pimco and/or its cast of characters. I mined public filings, court records, lawsuits, exhibits, and testimony; I drew heavily on countless news articles by reporters at Bloomberg News and the *Financial Times* and *Barron's* and *The Wall Street Journal*, Reuters, *The New York Times*, CNBC, the *Orange County Business Journal*, *Dealbreaker*, the *Los Angeles Times*, as well as *Vanity Fair*, *The Atlantic*, *The Bond Buyer*, Law360, Debtwire, and many others.

Because nondisclosure agreements are common in the finance industry, and Pimco is known to be litigious, most of the interviews that helped to shape this book were "on background," which means I can use the information a source gave me but not their names or identifying information. These conversations drew on the imperfect record of human memory, recalling events many years in the past. I carefully vetted and fact-checked all accounts, using contemporaneous documents and versions of events from other people. Some moments are just one person's recollection, and I make it clear whenever that's the case. I regret that I could not speak to every person involved; some were unreachable, because they died or they never returned my calls or, in a couple of cases, proved impossible for me to track down. The frame of this book is necessarily influenced by who would speak to me; I have done as much as I can to compensate for that. Everyone named who is still alive had an opportunity to comment or correct the facts presented here. After declining numerous requests to speak over many years, Mohamed El-Erian evidently obtained an unauthorized copy before publication, and his lawyer sent a very detailed letter with his specific objections to certain passages; I addressed those objections as appropriate. Everyone named who is still alive had an opportunity to comment or correct the factual information presented here.

After years of collecting scraps of information, old newspaper clippings and analyst reports and academic papers and interviews, I gathered them all and arranged them into what you now have in your hands. This is not a comprehensive history of Pimco; some things are missing, and I'm sure to some extent some things are misremembered—we all have our own numbers. This book has been professionally fact-checked and is the closest possible telling of what actually happened in this company's long rise and quick fracture—what they took and what they left us with.

1

The Housing Project

August 2005. Dan Ivascyn climbed into the passenger seat of his mortgage broker's car and buckled his seat belt. It was early on a perfectly pleasant August day, which he would get to spend riding around with this stranger. They pulled away from the Countrywide office—one of four new branches in the Boston area—and set off to explore a suburb, driving past cranes and bulldozers and Tyvek-wrapped house skeletons, signs that said IF YOU LIVED HERE, YOU'D BE HOME NOW.

They'd already talked about the state of the market a bit. It wasn't news to Ivascyn that things were frothy. It was slowing slightly, but that was normal for this time of year, with kids going back to school and the weather deteriorating.

The broker had a couple different neighborhoods he wanted to show that he thought would be interesting to Ivascyn. *This development,* he said as they approached, *we've done a lot of interest-only loans here. This next one is mostly adjustable-rate. If we turn here, down the road a ways, that's where we're doing a lot more "affordability" products.* As they drove further out into the suburbs, they clocked the rising prices: *The Worcester market only rallies when people are priced out of Boston.*

Ivascyn, an analyst on the desk that bought and sold mortgages and products tied to them, was friendly, personable, good at putting people at ease. But this wasn't really a charm offensive. He listened patiently as the broker chattered, dutifully taking notes.

He wasn't mad that he had to do this. He could see the marketing benefit. It was a story they could tell clients: Pimco didn't just trust the data, they actually went out and checked.

And anyway Gross had insisted: "We needed to get a feel for the rest of the country," he'd said. Some economists had begun to warn about a housing bubble, but the sound of money has a way of drowning out other noise. The price-appreciation party had raged on, even as Federal Reserve chair Alan Greenspan cited "a little froth" in the market. Pimco analysts thought they knew how out of hand things were getting, based on their customary intensive research and the black-and-amber figures on their twenty-thousand-dollar-a-year Bloomberg Terminals. But Gross wanted "real" data, information beyond what his mortgage traders had already begun to conclude. And Ivascyn was in no position to say no.

Gross, Pimco's mercurial front man and leader, cofounded the company in 1971 with two others. They'd taken a sleepy backwater unit of a life insurance company and turned it into the largest bond manager in the world. Now the lanky, mustachioed, and deceptively frail-seeming chief investment officer was the only one still charging ahead unabated. In 2002, *Fortune* magazine called Gross "the Bond King," and it had stuck.

Pimco had forty credit analysts covering companies like IBM and General Motors, so why not, Gross reasoned, send ten of those out into the world? "Instead of sending them to Armonk to interview the treasurer of IBM, let's send them to places like Detroit, Miami, or Vegas."

The brilliant idea had come to Gross in the middle of the trading day, while he was at yoga, his long string bean body upside down in the Feathered Peacock pose. *Aha!* The analysts would go out and pretend to be prospective homebuyers—they'd ride around with Realtors and get the real information about what was going on in the market.

So, now, one of Ivascyn's colleagues was in Detroit, one in Miami, one in Vegas. Ivascyn's boss, Scott Simon, the head of the mortgage group, was in Dallas because he liked barbeque. No one was going to buy a house. Or even pretend to. Simon and the rest of the team had objected immediately to the fake-homebuying idea. It made no sense. It just wasn't necessary.

So instead they called their contacts at various mortgage lenders— from whom Pimco bought millions and millions and millions of dollars of mortgages—and asked to be set up with local Realtors and branch officers, so they could go on these somewhat spurious ride alongs. Their lenders were wary, confused why Pimco would want this, what it was up to, but Pimco was an enormous client so, yeah, sure, meet my buddy at RE/MAX.

Later, Bill Gross would start saying they'd done as he asked, and posed as interested homebuyers. He told *The New York Times* that he struggled with the ethics of the subterfuge: "I didn't feel good about that, but I didn't know how else to get the real information," he said.

And sure, fine. It was a good story, and it wouldn't be the first time something got dressed up a little for show. It's not like the mortgage team was going to correct him on it.

Of course, Gross wasn't on the road. He hated traveling. He was at home base, at his desk in Newport Beach. The brilliant landscape of sun and sky and sea stretched out behind him, entirely unappreciated; he never turned around. Silent, eyes twitching and head twisting from one of his many blinking screens to another, like a hawk before a nest of mice, he monitored his Bloomberg Terminal. He scoured bond prices and news feeds and "MSG," the most popular terminal function, known in the external world as "email." This Housing Project caper was for grunts like Ivascyn and Ivascyn's boss, Scott Simon, people who at any other firm would have been treated with a modicum of respect. It was almost surprising that Simon had complied with the Project without a fight. He was among the few at Pimco with an external reputation, an indisputable ability to deliver returns, and a rascally streak, which, with his trading performance, magically insulated him from the insults and pettiness and pedantry, made him exempt from the standard humiliations at Pimco.

Simon found the Housing Project logistically annoying; it cost time to deploy the whole mortgage team across the country, to confirm what it was their *job* to know already—and the thing they were *not* rich in was time. But it's not like there had been a vote. Sometimes it was worth it just to do it and get the free barbeque.

The broker drove Ivascyn through several neighborhoods over the course of the day. They drove past this house for $225,000, that one for $360,000, another going for 80 percent over its last sale, a new build that went for 30 percent over the asking price, which was shocking for that property. The loan structures weren't too creative—a lot of those adjustable-rate ones, with super-low payments now that balloon in a few years. But those were increasingly ubiquitous. To be honest, the broker didn't think Boston was unique in that sense.

They returned to the Countrywide office. Ivascyn thanked the broker and shook his hand; they agreed to keep in touch. Ivascyn would call him at the end of every month just for a fifteen-minute chat to see how things were going. This guy seemed pretty informed on the state of the mortgage market, so it might be useful to keep a line open.

Ivascyn turned to walk back to his car. He looked on the bright side: He might get to visit his family in Boston, so that was nice. And he was building relationships with brokers and mortgage bankers, and getting access to their data. Other firms weren't getting that data. That was good. And, fine, he had seen with his eyes what his team had already begun to think: that the housing market had gone haywire and was now way, way, *way* too hot.

"The extent of the lending malpractice—to use a nice word—was shocking," Gross told *Businessweek*, in 2011.

Once all the analysts returned to Newport Beach with their on-the-ground research, they compiled their findings in a paper. Never shy about publicizing its thoughts, Pimco published "The Housing Project" in May 2006, walking through what everyone now knows about the early 2000s housing boom: low interest rates reduced monthly payments, which allowed home buyers to buy bigger, fancier, more expensive homes, at the same monthly installment. Prices rose and rose. To feed the market, lenders created interest-only and other delayed- or hidden-payment loans, which only bought borrowers time as they stacked up more and more debt. Eventually, they would owe too much; the only way out was to find another buyer for an even higher price. Someday that trick would stop working, and borrowers would stop paying. The market was "slowing under its own weight," Pimco's report said. The number of homes actually selling was falling; the number of homes for sale was increasing.

Pimco's head of corporate credit took it further: in June 2006, he predicted that housing would determine the direction of the economy and prospects for corporate borrowers, too. If housing cooled, he said, consumers would pull back on spending, which would cool the overall economy, which would make lending standards tighten. Asset prices would slow their climb, defaults would increase, trading would dry up, and price swings in financial markets would become more dramatic. "At that point, 'For Sale' will not just be a sign you see in front of your neighbor's yard—investors may also put a 'For Sale' sign on risk assets as well."

The corporate credit head's note added to the huge and growing pile of research on Gross's desk on the trade floor. It put him in the Pimco chorus, from Gross on down to Simon's mortgage team and Dan Ivascyn, calling the end of the housing boom and the start of something much worse. They mapped out what their conclusions meant for the rest of their business: if home prices were stagnating, Pimco should avoid buying too many things tied to them, like asset-backed and mortgage-backed securities, or the risky derivatives contracts that had flooded the financial industry, churned out by overheating machines on Wall Street.

On the one hand, a bet like this would be right up Pimco's alley. Pimco had been preaching that the world was in a state of "stable disequilibrium," good times about to turn bad. Its pessimism was natural, inherent: it was a bond investor. Bond investors are notorious downers. A bond is just a debt, a promise to repay money with interest. In the best case, bond buyers get their money back at the end, plus the promised interest payments along the way. Now, thanks to Gross and his fellow pioneers of bond trading, they might also get some extra profit from betting on the *right* bond. But even those prices moved in "basis points," fractions of percentage points that bond investors scraped together. Worst case, the borrowing company went bankrupt, but even then, bond investors could pick through the leftover assets in bankruptcy and recoup something. Being a bond investor was about seeking safety, calculable certainty. Optimism was for stock investors, people who had zero claim on the assets, who bought a story about growth, potential, and the future and hoped to ride it to the moon. Their upside was hypothetically infinite, but their investment could go to zero. They bet on faith in corporate management, instead of the black-and-white promises of bond documents, the covenants that limited the borrower's ability to make dumb choices.

Back when Gross started and bonds were pieces of paper living in vaults under insurance companies, you generally took your licks when a company went bust. But all those decades ago, when Gross convinced his boss to let him start a little pilot portfolio and—innovation!—*trade* the bonds, suddenly forecasting disaster became profitable.

And now, the entire housing market was looking like a disaster-in-waiting.

On the other hand, this would be kind of a major strategy reversal for Pimco after a decades-long love of buying mortgage-backed securities. Other investors had historically overestimated the extent to which home buyers would refinance or pay off their home loans the minute interest rates moved lower. Pimco was happy to pick up the extra money for what others perceived as risky, so it cheerfully snapped up mortgage-backed products. Over the decades, its enthusiasm and outperformance lured other investors to give mortgages a try, too. The market grew and grew, fueled by demand. Betting against the machine would be almost a change in identity.

Still, Gross's other lookouts told him trouble was brewing. Paul McCulley didn't present like the average suit that excelled at Pimco, with his thick drawl airlifted from the mountains of Virginia and his pet Netherland Dwarf rabbit Ms. Morgan le Fay, whom he rescued from a post-magician retirement. McCulley ran the cash desk, but really, he was an economist, a big thinker. Now, in 2006, he was mapping out what he called "the shadow banking system," a dense, invisible forest of transactions that bound together institutions from Goldman Sachs to insurance companies to Pimco. They'd all entered into contracts with one another, buying and selling bonds and swaps and derivatives. All those connections had them fully intertwined, the density masking who actually had what and who owed what. While nearly everyone else was blind to it, McCulley could see the rotten roots of debt and leverage winding underneath the entire global financial system. He was a disciple of Hyman Minsky, an economist who had preached in the 1960s through the '80s that too much calm, too much stability, sows the seeds of instability. When the economy is booming, people forget the bad times and reach a little too far, borrow a little too much. McCulley nudged Gross as early as 2002 to read these then-deep-cut papers. The economy was approaching a "Minsky moment," McCulley said, a tipping point into market chaos.

At Pimco's Investment Committee meetings—which could turn into a brawl at any moment, with Gross sometimes impassively overseeing the ruckus, other times actively leading the gang—McCulley bellowed about "the shadow banking system" in his drawling, backwoods accent. He'd bang his fist on the conference table, *It's all connected. The whole thing is going to blow.*

Pimco wasn't alone in seeing the crisis ahead; there were smart people in messy corners of the mortgage market biting their fingernails and staring at their Excel spreadsheets and their Bloomberg Terminals. Some people knew.

But it's not enough to know. Knowing is hardly the battle. The tricky part was that they all still had to make money in the meantime. Money managers aren't paid to hold on to cash and wait. If they sit in cash, refusing to take risks to generate returns, then their clients tend to take their money back and avoid paying the fees. If Gross and his team were going to act on their hunch that disaster was coming, they had to figure out how to navigate the period between knowing a thing would happen and its coming to pass.

Gross decided to trust the chorus of Ivascyn, Simon, McCulley: Pimco would bet against the market in a big way.

"Bill was to a large extent a trend follower, but he had a unique ability to know when it was time to lean against that trend and take a contrary position," former Pimco partner Ben Trosky remembers fondly. "There were numerous occasions where everyone [else] was scared shitless, and Bill put on his seat belt."

Gross was known for big contrarian calls, and he was right more often than not. In the early 1990s, in the aftermath of the savings and loan crisis, when the banks were limping along, the Federal Reserve tilted interest rates to their benefit, keeping short-term rates low while allowing long-term rates to rise. So, Gross decided to sell long Treasuries; he was right, and the trade worked.

Now, while their peers continued gorging on risk and derivatives and off–balance sheet vehicles, Pimco traders ratcheted down how many risky bonds they bought. And Gross geared up to make his pitch to the world.

He put the flag in the ground on July 7, 2006: rates had peaked, he announced on Bloomberg TV and in Reuters. Sometimes in finance, he knew, you need to grind your view into everyone else's consciousness, get people on board, *force* the market to turn. That was a Pimco specialty—in part why the firm put out paper after paper, interviews, TV appearances, McCulley's "Global Central Bank Focus." And always, Gross's—Pimco's—*Investment Outlook*. He had sent out this now-legendary newsletter to clients and whoever else wanted to read it since 1978. He'd inherited the job of updating clients on the market views of Pimco's then-parent company and started in the staid form of his predecessor. But he quickly figured out that if he wanted readership beyond a bunch of bond nerds, he'd have to give them something different, something interesting. So, the notes became 1,400 words of quirky personal anecdotes and confessions peppered with folksy colloquialisms, references to the babbling creek behind his childhood home in Ohio, his five-year-old son's humiliation at bat, his own failed attempts at college basketball as a metaphor for the market. One opened with a poem he'd written, in the style of Robert Frost, about investing; another his terror of the torture of Christmas parties; another, with his daydream of chatting with a Flavor Flav–costumed genie. He repurposed some of his favorites and tucked them into his 1997 book, *Everything You've Heard About Investing Is Wrong! How to Profit in the Coming Post-Bull Markets.*

The quaint, reflective persona of the notes' author was endearing, if eccentric, and Gross matched it in his frequent appearances on financial news television shows. He came across as surprisingly meek, his high-pitched, wispy little voice inspiring mockery on trade floors across the country.

Anyone who knew Gross in the flesh knew the façade didn't match up. In real life, Gross was exacting, uncompromising, unwilling to back down. And he had built Pimco in his image. Normal trade floors, at banks or other money managers, were jumbles of loud televisions and yelling and slamming phones and crude jokes and debates—but not at Pimco. Everyone emailed. The thick carpets muted the sound of any foot traffic; the clicking of keyboards was the only exception to the library silence. If a trader had to speak, to call a bank and get an order of bonds, he did so quietly, breathing words into the telephone. Occasionally, someone would put on a little show, emphasizing to the Wall Streeter at the other end of the line that he would give them an extra sixteenth, *because we're fucking Pimco.* But that was an emergency option, used only in dire situations. Emailing was always better, even if the email recipient was sitting three feet away. *Especially* if the recipient was sitting three feet away.

Gross sat at his desk, his tie draped open around his neck and his suit jacket on a nearby coat rack, from 6 A.M. until yoga, which was generally over by 10:30, and then again until late afternoon. His technician beat him to the office every morning to log him into his PC, his Unix operating system, his Reuters and Bloomberg Terminals, and run a printer test, so his Bloomberg Terminal screens were glowing in welcome upon his arrival. Most everyone else had to log into their Bloombergs using their fingerprint; Gross's terminal had no biometric login. And should he or his tech forget, he kept his password on a printed note Scotch-taped to the keyboard.

Gross broke for Investment Committee meetings four times a week, from noon to 2 P.M. or so, and whatever other pressing meetings were forced upon him. Preferably there were zero. Gross wanted to be in that chair.

He disliked small talk and would avoid eye contact or greetings in the hallways. But there was always a risk of more high-pressure interactions. For a Pimco trader, a day could easily be derailed by accidentally looking up from the screens and—disaster!—making fleeting eye contact with Bill Gross. Seconds later, an email might appear:

WHAT ARE THE TOP FIVE HOLDINGS IN YOUR PORTFOLIO— AND WHY?

GIVE ME THREE ACTIONABLE TRADE IDEAS.

Day, shot.

That panic flowed down the line, from the portfolio managers to the analysts below them to the traders who executed the firm's ideas in the market. The fear permeated the days of the client-facing portfolio specialists, the product managers tasked with inventing new things for clients to buy, the compliance people scrambling to keep things within the legal lines. No matter how well you were doing, it wasn't good enough. Do more, better. Your ass was *always* on the line.

He tested them constantly. He used to pace the trade floor, quizzing underlings on the price of an obscure security only vaguely relevant to their job, down to the decimal; or asking a half dozen senior portfolio managers to calculate, by hand, something they could easily type into their Bloomberg Terminals to find out. No, he wanted the longhand "bond math," which is just math, but worse. Or he'd leave little notes on your desk scrawled on trade tickets used to buy or sell bonds, sometimes complimenting you on a trade idea or more often asking you to justify why you held this much of that bond. It didn't matter how small the position was; or if you'd inherited it from the last guy, who'd imploded or quit, and you didn't know why he bought it two years ago. What mattered was "owning" the risk. It was yours now. Defend it. What did you think and what were your justifications, with fresh data points and prices?

The tension was reinforced by location: they were trapped. They were at the opposite end of the United States from Wall Street, from New York City, where employment in the finance industry was fungible, where competitors would happily snap you up should you realize you made a horrible mistake in job choice. Here, there was nowhere to go. The nearest major competitor was in Los Angeles, two hours away with traffic, and there was always traffic.

So, the money managers, analysts, traders, compliance people—they were all stuck there, in a gorgeous desert that ended in cliffs, their luxury homes perched precariously on top, dangling over the furious ocean. The location had really been an accident: Pimco's then-parent company, Pacific Mutual Life Insurance Company, had moved there in 1972 because it was cheaper than downtown LA.

Now, decades later, Pimco lived in a squat building with a gleaming white exoskeleton on Newport Center Drive, a four-lane lasso around a mall called Fashion Island. And now the sunny location was part of the company's pitch to potential employees: the landscape was stunning, obviously, meant for postcards; the weather was always sunny; but also, out here, they could avoid finance's self-reinforcing thought bubble; out West, they were free from the "same old discussions with the same old business colleagues at the same old lunches every day," as Gross once put it, from "all that hubbub and hectic atmosphere." Intentionally isolated, he said, "a quiet oasis of serenity."

Serene for him, maybe, but his personality mangled whatever peace the rest of them could have enjoyed. The place was suffused with Gross's clinical insecurity that someone might catch up, that someone might threaten Pimco's dominance.

No moment wasted, no dollar left unsqueezed. This was the dominant culture, trickled down from the trade floor: Gross's "Pimbots" ground their teeth in their sleep and woke up screaming; their marriages and livers disintegrated. It was precisely that they *were* so intensely obsessive, going beyond what everyone else did, that made them so great, they had to convince themselves. Their competitors weren't living and breathing this stuff like they were, no matter what they said in their marketing materials. In Newport Beach, there truly was nothing else—just money and making it into more money. Spotting a flaw, exploiting it. That was what Gross and, by extension, his firm did best.

Failure to deliver wasn't tolerated. Pimco would sniff out anyone's weakness.

The market refused to respond to Gross's July 7, 2006, announcement. Maybe he'd been hasty in declaring it. He'd spoken "brashly, and perhaps recklessly," he wrote a couple weeks later in an *Investment Outlook* titled THE END OF HISTORY AND THE LAST BOND BULL MARKET. "Sometimes I just can't help myself when it comes to the press." Since then: "too much tension, too many sleepless nights. Market turning points have a habit of doing that, and this time has been no exception."

These lines had a practical implication for every Pimco employee who wasn't Gross. Pimco's flagship Total Return Fund was underperforming, and this meant steering clear of Bill Gross. More, even, than usual. Total Return was Gross's fund, his baby, the one he'd overseen personally since its inception in 1987. Total Return was his life's work: Gross had helped to pioneer active bond trading in the 1970s, when bonds lived in vaults and rarely changed hands. He and his peers revolutionized that, trading ownership of company debt among themselves, buying the debt of companies that looked promising, selling the opposite. Total Return was the result: the culmination of Gross's carefully built rejection of the traditional, low-risk approach to bond management; his hard-won innovations and inventions mucking through the market; his creepily prescient market calls; his instinct and skill; his years of intense work hunting, scouring the markets for underpriced bonds or smart derivative plays—all of it. The fund's endurance for decades had built, was building, Gross's legendary status. That track record was why they called him "the Bond King." It was his measuring stick for self-esteem, and had been for twenty years. It was the biggest fund at Pimco; at times, the money in Total Return accounted for more than half of what the firm managed. And when its performance fell behind that of its peers, Gross became a monster.

He had to avoid people entirely; they could only remind him of the acute and immediate pain of failure, the humiliation of underperforming. The legend went that his wife, Sue, kept a spare bedroom in their sprawling Laguna Beach compound for her to sleep in when Total Return wasn't doing well (this rumor wasn't true).

"Anonymity, not notoriety, is the watchword," Gross said of stretches like these, in a 2001 note typical of his unorthodox, oversharing approach to market commentary. "You mope, hang your head, chew out your wife for no reason at all, wake up at 3:00 A.M., then take the stairs instead of the elevator up to work. It must be the equivalent of PMS[,] except in this case it's the 'Performance (is) Missing Syndrome.' Don't talk to me, don't try to be nice to me, Just Leave Me Alone!"

For traders at Pimco, where a normal day was a minefield, the field was now all mines. Stay silent and avoid Gross's eyes. Minimize interaction and pray that performance improves. *Lord, let the market turn. Lead us to safe havens. Grant us mortgage delinquencies.*

It hardly mattered that, this time, the poor performance was incurred almost on purpose. Pimco was playing it safe, waiting for the market to sour, not "reaching for yield" like everyone else. This should have provided some comfort. The market *had* to turn, sooner or later, and when it did, they would be vindicated. Everyone at Pimco knew that, rationally.

There's a saying in finance, often attributed to John Maynard Keynes, an economist whose portrait watched over Paul McCulley as he sat at his desk: "The market can stay irrational longer than you can remain solvent." Turning out to be right doesn't do much good if you run out of money first.

Solvency wasn't Pimco's problem. With over $600 billion in management-fee-generating assets, from slow-moving pension funds and mom-and-pop investors, it had no real worry about running out of money. It had a lifeline, should it really need it, in its sort-of distant parent company, the German insurer Allianz, which had bought a controlling stake in Pimco in 2000. And, so far, the underperformance wasn't so bad. Everyone underperforms sometimes. But the longer Pimco underperformed, the itchier its clients got, and the more confidence waned. And the itchier the clients got, the less sticky their money was. Once clients start to pull their money, things can snowball.

Nothing like that had ever happened at Pimco, but the huge vulnerability it was now betting on—the entire U.S. economy, maybe the globe—was refusing to be exploited. Pimco could not bend it to its will or bully it; it had to *wait*.

The market optimism persisted. Everyone was maintaining that any problems—sluggish sales, delinquencies here and there—were contained. The Fed was anxious; it had been using its primary tool of fiddling with interest rates, hiking them higher, again and again, to dampen the exuberance in housing—operating, as McCulley said, "on the thesis that an unresponsive mule is not really unresponsive, just in need of additional whacks on the head with a two-by-four."

Pimco bought bonds that would benefit when the Fed finally cut rates, as it knew would happen when the housing bubble burst. It stockpiled cash and pared asset-backed securities down to mostly the safest stuff. It avoided the flood of new bonds issued by the riskiest companies; it passed up the (relatively) juicy coupons such bonds offered, abstaining from risk because it was sure the economy was about to blow up. But companies that should have been experiencing financing difficulties were met with enthusiasm in the market. Instead of going bust, they could easily refinance. So few companies were going bankrupt, the corporate default rate hit a twenty-five-year low. Pimco watched as the juicy, risky bonds, the ones it had not bought, rallied and rallied. The Dow Jones Industrial Average kept hitting new highs. Pain.

The year 2006 would turn out to be the first in more than a decade that Total Return lost to its peers. "Reality is a delicate fabric," Gross wrote, opening his December 2006 *Investment Outlook*. "Even in the face of hard facts, people resort to self-deception in order to protect treasured illusions."

"Timing is everything," he said later. "There was a lot of internal questioning and debate. Maybe we should jump in the pool with everyone else. Every investor has an alarm clock. I wish I could get up at 6 every morning and time things just right. I probably get up at 4:30. There's a cost to that hour and a half, where you sit around the table and acknowledge your competitors are having your lunch. But it's better than getting up too late."

In finance, the cliché goes that being early is the same as being wrong. There's another truism: trying to time the market is a fool's errand. Gross's track record in that impossible arena was better than most. So, a little bit too early, Pimco was ready, traders in position. They could survive these lean days, watching reckless risk-taking reap fat profits as they hoarded all the basis points they could scrape out of the market. They knew they'd be proven right. The chaos couldn't come soon enough.

2

In the Beginning

In January 2007, no one thought the U.S. economy was on the precipice. Steve Jobs introduced the iPhone at just $599. President George W. Bush addressed the Union, predicting a balanced federal budget by 2012. "Subprime" borrowers were failing to make payments on their mortgages, but investors continued to fight one another for the privilege of buying riskier and riskier bonds, asking less and less in compensation. The stock market chugged ever higher.

Bill Gross felt like he was watching the euphoric rise of some dumb new religion. Everyone in the market seemed to think that adding debt would always produce positive returns, no matter what. He knew it was bullshit, but Pimco was still missing out on the rampant returns that stupidity was generating for everyone else. Gross was transfixed, watching Pimco slide farther down the rankings against its peers.

Outwardly, he projected certitude. He used his intensely confessional monthly *Investment Outlook* as a vehicle. People loved his *IO*s. Everyone in the investment world knew his writing voice by now and gobbled up the new notes within minutes of their being posted on the website. National newspapers sometimes wrote them up. It was confirmation that Gross's openness in these notes, his eccentricity, was working: He was interesting, extraordinary. He was a legend, a genius.

"There's an ill wind blowin'," he warned in his January 2007 *IO*. Quietly, though, he wondered if the markets had moved past him. If he had failed to see some greater seismic shift. And if so, if that meant he'd seen his best days. Had he been premature in declaring himself a legend? Had he lost his touch?

The moment felt like the end of something. His third and last child, Nick, had left for college that September 2006, and the family's Laguna mansion went from vibrating with teen angst to a deafening emptiness, just two thin, late-middle-aged bodies left in a vast, silent, negative space. Parents, but done parenting.

A few months later, Gross shaved his signature mustache. To look younger, he said. It was going gray, and Sue said the dye was poisonous. Maybe it was a little bit of superstition, too: a new look, to break the streak. Maybe now the markets would sober up.

Gross had stewed for decades on what made a man great, and by now, he felt he had a handle on his need to be extraordinary, his compulsions, his fear. He thought his undergrad degree in psychology, from Duke University, had helped him see the human expectations that made up financial markets, but it also was reflective of his introspective nature, unusual for a finance guy. Years ago, he'd figured out why he was so afraid of stopping during his then-noontime runs: if he didn't shake the urge to stop, he might stop, and stop again, and again, until he lost the ability to run and, then, somehow, lost himself. He had to keep going.

"My life's plan has always been to outlive and outlast 'em," he'd written in an *Investment Outlook* in 1993. "To persist. To persevere. To land on my feet, keep on running, and never stop." Even then, at forty-eight, he'd felt himself slowing, mind and body. But he knew that this was normal. "Excellence for most of us blossoms and flourishes for only a brief flicker of time. Either because of human frailty, maturation, or simple outright exhaustion, it's difficult to perform at a crescendo for an extended period. Very few stay at the top for very long." The intervening fourteen years hadn't mitigated that anxiety.

Bill Gross, and Pimco, started small. After struggling to find a job out of business school, Gross landed at the staid old insurance company

Pacific Mutual as a securities analyst and loan officer in its fixed income department. The business of life insurance necessitates knowing generally how many customers will die each year, how much an insurer will need to pay out, and when-ish. Usually it's not for a while. So Pacific Mutual could take its customers' life insurance premia and invest the money in bonds that throw off interest payments until they mature (and return the money) approximately when the insurer expects to need it back. It could pretty safely buy a thirty-year bond, and earn the interest, with money from customers who most likely wouldn't die for another thirty years.

Gross was hired to the fixed income department because, by happenstance, he had written his thesis on convertible bonds, so named because they can convert into stocks when the company's shares hit a certain price. His interviewer thought this was impressive and just what they needed.

It was not stimulating work. Gross found himself with uninteresting jobs like clipping bond coupons in Pacific Mutual's vault, snipping the little tags off the bottom of corporate certificates and mailing them in for interest payments. That was all a person would do with bonds at the time. For the first few years, Gross couldn't wait to get transferred into the stocks division. But then, at the start of the 1970s, he convinced his boss to let him try a radical concept: *trading* bonds.

It started when a broker in town, Howard Raykoff, pitched Gross's boss over lunch: there was money to be made trading bonds. Raykoff had stumbled into it, and it got stuck in his head like a song. When he started out, buying new bonds when a company issued one to manage liabilities at a bank, he'd been studying the four-inch-thick book of bond yield tables, which listed every bond, every price, every yield, every coupon. He took it home at night to study more, and eventually the numbers started to make sense, to organize themselves.

"I memorized the price changes of the bond, whatever that bond may be or was, so for every basis point change, or five- to ten-basis-point change, how that would affect the dollar price of the bonds," Raykoff says. He started to get a feel for the numbers, their relationship to one another, that they behaved in a certain way, almost predictably. "Each bond has a different characteristic based on its coupon, its maturity, and its indenture agreements," he says. Watching the yields breathe up and down as their environment changed, the market became, to him, a living, breathing animal. "The tables *read* to you. There's a story, and the story is volatility."

Interest rates were climbing, and rates and price move inversely, like a balance, so whenever a company sold a new bond to investors, the price would immediately fall. Very annoying for anyone buying new bonds.

Raykoff wanted to sell the bad bonds and buy better ones, but his employer, a bank, was firmly against this. It wanted him to buy up different bond maturities so it would have a reliable schedule of when that money would come back, when the bonds matured. Raykoff saw this as a waste of a perfectly good opportunity, so he did what he wanted to anyway: He recorded each trade and its outcome in a detailed spreadsheet. Then he slipped that spreadsheet into a brown binder with a thin, hard cover and carried the binder to show to people who might be convinced—a blueprint for the why and the how of trading bonds.

He soon got a new job at a brokerage, where he needed to drum up business. Business meant he needed trades to broker, other people to trade *with*, so Raykoff needed to become an evangelist for his new religion of bond trading.

"I went around to all these companies, saying, 'Here's what you can do to improve your portfolio! And if bonds are at 8 percent, you can improve your portfolio overall by 1 percent, you're doubling your money in eight years as opposed to nine—the power of compounding!'"

Raykoff got little traction. Most people were like his employer and just wanted to "ladder" their portfolios, keeping a bunch of different maturity bonds that would pay back their principal at a predictable time. What Raykoff was proposing might yield losses, which was unthinkable.

"Nobody listened. It was a real hard sell."

Undaunted, Raykoff saw bond trading everywhere. He'd be driving home from work on the Los Angeles Freeway, traffic stagnant in one lane but "moving slightly more in another lane, so, I'd get in the other lane and get ahead of where I was," he remembers. "And I'd say, *That's what bond trading is! I'm trading one bond for another to get another return. And if I keep doing that, I'm going to continually not be stopped. That's what I thought. It's like bond trading.*"

So far, there was a guy at Valley National Bank of Arizona who traded a little, and another guy at Scudder, Stevens and Clark. Still, at their lunch, Gross's boss told Raykoff no thanks, they couldn't do it—but it was interesting, so why didn't he come down and tell his portfolio analysts about it?

"That sounds great to me," Raykoff said. "I'll talk to anybody about the mathematical volatility of bonds!"

So, he brought his brown binder to Pacific Mutual's offices, on Sixth Street between Grand and Olive, passing under a giant clock and a sign beneath it that read TIME TO INSURE. He gave his presentation to two young portfolio analysts, Les Waite and Bill Gross. They shook hands at the end. Nothing committed, nothing lost but time. Raykoff left not really expecting any follow-up.

Gross saw opportunity. So, he asked his superiors: Why don't we try it? We could take some of these bonds sitting down in the vault and sell them. Inflation was eating away at them anyway; what was there to lose? If they tried it, with just a small account with PacMutual's money, they could start a track record, and if they did well enough, they could show external clients how much money there was to be made.

He was persuasive. His boss was older than Gross, but "young enough to recognize a good idea," Gross says. "He said, 'Oh, let's try it.'"

PacMutual gave him $5 million to play with. This was throwaway cash for the firm, yet the experiment was radical. It was "very avant-garde," Raykoff said, "for an insurance company to set up a pilot portfolio to trade bonds." They were going to put ten bonds, of $500,000 each, he remembers, trade them, and see how it went. Waite and Gross alternated managing the little portfolio. Gross took a liking to it, and eventually, Waite fell away.

Raykoff and Gross sparked a little friendship, bonding over their shared love of bond trading. They were both pretty new in their jobs, with newish wives and new babies, newish similarly priced houses. Raykoff called Gross "Billie"—sometimes "Billie at the Beach," because, by then, Pacific Mutual had moved to Newport Beach—and Gross called Raykoff "Howie."

Even Raykoff was impressed by Gross's dedication to bond trading. He remembers getting a call while Gross was vacationing in Hawaii with his then-wife, Pam; he wanted to trade some bonds. "That's how interested he was." Raykoff respected that.

The little team included another young sprout, hired a few months after Gross, who'd worked at a stock brokerage firm. Jim Muzzy had a friendly face, his perennial smile framed by pointy ears that gave him an elfin air. He'd applied because he lived in Newport Beach and had heard the company was moving down there, so he wouldn't have to drive two hours round trip every day. His job was the same as Gross's, researching companies, helping underwrite debt, and, when it was time, going down into the vaults and signing the coupons and taking those coupons to the borrower to get the interest payment.

PacMutual was a small-time regional player with a credit portfolio of well under $1 billion. But it happened that the company had gotten back a recommendation from management consultant McKinsey on how it should grow: by investing. Gross's superiors had created a corporate shell in answer to that recommendation, Pacific Equity Management Company. That quickly became Pacific *Investment* Management Company.

PacMutual would eventually assign them a grown-up to babysit the "skunkworks," as they jokingly called the backwater investing operation (if they knew about it at all): Bill Podlich had joined the company in 1966 as a credit analyst. He watched over the senior staff on all the planning and strategy for the investment operations at PacMutual, and was seen as a rising star.

So they took the $5 million and the empty corporate shell and ran with it, a stealth project inside a sleepy insurer. The three fell into different roles naturally: Muzzy didn't love investing, managing portfolios. But he was warm and good with people, and he had some ideas to jazz up marketing (i.e., actually explain to the clients what they did with the money). Gross hated traveling, talking to people—he could do it, and clients found him charming, but it took him away from his desk and the more pressing business of trading. Podlich was so obviously brilliant at business strategy that adding any other function would have been a glaring misallocation of his time.

Thus, they easily became a "three-legged stool"—Gross in bond trading, Muzzy in client services, and Podlich in business strategy. They had balance.

As the skunkworks proved they could make money trading bonds, they looked for ways to get clients, to manage money for companies beyond PacMutual. Corporations wanted to invest money for their future pensioners, and many wanted outside managers to do that investing for them. With its expertise in bonds and the track record from that $5 million portfolio, Pimco pitched itself to do just that. So from the early 1970s to the mid-1980s, Pimco found growth in scale as, one by one, it added big companies to its client roster, beginning with Southern California Edison, then Albertsons, the grocery chain. Pimco was buoyed by the 1974 Employee Retirement Income Security Act (ERISA), which set standards for corporate retirement accounts and formalized money management as an industry. Then in 1977, Pimco got its big break: AT&T.

The next year, the pension manager for R.J. Reynolds Tobacco Company visited Newport Beach, interested to hear from these young bucks, but also apprehensive: "We were talking about giving this vast sum of ten million dollars—which was a lot of money to us, and I think a lot of money to Pimco—and here we've got these guys who look like children," he recalls. Their sincerity was striking.

"They weren't slick. They had worked hard and looked like an up-and-coming shop." And Pimco's fees were among the lowest of those of all the managers they were considering. So, RJR signed on. "I think Pimco was really appreciative of getting a ten-million-dollar account and being able to put R.J. Reynolds Tobacco in as a client on their masthead."

At the outset, the "Pimco" operation was not glamorous. No one wanted to be a portfolio manager in the 1970s, in stocks or bonds, Gross recalls: "All the money was on the sales side." Portfolio managers made fifteen thousand dollars a year; salesmen made one hundred thousand and up. And for years, the skunkworks didn't make any money; it was perennially at risk of being shut down, whenever the PacMutual executives got tired of unnecessary risk taking.

But the runaway inflation of the 1970s helped keep the operation viable. It created the kindling for the beginning of active bond trading. By just sitting in vaults, bonds lost value. That made Gross's boss amenable to the idea when he heard of a couple guys trading bonds, making money buying the better bonds and selling the worse ones. If inflation hadn't been burning value off those precious pieces of paper, Pacific Mutual might not have given him that little pile of money.

From the 1970s, with a few hiccups, taking risk made money. When the dollar was untethered from the fixed exchange rate for gold in 1971, and the boom in credit creation began, taking risk smartly, adding "leverage," and avoiding a few dips turned money into more money.

The first year for the little three-legged stool didn't demonstrate greatness; they lost money. But late that year, they decided to go all-in on bonds, investing more aggressively, in anticipation of a major rally. They were right, and they timed it perfectly. In 1975 and 1976, Gross's portfolio banked stellar returns as notches in an increasingly impressive track record, right as ERISA sent pension managers and consultants calling.

They navigated the 1970s nimbly, and then Gross correctly called the end of the mini-recession of 1981, and the regular recession of 1983, which kicked off a multi-decade bond rally. That's what earned Gross acclaim in the 1980s on *Wall Street Week* with Lou Rukeyser, the Friday-night PBS show that minted the industry's celebrities.

In 1980, Bill Gross hired Chris Dialynas, a recent graduate from the University of Chicago's business school. The dark-haired, dark-countenanced weirdo quickly became Gross's understudy, devotee, friend, and a princeling on the trade floor. Gross thought Dialynas was brilliant, even if Gross laughed at his rants and his ability to ferret out conspiracy at every turn. Dialynas and Gross shared many similarities: hyper-attention to detail, interest in complexity and novelty. Dialynas surpassed Gross in his ability to see all possible future disasters, perhaps beyond the point of utility. The three-foot-high stack of research reports, notes, and bond documents on his desk was so heavy, so entrenched, that when it came time to move offices, the bottom pages had become embedded in the desk's varnish.

Together, they made an odd little band. Podlich's composure and formal, tall-white-man bearing gave things an official sheen. Muzzy's geniality helped to bind the little troupe, his pinch of mischievousness reminding employees that they were living humans capable of joy. He was the firm's culture keeper, starting a tradition of rewarding people for a job well done with "Muzzy bucks," little dollar bills with his face on them, and inviting the floor to smoke a cigar when they signed up a new client. He'd walk around saying "We got a new one!" and people would come up to the fifth floor, the smoke wafting around the building having brought them the good news.

Gross hated smoke and hated smoking, so that tradition didn't last. But then came cash.

Pat Fisher, who joined in 1976 and ran the entire back office, pointed out that every time the skunkworks got a new account, it was more work for her employees, who had to record and process every new trade without error. They needed some incentive, something to make them excited, too. She suggested a new tradition.

There was a little bell on the secretary's desk in the reception-ish area, near the stairwell that connected the company's two floors. One day, they rang that little bell to gather the staff around the stairwell. They announced the name of the new account, what kind of portfolio it had, and for how much money. And Fisher reached into her pocket and pulled out a huge stack of one-hundred-dollar bills. She fanned them in front of her face. Everybody's eyes got as big as saucers.

She doled the bills out, one by one, to all back-office employees, a bonus equal to one dollar per million of the new account.

Eventually, this got to be too time-consuming, so they opted to hand out envelopes stuffed with cash.

"That little extra really meant a lot to me," Gross's trade assistant remembered; those bonuses furnished her house. She'd hold each bonus in her hand and tell it something like "You are a lamp."

Technically the head of operations, Fisher made the place run. She was in charge of HR and payroll and technology, and for a time, she also invested short-term cash, little spare bits of money that didn't have a permanent home yet, getting yields of 20 percent overnight. She also orchestrated the company's move to a new office, adding pneumatic tubes from the trade floor to the back office for processing, so her employees wouldn't have to venture into the hot zone of the trade floor and risk getting scorched. Her primary job was to make sure there were no mistakes, no trade errors, no numbers transposed or trade tickets lost. She bent the inefficient banking system into the shape that worked best for Pimco, badgering all the custodian banks into getting fax machines in the 1980s to improve accuracy, and further improving it by pitting them against one another for Pimco's business.

Which was increasingly important as trading volumes surged. With the ballooning of pension funds and mutual funds, products that exploded in the 1980s, money was starting to stream in. In 1975, five hundred mutual funds (i.e., pooled money from smaller investors that added up to big investors) oversaw less than $50 billion, with fat, double-digit commissions for the salesmen peddling them. By the mid-1980s, mutual funds were becoming the go-to product for "retail" investors, regular mom-and-pop folks. By late 1985, mutual funds oversaw well over $200 billion. Pimco rode the wave, a little, but they focused on big pension clients to grow faster. By 1987, the firm over-saw about $15 billion.

Gross's success firmly established "Total Return" as a style, a cat-egorization of a type of strategy, one that centered on the idea that a bond could do more than just throw off interest payments; it could also go up in price. Interest payments plus capital appreciation com-bined to produce "Total Return." Gross's invention, the marketplace for bonds, had flourished.

Total Return's success was not a fluke. The bond market's flourish-ing in turn had given rise to the thousands of professionals who fed on it, more and more over decades; all those professionals fighting to lend to companies meant those companies had access to increasingly cheap money, vast and vaster pools of capital with which to finance a new plant, a new project, a new business line. Those professionals, those traders, would tell themselves: *We make markets more efficient. We are lowering the cost of capital for companies. We make it cheaper for them to operate.*

All while making their own more-than-healthy living as they tried, year in and year out, to beat one another at this simple game of mak-ing more money, for clients and for themselves.

People who self-select into finance often share character traits: they enjoy working with numbers and predicting the economic implica-tions of everything from current events to playing lacrosse. Pimco was more specific. The environment seemed to attract one particular breed of human, and those weird, intense, paranoid men (and the odd woman) seemed to thrive in direct inverse proportion to the depth of their emotional problems. Ben Trosky, the feral cowboy who built Pimco's high-yield business in the 1990s, used to say the new-hire in-terview should be two questions: "Were you abused as a child?" and "Did you like it?"

The early crew had seemed to enjoy tormenting each other on the trade floor. They rotated who bore the brunt—though, more often than not, it landed on the same people. For much of the 1990s, that was Frank Rabinovitch, the portfolio manager and technology specialist they broke. He arrived a sweet statistics nerd, and left twisted, full of rage. They'd doused him with bug spray, saying he smelled bad; when he wore an expensive new tie to work, they cut off the bottom of it with scissors. *It was an ugly tie; we're helping you.* They tackled him on the trade floor playing touch football, even after he instituted a rule that you had to count to three after snapping the ball. ("He was not real athletic," one partner recalled. "The guys would go and crush him anyway. It was their mindset. You had to make a really aggressive argument to win the day.")

They called it good fun, but it was kids pulling wings off a fly—because they'd all arrived missing wings themselves. The abuse demonstrated their strength, proved that they deserved to survive. It sharpened them, prepared them for the field. It was Gross's chant in the 1990s: "Grow or die, grow or die!"

That chant had become acutely relevant to one leg of the three-legged-stool in the early 1990s. Bill Podlich had had a health scare—in addition to what necessitated his desk drawer full of Maalox—and suddenly it was confusing why he continued dealing with all this when he had all the money he needed and could easily go do what he wanted, like ride trains all day. He and Pat Fisher had gotten married in '85, and she'd started to pull back at the office, frustrated by working with people who were less effective and yet seemed to look down at her.

Pat and Bill Podlich had a "no Pimco in the bedroom" rule, but at 5:30 one morning in 1990, she was getting ready for work and started absentmindedly complaining about how she wasn't getting any support from Dean Meiling. Bill looked at her blankly. Later, on her drive to work, she realized that not only had she broken the rule, but also that the agita just wasn't worth it. By then, she had slid into being a consultant, as Meiling and the others were made partners. Maybe it was time to move on.

A few years later, Bill Podlich figured the same thing. He couldn't sleep, and when he did, he ground his teeth. Too much stress. Time to move on. Time to board a train and ride across the country and enjoy this big pile of money. Otherwise, what was it all for?

Podlich would stay close and consult for years, but they needed to replace him. Which was difficult, largely because there were so few people Gross respected enough who could tolerate his sharper edges. But a few people knew that basically the only Wall Street firm Gross respected was Salomon Brothers, in no small part for its aggressive, swaggering, dick-measuring culture. And some of them also knew a good guy there who'd just left, who might be just right for the job of handling Pimco and, more to the point, Gross.

A few phone calls and visits later, and in 1993, Bill Thompson stepped in as Bill Podlich departed with his pile of money and an acid-stripped esophagus, riding his train into the American Plains. (Yes, there are many "Bills" in this story.)

Thompson wasn't a fly missing a wing in the same way as his new colleagues. He was unfailingly positive and respectful, his sky-high eyebrow arches punctuating a joyful bearing. His easy humor helped him defuse tense moments. He remembered colleagues' children's names and inquired after their well-being; he remembered who loved baseball, as he did, and which team. He and Gross had similar backgrounds—simple Midwestern boys with middle-class fathers, abruptly rich in confused California—but Thompson had the patience for Gross's eccentricities, could tolerate his mood swings, appreciated his strange little sense of humor, and possibly projected it when doing so was useful. He provided the antidote to Gross's insecurity, a balm to the open wound of Gross's psyche and the culture it created.

While Thompson was careful to observe that culture, he also sought to balance it. As he got his footing, he realized this band of unruly wild animals was actually a bunch of self-serious purists. At one point, Frank Rabinovitch threw a chair at him. He could feel that they weren't sure of him and his polish.

So, after a little while on the job, Thompson decided some team building was in order. Some way to get them laughing together. But it couldn't be a normal corporate "trust fall" thing. He had something in mind, but it was a bit of a gamble.

When they announced the newest partners in early 1994, Thompson arranged a big, celebratory dinner for all the managing directors, the new with the old. A chance to loosen up.

In those days, Pimco's core was mostly young, and they still sometimes socialized. Drinking activities were largely spearheaded by the hard-charging Bill Powers, who had to keep his tolerance up for his role as good cop to Wall Street. Gross only occasionally partook in these nights—he wasn't a big drinker or a big "team" guy, but in the very early days, even through the early '90s, he showed up occasionally. When the partners all went to Vegas, he went, too, but he ducked out early to fly back so he could be fresh on the trade floor in the morning.

Gross showed up for Thompson's gambit. It started off as a standard dinner, in a staid conference room at The Pacific Club, not five miles from the office, with hotel steak and red wine.

Once they were good and limber, Thompson rose. He took out a stack of pictures, head shots of each of the managing directors gathered before him. His audience emptied their wineglasses and grinned their purple teeth, listening between whispers. They were going to do an exercise together, Thompson told them. He held up a picture: John Hague's beautiful tanned face. Robust, bushy eyebrows. Blinding Hollywood smile. "The closer," they called him, for his uncanny track record of closing new client accounts. Thompson turned and pinned the picture to the wall behind him.

"We're gonna tell him what we really think of him," he said, as he pinned up more pictures. "Go ahead, get it out. Call him an asshole."

The men looked at one another with some discomfort.

Thompson gave them a beat. "Go ahead!"

"He's . . . an asshole!" one man, from the back of the room, finally said.

"ASSHOLE!" another joined in.

Thompson held up another face: Chris Dialynas, mouth frozen in what seemed to be his perpetual smirk. The response came more naturally this time: "ASSHOLE!"

Ernie Schmider. Actually a lovely guy, which of course you couldn't say at Pimco; that would be a career ender: "ASSHOLE!"

Meek, fastidious Dean Meiling: "ASSHOLE!"

This was fun. Cathartic.

"There were people at that table who looked at other people at that table and thought they were assholes," says one former partner. "This was the vocalization of it, and everybody got a shot. It's like, 'Yeah, he's an asshole!' and he's sitting right there, but you're looking at his picture, not at him."

Thompson's gamble was on-key, perfectly Pimco.

"People actually loved it," Gross says. "It was Thompson's way of introducing himself to the group and being one of the boys."

And so, Bill Thompson was on his way to being accepted as their leader, a first step in becoming beloved and respected almost throughout Pimco, a hard-won and basically impossible achievement. He would go on to lead the firm to explosive growth, with that same artful appreciation of how to calm and wrangle the unruliest factions of the organization, including and especially Gross. Cohered and stable, they could focus their aggression more constructively—toward digging out market quirks and bond document loopholes to exploit to the hilt, toward bullying banks and competitors, toward straining the legal and social limits on definitions and conduct—all to scrape out more basis points for clients than the next guy.

Pimco's willingness to dance on the edge, its dedication to it, would show up again and again over the years in its investing—eternal paranoia about falling behind wed to a love of risk taking. Inside its walls, the mood was the same: a pressure cooker kept just below the boiling point, a delicate tension that, with careful, canny management, could continue to bear that outperformance.

Toward the end of May 2007, Pimco's managing directors convened in an over-air-conditioned conference room at The Pacific Club. It was time to talk about the future.

A housing slowdown had finally caused a market downdraft—the word *subprime* was abruptly everywhere, as Americans who'd happily bought homes they couldn't afford realized that they could not pay—but as Fed chair Ben Bernanke had said in a speech that month, the mess was contained: grave, but small. Meanwhile, Pimco had missed buoyant growth outside the United States and remained behind its peers in returns.

Thompson had no imminent plans to depart, and Gross planned to die on the trade floor. But both still-vibrant Bills had to start thinking about their futures, and the firm's. Gross had just turned sixty-three in April; Thompson was around the same age. To some extent, their most important job now was making sure the company continued, with certainty and stability, beyond them. For years, clients had clamored for a clear plan detailing life after Gross, the proverbial bus always looming, at risk of hitting the "key man" and sending them panicking. A business built on the mind of one man is too fragile. To be a real company, clients needed the institution to grow around and beyond that man, to defray the risk that he might end up being mortal.

What's more, Jim Muzzy was eyeing retirement. Pimco's top managers, Gross included, knew they needed someone at or near the top who could gently amplify the good parts of the firm and its intense culture. That person also needed to try to contain the extremely negative parts, mostly Gross's personality and its effects.

There were also more immediate concerns: compensation for all the Pimbots. They showed up before 5 A.M. to make money into more money—for clients, yes, but also for themselves. Anyone who joined post-Allianz in 2000 had missed out: the real money had been the payouts Gross and Pimco's negotiators brokered in the Allianz deal. Pimco's executives long attributed its success to proper incentives, making employees owners. Now, the company needed to build a new incentive plan to lure and keep the next generation.

They had to get this right. The pressure was particularly acute because of the "war for talent" raging outside. If the company was going to keep growing—the old-timers could still hear the chant from the 1990s, *Grow or die, grow or die*—they would need a real plan.

Now the thirty-odd partners sat wrinkling their suits around a large table, sipping water and coffee as they watched Bill Powers, one of Gross's favorite fixers, the stout also-mustachioed head of mortgage trading, present on the state of "talent management."

The outside world was booming, Powers said. Despite Pimco's terminal diagnosis for the mortgage market, mortgage-backed magic on Wall Street was still throwing off tons of money that traders happily scooped up from their seats at JPMorgan, Citigroup, Deutsche Bank, and at the hedge funds that seemed to pop up everywhere.

The competition for brains was expensive. In the washout they knew was coming, that talent would spill forth at a discount, but until that happened, way too much money was still sloshing around, and they were stuck bidding up already inflated salaries from Los Angeles to Hong Kong. They could do it, but they really didn't like to.

Another issue: Pimco needed to dream up new products to sell clients. New York was increasingly a cleared forest: the biggest investors all had money in Pimco's bond funds. Where would the next wave of growth come from? Who would buy if they'd all already bought? Pimco proudly kept advertising very light. Its primary and most effective advertising was Bill Gross on TV, in *The Wall Street Journal*, along with its network of salespeople pushing its products to wirehouses that sold to the mom-and-pops; and its army of salespeople targeting pensions, insurance companies, and consultants, with their own vast institutional networks. The firm could tap more into sovereign wealth funds, the mega pools of money belonging to Singapore or China or Saudi Arabia, or the UAE. Or it could focus more on high-net-worth individuals. But to help with any of that, it needed something shiny to sell.

That could be hedge funds, those high-fee vehicles that had proliferated after they emerged from the dot-com bust unbloodied and victorious—by 2007, it seemed a new one was founded every minute. Pimco had some small offerings, quietly launched with loyal institutional clients, but few outside knew about them. Should it do more? Or, on the opposite end of profitable, should it build one of those cheapo "exchange-traded funds," vehicles creeping from the stock world into bonds? The fees for such funds were so low they threatened to cannibalize business from elsewhere, but clients loved them. Maybe too much. Or should it . . . do stocks? Pimco had always been bad at stocks. They were bond guys, too pessimistic and paranoid to believe the stories stock guys told themselves. The firm had tried a few times over the decades, and each time, it had ended up as just a bond manager again. But maybe now it was time to get back in. It wouldn't buy an existing fund manager; not Pimco's style. You do that, you end up paying for it twice, they always said—once, to buy the outfit, and again a few years later to replace the traders who had made the operation and who inevitably left the second any handcuffs in the purchase agreement came off.

The partners decided to table the discussion, a very bureaucratic conclusion, the kind that always tweaked Gross. He had to let these jokers hold the reins. The firm was bigger than him; he knew that. But it was hard to sit back and let them spout off, remembering how silly and unwrinkled each had looked on his first day at Pimco, their puttyish faces fresh like babies'. He had let them on his platform, brought them up. *He* had built this—with Muzzy and Podlich and now Thompson. *He* knew how lean they needed to run, how hard everyone had to work, how proud they could be of all they'd accomplished. They did not need fatty layers of committees, everyone chiming in with their contribution, speaking just to hear themselves speak. Gross knew that consensus thinking would slow them down at best or glide them to mediocrity at worst. But he had to let them lead.

On the bright morning of the last Saturday in May 2007, right around the time of the off-site meeting, Gross and Thompson walked up to the entrance of the Montage, a sprawling luxury hotel on the Laguna coast.

Gross, nerves jangling in his weekend wear of a golf shirt tucked into slacks, greeted Thompson gingerly. Thompson was used to Gross's sheepishness; this was normal, despite the near-constant contact of their now-fourteen-year relationship. Gross approached every social contact like he was inching up to pet an irritable horse. Thompson would put him at ease, ribbing him with gentle, harmless jokes, to show his good intentions. It didn't take as much anymore, because Gross trusted him now. But this was an important breakfast, or could be. Gross needed to be maximally limber, as relaxed as he could get—but also not too relaxed, as they were about to meet the world's most formal, most mannered investment professional.

They walked inside to find Mohamed El-Erian already seated.

El-Erian, an old Pimco fan favorite, was in town by coincidence. He lived in Boston now, but he came back to Newport Beach regularly. To local residents this seemed immensely understandable.

The diplomatic son of an Egyptian diplomat, El-Erian had been a rising star in his first stint at Pimco, from 1999 to early 2006. Now he was just a star. He had led Pimco's "emerging markets" team, buying and selling bonds issued by developing economies, Indonesia or Colombia, generating impressive returns, and building the team to success and dominance. He was best known, within Pimco and without, for one trade: Argentina. In the late 1990s and early 2000s, everyone owned Argentina's debt. So, they were all slow to acknowledge when the country was teetering on the edge of bankruptcy. El-Erian was not. He ushered Pimco out of the investments, avoiding showing his hand by quietly selling the bonds little by little to local brokers in Argentina, who largely sold them to Argentine pensions. When Argentina defaulted in 2001, those pensioners and the vast majority of emerging market investors lost their money—while El-Erian's fund generated 27.6 percent. El-Erian looked brilliant.

Capitalizing on his fame, El-Erian had left Pimco in 2006 to run Harvard's $26 billion endowment fund. He planned to pop back to Newport Beach about once a quarter, visiting his wife's family and keeping up with friends. He still had his house and his cars in Orange County, which raised some eyebrows in Cambridge about the degree of his commitment. But why would anyone give up a beautiful home near the coast, especially while enduring long Massachusetts winters?

Sitting with him now at the breakfast table at the Montage, as crooked palm trees outside swayed against a cartoon-blue sky, the Bills asked El-Erian about the culture at Harvard. Was it very different? Were people very competitive, or was it more laid-back?

El-Erian explained that he'd walked into a leadership vacuum. His predecessor had taken many of his most talented colleagues with him when he started his own hedge fund, sick of the scrutiny of the endowment's nontraditional investing approach and the constant furor over his and his colleagues' outsize pay.

As tough new jobs went, it was okay. El-Erian had brought in new talent, morale was recovering, and performance was good. In this business, the performance was all that mattered. El-Erian had just gotten written up in *The New York Times* for selling stocks, 5 percent of the endowment, right before a market dip.

This was irresistible to Gross. He turned the talk to what was on everyone's minds. "Would you consider coming back to Pimco?"

El-Erian's bushy eyebrows flickered. He sat forward in his chair.

Gross didn't have to explain much of their thinking. El-Erian knew they were interested. The idea had begun to take root in Gross's mind: El-Erian was an obvious answer to their long-outstanding question of who could shepherd Pimco after him.

Gross planned to leave the trade floor boots first, but he understood what Thompson sometimes told him: that they had to figure out where the hell this thing was going. They needed to show clients that Pimco was serious about managing its own business, its future. Gross's time was stretched so thin. He was the public face of the firm and the first name on so many different accounts. If he wasn't showing wear yet, he would. Gross also didn't love all the managerial duties he'd accrued. He was amenable to letting somebody else do the onerous work of helping run forums, traveling abroad, holding the hands of needy clients. If someone could keep Gross free to trade, to do his work, that would be an improvement. As long as no one was confused about Gross's role and his intention to die in it.

El-Erian seemed to have some of the necessary characteristics. He was a proven investor. A classically trained economist with degrees from Oxford and Cambridge, he could do the big thinking, the "top-down" economic analysis Gross loved. At Harvard, El-Erian over-saw strategies that went far beyond bonds, into "alternatives" like locked-up long-term investments in private equity, or nimble hedge funds that embraced higher risk across different types of assets; Pimco probably should be looking more seriously at those areas, especially if its catastrophic forecast for the U.S. economy came to pass. El-Erian had managed people before, both at Harvard and in the 1990s, at the International Monetary Fund, a heavily bureaucratic institution focused on international trade and helping developing economies. An economist, investor, *and* a people person, he could bridge the di-vorced sides of Pimco in a way they'd never been before. Maybe it would look like stability.

Plus: Harvard's endowment fund had generated 16.7 percent in the twelve months ending June 2006. Very good. Fiscal 2007 was shaping up to be even better: in a few weeks, at the end of June, the fund would clock in at 23 percent.

This meant that El-Erian was outshining Gross. In the first half of the year, Total Return was basically flat, while the benchmark bond index generated almost 1 percent.

The three men knew all this as they conducted their cordial con-versation. Gross and Thompson wanted to make it clear: There could be a good opportunity for El-Erian to come back, to step up. He was the right idea at the right time.

El-Erian was clearly interested. There probably wasn't much to con-sider. Among the likely factors: yes, he would have to do the hard work of wrangling the ornery, seditious traders and somehow lead them. But there were plenty of freebies: He'd be all over the financial TV net-works as a brilliant expert, almost no matter what he said. He'd speak at all the industry conferences and the big ones that transcended finance, with every important person from politics and money around the globe in attendance. All while clipping a multimillion-dollar salary. Harvard had that prestigious academic brand, but Pimco's reach was far greater, with more than twenty times the assets and—thanks in large part to Gross's legendary status and decades of cultivating his "approachable bond savant" image—even more influence. Very worst-case scenario: El-Erian did it for a few years, clipped that fat coupon, and was minted in that big, broad world of thinkers and influencers. From there: CEO somewhere even bigger, or chair of the Federal Reserve? Even if the thing went maximally poorly, he would have lucrative consulting gigs and prominent newspaper columns for life.

No one made a firm offer, nor did anyone ask for one. But they seemed on the way to working something out.

El-Erian got back on a plane to Massachusetts. Ben Bernanke gave another speech about subprime mortgages. The S&P 500 hit three record highs in four sessions. Gross took a mini vacation.

3

The Turn

On the first Thursday of June 2007, Bill and Sue were at their home in Indian Wells, near Palm Springs, desert towns about two hours from Orange County, depending on traffic. It was hot, maybe 105 degrees, and Sue wanted to stay at home and drink a lemonade in the air-conditioning. But Bill wanted to play golf. He needed exercise. It might provide respite from the market euphoria occupying his mind. On the course, he could pour his frustration and his intensity into that tiny ball, and maybe some of it would stay there when he left.

There was another reason Gross needed to play, which was sort of a joke but also not: on the bookcase in the family room of the couple's Indian Wells house sat a six-inch-tall trophy, a chartreuse ball atop an ebony base; the plaque read, HOLE IN ONE, MARCH 15TH, 1990, 14TH HOLE DESERT COURSE, 155 YARDS. Above the inscription: SUE GROSS.

Sue.

"It was a great shot but it wasn't *my* shot, and I guess therein lies the explanation for why I continue to tee it up," Gross wrote in an *Investment Outlook* years later.

He suited up and went, all alone, to the Mountain Course nestled at the base of Eisenhower Mountain. On the par-three seventeenth hole, he struck the ball just right. It arced perfectly across the sky, landing near the flag, and rolled into the little hole, 139 yards away.

A hole in one.

With no one around to see it.

Good God. Did it even count?

Yes. Yes, it did, he decided. *That damn ball went in.*

When he told Sue later that day, she agreed that it counted, though he thought he detected a funny look in her eye. Though, he noted, she didn't know the first thing about golf.

No one else, not one non-wife person, agreed.

"I suspect they're jealous," Gross said. "I've seen a few of them hitting buckets of balls at dusk from that very same tee when they think nobody's looking. I'm watching, though, which brings up a funny question. If they sank one, would theirs be a hole in one because I was a witness? A damnable game."

A lifetime achievement, even if self-declared. Perhaps a propitious sign. Maybe there could be some daylight through the cracks of his persistent bad mood. Only one thing could really dispel that mood, and day by day, that thing looked nearer.

The market was finally starting to turn. Mortgage delinquencies were climbing. A new tangle of words had appeared alongside *subprime*: *collateralized debt obligation*. CDOs were bundles of many bonds—often, mortgage-backed ones—that were then sliced into "tranches" of risk, ranging from super-safe to super-risky. Any problems in the bonds would affect the more "junior" tranches first; the senior tranches would lose money only if there were many defaults at the same time. The odds of this happening had been near zero, according to the companies that graded bonds, Moody's and Standard & Poor's, which for years had given the senior tranches spotless "AAA" reviews. Many investing judgments were pegged to those grades, so much blind faith in lieu of doing the homework.

Those structures were now falling apart, the AAA label peeling off. Mortgages with past-due payments were surging, and defaults were rising. The payments no longer coming from mortgages meant trouble for the waterfall structure of CDOs: Money was supposed to flow down, from top to bottom, reaching the last tranche last. If the money ran out before then, so be it; the last tranche was the riskiest slice by design. But it was becoming clear that losses would be far worse than the ratings companies had calculated, the money running out far sooner, way higher up on the structure than expected. Moody's and Standard & Poor's would start frantically cutting their ratings.

The investment bank Bear Stearns noticed a growing problem in two of its hedge funds, invested in CDOs backed by subprime mortgages. Declines in those markets were carving huge holes in the funds. In June, Bear poured $3.2 billion into one, hoping to fill in the hole.

Things were getting scary. Just what Pimco had been waiting for.

Gross was downright gleeful in the next *Investment Outlook*. The ratings companies had been duped, he wrote. They'd given out top ratings to what was now turning out to be worse than junk. In turn, they'd duped investors, who were now at risk of losing much of or all their money.

"AAA? You were wooed, Mr. Moody's and Mr. Poor's, by the makeup, those six-inch hooker heels and a 'tramp stamp,'" Gross wrote, with trademark subtlety. "Many of these good-looking girls are not high-class assets worth 100 cents on the dollar."

Yet, amazingly, the stock market climbed. In late June, private equity giant Blackstone went public in the biggest initial public offering in five years, as debt-laden buyouts that they and their cohorts propagated raged on. The markets were split, seemingly ignorant of one another, stocks charging forward in endless optimism while credit markets fell apart, as if their fates were not bound.

Policymakers and regulators tried to keep up. In the Fed's midyear checkup, Bernanke informed Congress that foreclosures were causing "personal, economic, and social distress for many homeowners and communities—problems that likely will get worse before they get better." A glut of unsold homes weighed on the market.

The day after Bernanke's testimony, the Dow closed above 14,000 for the first time ever, as traders took his "before they get better" to mean that housing demand would, probably, stabilize, and decided not to worry. But in credit markets, Bernanke's delicate phrasing did little to soften his message: subprime was leaking. Paul McCulley's horrible vision—those rotten roots spread underneath the markets, the economy, everywhere—was beginning to come into focus.

In July 2007, Bear Stearns told clients that its troubled hedge funds held "effectively no value." The extra compensation that investors demand to hold high-yield corporate debt instead of Treasuries had hit a record low in June and then climbed; now it went vertical. That "spread" over Treasuries, which moves 0.01 percent at a time, surged almost a full percentage point, to 4.3 percent, by August 1.

As August began, Bill Gross faced a decision. He and Sue had planned their annual cruise for that month, through the Panama Canal. A cruise was his preferred method of relaxation because he didn't have to pack and unpack. He took his vacations seriously; he kept the time sacred, uncontaminated. If they went to New York or Beijing, everyone would say, *Bill, you've got to stop by Merrill Lynch, go see this-and-such client*, and he would not do it. On a cruise, he got to be fully, physically, cut off, in the middle of the ocean. No one to visit, no employees or clients to bother him.

But it was becoming apparent that August 2007 was not a good time to be cut off. CNBC's Jim Cramer had just had a full-on meltdown on TV, waving his arms and yelling about how everyone he talked to was freaking out and the "know-nothing" Fed was missing it. The market was finally providing opportunity for Pimco's Total Return to claw its way back. The firm had positioned itself accordingly, preparing for when the Fed had to lower interest rates, and avoiding or selling riskier corporate bonds that might default in a downturn. Gross couldn't take a break now, right when it was all happening.

"It was a time not to lose money, and start making it," Gross said later. He and Sue deferred their cruise to December.

The troubled Bear Stearns funds filed for bankruptcy. Never one to pass on a bargain, Pimco bid on some of the holdings the fund and its creditors auctioned off.

On August 9, BNP Paribas, France's biggest bank, announced that it was freezing three funds. Investors had been pulling in droves, and the bank had to stop giving them their money, for a reason that cast a chill over the market: BNP could no longer figure out how much the holdings were worth. The price swings were too wild. It was impossible to calculate what to give back to investors. A couple of weeks earlier, the cumulative value of those holdings had been €2.1 billion; now it was €1.59 billion. Or thereabouts. "The complete evaporation of liquidity in certain market segments of the U.S. securitization market has made it impossible to value certain assets fairly, regardless of their quality or credit rating," BNP said.

This was it. This was McCulley's "Minsky moment," when increasingly reckless risk taking culminates in the bursting of asset price bubbles. Market collapse.

"I remember the day like my son's birthday," McCulley said later. "Game over."

After months of teetering, hoping the subprime problem wouldn't spread, stock and bond markets began to swoon in earnest, together. Hedge funds with "quantitative" strategies that didn't bet on a market direction—they bought what mathematical models dictated, and so were supposed to be uncorrelated, insulated from this mess—suddenly had huge losses in their normal, not-subprime-related stocks. Everything was contaminated.

The Fed cut how much it charged banks to borrow. Along with the European Central Bank and the Bank of Japan, it pumped cash into markets to assuage fears and keep order. Japan's economy minister told reporters that "the effect of U.S. subprime loans is spreading to financial markets around the world."

The moves did not reassure market participants, just reinforced their greatest fears. By mid-August, the S&P, the Dow, and the Nasdaq were down by about 10 percent since that year's highs, formally qualifying the turmoil as a correction.

It was against this stressful backdrop that Paul McCulley took questions at the Kansas City Fed's annual symposium in Grand Teton National Park, near Jackson Hole, Wyoming. When the organizers had picked the theme of "Housing, Housing Finance, and Monetary

Policy" for that year's gathering, some invitees grumbled that it was too boring, unimportant, irrelevant.

Now, not so boring. Central bankers, finance ministers, professors, and the most important market participants checked into Jackson Lake Lodge in late August 2007, passing the lobby's huge picture windows where the Teton Range lined up at the horizon.

Every evening, amid the "howls of coyotes and bugling of elk," as Yale economics professor Robert Shiller recalled, regulators and economists tried to gauge just how bad the current housing slowdown was. It looked like a classic bank run and yet was worse, scarier. Was it *just* a correction? A bubble popping? Whose fault was it? Should the Fed do something? What?

Part of the problem: the Fed could touch really only the banking system. But much of the current troubles were roiling things that were not banks.

McCulley, sporting a "professional professor" look, his thick mustache halfway to walrus, his orderly brown hair graying in the front, adjusted his rimless glasses, cleared his throat, and began.

The economy was suffering not from a run on the *banks*, as others were suggesting. No, this was a run on the *shadow banking system*, on that veiled, interconnected web of unregulated institutions and corporate shells, he said, "the whole alphabet soup of levered-up non-bank investment conduits, vehicles, and structures."

Real banks had insured deposits from their customers, and access to the "discount window," supercheap financing from the Fed. But shadow banks used other leverage, like commercial paper, the shortest-term market for corporate borrowing, where quick-trigger investor nerves are expressed the fastest. If an institution needed to roll that short-term paper into new paper, and abruptly no investor wanted to lend to it, *zoop!* Funding would be gone.

That's exactly what was happening, McCulley said: The asset-backed commercial paper market had already shrunk by almost $200 billion. Evaporated. The shadow banking system had $1.3 trillion in assets that now needed to be offloaded. The system needed to borrow from real banks, and/or have a fire sale of anything it owned.

McCulley had been mulling this concept for years. So, by the time he opened his mouth in Jackson Hole, he could name the thing, precisely and concisely. From the moment he spoke the term, *shadow banking* flew across the financial landscape.

He'd articulated something everybody had felt, had glimpsed but hadn't seen in its entirety. Shadow banking was the system behind why markets had been, until weeks earlier, eerily responsive, imbued with an electric demand for new credit, new products, new anything with yield. Whatever you could dream got tranched and bought faster than you could say "due diligence." This was why, and how, so much debt had been absorbed so quickly in those previous years.

That fall, the U.S. government struggled to respond. The Bush administration tried to roll out new programs to help struggling homeowners. The Fed lowered interest rates by half a percentage point in September and, the next month, by another quarter of a percentage point. Subprime lenders went out of business. The job market started to shrink. There was a run on deposits at Northern Rock, in the United Kingdom. U.S. banks hit the Fed's discount window. Merrill Lynch announced a $5.5 billion loss. No, wait, *$8.4 billion.*

The U.S. Treasury pushed some banks (JPMorgan, Citigroup, Bank of America) to combine forces for a $100 billion "superfund" to signal support in the markets. Representatives convened to figure out how. But no one actually wanted to do it. The group disbanded by Christmas.

Everyone else was scrambling, and Pimco's smart positioning finally started to pay off. As the portfolios of competitors lost much of their gains, Pimco Total Return returned.

By the end of the year, Total Return had generated 9.1 percent. Morningstar, which rates fund performance, said Total Return "smoked" competitors and beat its benchmark by almost 2 percentage points—"an astounding margin of victory in the bond world."

Riskier high-yield bonds, like the ones Pimco had eschewed in the run-up, eked out less than 2 percent.

"When Humpty Dumpty cracked, our performance was excellent," Gross said years later. People outside his own market started to hear about the bond savant who'd seen the crisis coming. The legend of Bill Gross grew. Name checks in the financial press spilled into the mainstream. He'd been the *Financial Times*'s MAN IN THE NEWS the week Lehman fell, called "an unlikely master of the universe"; *The Washington Post* ran a profile titled "BOND KING" CAN REALLY THINK ON HIS HEAD, spotlighting how Gross's enlightenment arrived in inverted yoga poses; and *Time* magazine called him "the guy you want to hear from more than anyone else, especially when everything debt-related in the world seems to be falling apart."

"From that point on, the one trillion went to two trillion," he said, "because we'd done so well, and the trust in Pimco was doubled as well."

Gross remembers: "We proved ourselves long before, but this was a confirming." Clients felt vindicated for sticking with him, that "even during disaster, Pimco can beat the market and save us money."

That December, six months after his witness-less golf victory, Bill and Sue went to Panama, their shining white colossus of a ship cruising serenely between the banks of the jungle.

4

The Crisis

At the dawn of 2008, as the financial world tried to caffeinate away persistent eye twitches, Pimco received an auspicious blessing: Morningstar named Bill Gross Fixed-Income Fund Manager of the Year for 2007, his third time winning. Gross was elated.

This was the kind of thing he lived for. When he interviewed potential Pimco employees, he liked to ask, "Which would you like to have the most: money, power, or fame?" Candidates would shift nervously, wondering what he wanted them not to be. "It was always a delicate answer, because whichever one you said would open a vulnerability," Gross says. They were always embarrassed, and they always said money or power. Gross would then gladly share his own answer. He would tell anyone who asked. "I was obsessed from the beginning," he says. "From the get-go, my motivation was to be famous."

It was a matter of finding an edge, Gross had figured out young, a way his excellence could rise above that of all the others. Despite being tall, he learned his freshman year at Duke that he wasn't going to be exceptional at basketball; he got cut, an insult he would nurse for decades. His collegiate attempts at business, scalping basketball tickets, yielded more success: he'd buy ten or fifteen and hope that Duke made it to the Final Four, and it happened that three out of his four years, they did. "It was always a lucrative business, by luck," he says.

But luck was not edge. It didn't scale, and he couldn't trust it.

Bad luck showed him he was good at risk taking. He found a more reliable system than scalping tickets, thanks to a horrifying car accident his senior year.

On a Saturday night in 1966, Gross's Phi Kappa Psi brothers sent him out to get donuts for potential recruits—"nobody trusted me to do anything but buy donuts"—but, speeding, he lost control of his Nash Rambler and smashed into oncoming traffic. He went flying through the windshield, which sliced off three quarters of his scalp, detaching it entirely.

He was rushed to the hospital. A state trooper found Gross's scalp on the side of the highway and escorted it to the emergency room, where it was reunited with Gross's head. The incident gave Gross lifelong anxiety about his hair and reinforced his obsession with good health and physical training that started in high school basketball and track: almost every day, for almost the rest of his life, he would leave work for one hour of yoga and/or stationary biking. But for much of his senior year, he was stuck in a hospital bed with a collapsed lung and in need of multiple skin grafts.

In his boredom, he picked up a book he'd bought after spring break the year before, when he'd lost fifty dollars at blackjack that he didn't have to lose. He was skeptical that Ed Thorp's *Beat the Dealer: A Winning Strategy for the Game of Twenty-One* could work, but he was stuck.

He read the whole thing. When he finished reading it, he got a deck of cards and started testing Thorp's strategy in his hospital bed. "I had to prove it, because I didn't believe it," Gross recalls. "I had nothing to do, so I proved it."

Then he practiced. Thousands of practice hands later, his shaved-bald head scabbing over, he decided he was ready for prime time.

He had to report for training for the navy that October 1966—his wartime risk-mitigation strategy, front running the most likely alternative to being drafted and getting sent straight to Vietnam—so, in the intervening months, he figured he'd test out Thorp's theories. He took two hundred dollars he'd saved up and went to Vegas.

His parents sneered when he told them his plan. "You'll be back in a day and a half," they said. Just as well; going east for college was his first getting-out-from-under-them, and this was another. He wanted to see what he was capable of.

He got a room at the Chief Court Hotel for six dollars a day; it was so grimy he wouldn't sit down to watch television. The room had been used for a multitude of illicit encounters, he figured, the office of working women. But it was six blocks from the casinos, and he was only ever there to catch a few hours' sleep in between playing black-jack. Plus, the hotel gave visitors ninety-five cents' worth of free ca-sino nickels.

He covered his still-bruised and bloody-looking head with a bucket hat, to avoid grossing out fellow gamblers but also to change up his appearance, keep casino security a few steps behind. The hat had the added benefit of making him look poor; he didn't want management suspecting he was some rich "wheel."

Gross would watch revelers buzzing around the hundreds of slot machines, Keno games, and fuzzy, green, semicircular blackjack ta-bles. Rows of clean-cut men in suits and women in demure dresses and helmet perms mindlessly pulled levers, over and over. He couldn't tell if he felt sorry for them or was disgusted. They were pouring their savings into these machines; they gave no thought to their approach and, so, had no hope of winning. Did they know that? Did they know they'd already lost? It made him almost sad, this testament to the com-pulsive, negative side of human nature.

I hope you're having fun, he thought, *because you're not making any money. Just as long as you don't lose your paycheck and your kids don't go hungry.*

His fellow gamblers at blackjack, cackling and sipping their drinks, were no more strategic. They were all suckers. *I'm a winner, and you're a loser*, Gross thought. He'd clutch his little pile of white, one-dollar chips, eyeing their piles of one-hundred-dollar black chips.

We're playing the same game. The only difference is the color of the chips.

In other games, he would have been lucky to be surrounded by so many morons, but Gross was playing only the house. He had a system. That entire sweaty summer, he would sit stick-straight in the air-conditioned casinos counting cards at the blackjack table. Fifteen or sixteen hours a day, from 7 A.M. until well after dark, seven days a week.

He sometimes felt gratitude for the casino's losers: He could learn from them. He could incorporate lessons from their mistakes into his methodology. Like their excitement: they'd get on a winning streak and start to make reckless bets and—*boom*—they'd get wiped out.

They had no feel for the table's heat. They were always upping bets when they should have backed off. Gross used only incremental bets, to "probe" the dealer, never putting down more than 2 percent of his chips at a time. And he would bet big only when the cards clearly showed he had an advantage—which was, relatively speaking, a lot of the time.

In blackjack, a gambler starts out with two cards and hopes to end up with cards whose value adds up as close as possible to twenty-one, but not above. The randomly shuffled deck makes or breaks that total. You can't know what card the dealer is about to draw—unless you have been keeping a close eye on what cards have come out already.

A player can track how many "face" cards or high-number cards have hit the table versus low-number cards, simply by counting—plus one for every high card, minus one for every low card, depending on the system. A card counter will hold that number in their mind to inform themselves—and the mathematicians among them can calculate the actual probabilities—whether the next card might be high or low.

Sometimes, the odds were against him, for long stretches, and Gross learned he had to protect his pile of chips to "avoid ruin," as players say. If he still had chips, he could play the next day.

Card counting builds intuition. Gross was learning to feel risk, when to lean in harder and bet more when the odds were in his favor and when to lie low and wait for the deck to heat up. Bet small; hold off. Hold off. Bet big; double down. It was like driving stick shift, or dancing.

"It gave me a sense of risk that was unusual in the 1970s, because there were not enough quantitative risk models at the time," Gross told the *Financial Times* in 2010. Computers couldn't yet spit out mathematically robust answers; you had to use your brain or instincts.

It was a hazard of the job that Gross would occasionally feel a hand on his shoulder and that some oversize man in a suit would say, *Casino management would like you to leave, immediately.* He was never surprised or unnerved when this happened; a hum of anxiety told him it was about to happen at every moment. Casinos hated card counters. This moment was always so close at hand that, whenever a casino actually kicked him out, it was almost a relief. He'd feel oddly proud. Because it showed that his plan was working, that he was succeeding in following Ed Thorp's path.

Counting cards isn't illegal, but a casino aims for volume, to exploit its slight statistical edge over its customers' hands. If a customer ruins the randomness of the game, it ruins the model. Casinos can deny anyone service, and they don't like when a player exploits a slim mathematical advantage; that's *their* game.

Gross's sort-of disguises did only so much; counting was hard to mask. He varied his wagers in funny little increments—tight, compulsive, carefully chosen—but to those who knew, his trick was obvious.

He wasn't a problem to the casinos money-wise, playing with one-dollar chips and winning twenty-five dollars at a time. But he understood that his trick was a threat to their system. It was unfair, but unfair, in his mind, in a rigged system.

Whenever he got kicked out of one casino, he'd step out onto Fremont Street, walk the few blocks to the next casino, and start his process over again. He rotated between the Fremont and the Four Queens, sometimes the Mint or the Golden Nugget.

Slowly but surely, Gross's plan worked; his little pot of money grew. So did his confidence in his ability to see patterns. This confirmed something he already suspected: that he was different. He saw through things, saw around corners. He could stay calm and use his system and outsmart the machines that tripped up everybody else.

Thorp's system mandated playing as long as possible, so the player got the "true odds" and not a random slice that might contain a losing streak. Gross embraced this and learned that his focus was best unbroken. At the beginning, he took breaks, temporary relief from the depressing people crowding the tables. But breaks bungled his rhythm, so he stopped taking them: he stood longer and longer, and got comfortable with sixteen-hour days.

After that summer, Gross went off to Vietnam, serving in the navy, and when he got back in 1969, he put the ten thousand dollars he'd generated in Vegas toward business school.

In 1967, Ed Thorp published another book, *Beat the Market: A Scientific Stock Market System*, about arbitraging convertible bonds and stocks and warrants. When Gross got to business school, he picked the book up. The topic happened to line up with what they were teaching in his program at UCLA, its professors on the cutting edge of warrants and options. Plus, it felt familiar.

"It was like blackjack," Gross says. "It was all very crude and rudimentary, because there was no liquidity, but that actually made it even better."

Again inspired by Thorp, Gross wrote his master's thesis on convertible bonds, securities that can transform into stocks under certain circumstances. Which then got him in the door at Pacific Mutual.

The cardsharp story stuck with clients, and he never tired of telling it. "You have to have that gambling instinct," Gross told *The Orange County Register* in 1992. "This business, if it's done properly, isn't gambling. But it entails some of the gambler's spirit."

In 2002, he told *Fortune*, "Vegas taught me that I could beat the system with a combination of hard work, ideas that no one has thought of yet, and the ability to tolerate a constant routine that to many people seems monotonous. But to me, it's the most exciting thing in the world!"

Years later, Gross met Ed Thorp, at a lunch set up by their mutual attorney, at an old favorite local restaurant, the Ritz; Thorp lives in the area, and in the early 2000s, he was involved with the University of California, Irvine's search for a lead donor for a stem cell research center, and by then, Gross was an obvious great candidate. He walked the hundred feet or so from Pimco and said he had only half an hour. So, they chatted, and after about thirty minutes, Gross's phone rang. It was his secretary saying he had to come back; he said no, give me another thirty minutes. Thirty minutes later, it happened again.

"We ended up talking for two and a half hours," Thorp says.

From there, Gross and Thorp struck up a casual friendship, with occasional lunches, two obsessive numbers brains on Southern California verandas. At some point, Gross told Thorp that same story, about the questions for prospective Pimco employees, how his right answer was "fame." "He wants to be a successful, well-known person in life," Thorp says. "Bill was driven more by fame than anything else."

For Gross, these weren't insignificant hallmarks of success. He'd won the friendship and respect of Thorp, who'd been such an inspiration. He had money enough for courtship from institutions in his community. They were signs that his diligence was paying off. Over the decades, in pursuit of his goal, he was learning, testing, watching which parts of himself, of his experiences, got the best response. He would iterate on them and then add the best ones, the most successful ones, to his legend. People liked and remembered the scalp story and the basketball failures reasonably well—but, he was learning, Vegas was absolute gold.

The announcement had gone out on September 11, 2007: Mohamed El-Erian would leave Harvard after twenty months on the job to become Pimco's co-CIO and co-CEO that January. "We welcome him home as a proven leader, an exceptional investor and one of the most respected names in the investment world," Thompson said in the press release, adding, "Neither Bill Gross nor I at this time have any plans to step down."

Officially, Pimco's partners chose El-Erian. That was the protocol, anyway, which dictated that management ask the partners to vote on their new leader.

Usually in these votes there was a clear right answer, and it was advisable to cast your ballot that way. The votes were "anonymous," but it seemed dicey to trust that assurance in the Pimco pressure cooker. Someone had to tally the votes. If it came out that you had voted incorrectly, you wouldn't know when or how, but you knew you would get dinged.

In the eleventh hour of their negotiations, according to people familiar with the conversations, El-Erian had demanded co-CEO, too. (El-Erian says, through his lawyer, that it was Gross's idea, as part of a succession plan.) Thompson thought that was a bad idea, two jobs in one person. And it was a departure from what made Pimco a deviation from that separation-of-duties three-legged stool that had been their defining trait—first Gross, Muzzy, and Podlich, and then Gross, Muzzy, and Thompson. But by then it was far too late to reverse course. Gross didn't love the new idea, but he still wanted to proceed. As long as the division of labor still insulated him from everyone and (more or less) everyone from him, as long as everyone did their job and let him do his, they would flourish as they had for the past four decades.

El-Erian seemed able to fill Bill Thompson's "people person" shoes, at least. His manners were the stuff of legend: no one could make contact without a barrage of "Best regards," "Wishing you the very best," "Hope you had an amazing day," "Great dog Halloween photo!" or "Congratulations on your great TV segment."

The partners voted twice, the second time unanimously, to ensure a warm welcome. So, forty-nine-year-old El-Erian became the firm's first co-CIO and co-CEO, overseeing all its portfolios and helping Pimco transition to new products and, one day, new leadership. Just as the whole world was melting down.

In New York, London, and Hong Kong, the disaster scenario Pimco had planned for was here. It had to tackle it.

After his win as Fixed-Income Fund Manager of the Year, a jubilant Gross went on CNBC, leaning in, wearing a bright red hat.

"Nice hat," said host Erin Burnett. "Bill—is that—'Think Pimco'?"

"It says, 'Think Pimco!' We're in party mode here, Erin."

Burnett smiled and asked whether the United States was sliding into a recession.

Gross danced confidently between his by-now well-worn points: emphasizing shadow banking and urging the government to inject money into the system. "Opportunity is coming," he said. "Pimco expects to be able to take advantage of it. But we still have a situation where risk assets are still at risk."

He was correct. That month, the CEO of Bear Stearns had resigned as the hard-charging investment bank struggled with soured mortgage investments. Rumors intensified that Bear was on the brink of insolvency, which became self-fulfilling as investors freaked one another out and pulled their money. By March, it was all over: JPMorgan had bought Bear for just $10 a share, with the Fed taking over some of Bear's riskiest assets to get the deal done.

At that moment, Pimco knew to pull up its direst forecasts: "We decided that things were critical and that the *unthinkable was thinkable*," El-Erian told *Fortune* magazine a year later, using a phrase that would become stuck in his mouth like peanut butter. "We went so far as to cancel everybody's holidays for the year."

"I'm not used to setting my alarm for 2:45 A.M., but these are extraordinary times," Gross said.

The rank and file started to adjust their schedules from the regular 5 A.M. to an ungodly 3:30 A.M., leaving to go home at 6 P.M., but they did not stop working once there. In the coming months, some would start sleeping in their cars in the parking deck. Sometimes that was just easier.

The conference room became a war room. With the blinds drawn to keep out the sun, Pimco's top money managers and traders put away their BlackBerrys to meet daily that summer, after Bear Stearns, "to make sure the ark doesn't have any leaks," Gross told *The New York Times.*

The war room's whiteboard hosted a "lesson plan," the multipoint process of "What Happens During Delevering." One, people abruptly demand to be paid more to take risk; spreads widen. Two, people panic-sell until they raise enough cash to feel calm again. Three, raising money now depends on the arrival of clean, new balance sheets, heroes showing up. Without that, prices will keep falling.

The great fear radiating across the market was *counterparty risk.* Pimco traded with many banks and other firms; when those trades made money for Pimco, it relied on those counterparties to pay up. It was unimaginable that an institution like Morgan Stanley or Goldman or Lehman wouldn't have the money. But who knew anymore? Bear Stearns couldn't pay, at least not without JPMorgan's and the Fed's help. Pimco's counterparties were thinking the same thing: no one trusted anyone, and counterparties who had once relied on confidence in each other now demanded ready cash. So, in case counterparties demanded payment, Pimco stockpiled $50 billion. "Bear Stearns has made it obvious that things have gone too far," Gross said.

The chaos reached Pimco's trading tricks. The magic that had helped the firm outperform for decades—Ben Trosky remembers one or two influential consultants who did not understand the magic calling its results "Gross cash"—required functioning markets, and these were increasingly hard to pull off as the outside world cramped with fear. One trading practice that was running too hot: what they called "Lambda Cash." Despite the fancy name, it wasn't that complicated: fund mandates limited how much Pimco could use "leverage," and it had figured out a workaround.

It developed this practice in the 1980s, when Pimco began what would become a habitual, persistent, extra-enthusiastic embrace of derivatives, long-established tools that took center stage in the financial crisis. Derivatives are tied to real things like bonds or stocks, but are not quite those things. Futures contracts, agreements to buy bonds at a future date, at a fixed price, are derivatives; so are options, financial instruments that give the right but not the obligation to buy or sell at a fixed price in the future; and so are swaps, financial instruments that exchange one series of cash flows for another. Because derivatives don't involve buying the underlying thing *now*, they require much less money up front. Using derivatives let Pimco get the bond exposure it wanted, without having to pay for it right away, and in the meantime it could take that leftover cash and invest it in anything that yielded more than zero, to generate more money, while competitors sat around *not* doing these things, lazily missing opportunities to wring pennies out of their dollars and days.

Gross loved a bargain, so he took to derivatives wholly and vigorously.

They gave this practice a formal name in the early 1990s, while perfecting the accounting system that tracked holdings, "Bonds Under Management," or the "BUM report." John Brynjolfsson, a trader who loved inflation products, was working on how to account for futures contracts. If you have a futures contract to buy, say, $2 million in bonds at a certain date, you don't own the bond, and the market value of your contract is close to zero. But the value will move as the bond's does, and when the time is up, you'll need that $2 million to buy the bonds as promised. Pimco figured out that, in the meantime, you could take the cash backing the future and count it as part of the position.

You don't need *all* the cash—at least not until the contract expires. You could buy futures contracts on $2 million worth of bonds, but keep only $1 million in cash. "In the first cut at it, we presented it as leveraged cash," says Brynjo, as he was known. "If you have a million, and you buy two million, that's leverage."

In this and in other cases where the position required managers to hold cash, Pimco figured out it could exploit the difference between cash and "cash equivalents," market instruments that basically count as cash, because they're so reliable and liquid. Like short-dated corporate bonds—they're about to mature, so they're almost as good as

cash, but they have a little bit of yield to them. Buying short-dated corporate bonds yielding just a few basis points more than cash locks in a
little stream of money that your competitors, with their normal cash,
don't have.

Sitting on the trade floor in the early 1990s, Brynjo explained this
accounting system to the members of the Investment Committee.
". . . So, we'll just call that leverage," he concluded.

Every face went white(r). "That's not going to work," one of them
said.

"You want me to change the formula?" Brynjo asked.

"No. No, the formula is fine. It's the name."

"Well, what else are we going to name it?"

Leverage, borrowing money, can amplify returns because you can
invest more, which is great in good times. But leverage only ups the
stakes; it can also help you blow up spectacularly. The cocaine of investing, leverage adds juice, but the price for using it might be higher
than you can pay. That's why its use is restricted in funds meant for
pensioners, who cannot afford to lose all their money. Even using the
word *leverage* can make conservative managers of mutual and pension funds nervous.

Brynjo cast around in his mind. *Leverage* . . . Finance loves the
Greek alphabet, and Brynjo was vaguely familiar with it. "What about
'Lambda Cash'?" Because *Lambda* also started with an *L*.

The Investment Committee approved.

Just Lambda Cash could add 0.25 percent, 0.4 percent a year—which,
in fixed income, is everything. And Pimco could do it forever. In any
asset class, that's how you win: if you just don't lose all your money on
some big, dumb trade gone wrong; if, instead, you steady-eddy along,
eventually you'll be number one in the long-term rankings. "Strategic
mediocrity," Pimco's self-deprecating junk bond manager Ben Trosky
used to call it, his own plan never to be number one in a given year,
but also never to blow up. Simply staying in the game long enough
meant you won. And that's what clients wanted: a good track record,
over time; a manager who beat those arbitrary benchmarks, even if

sometimes that meant gaming them a little—how would the clients know better? Or, rather, what did it matter if it was working?

There was only one problem. Pimco's tricks—using derivatives, extracting Lambda Cash, delaying settlement—gave it bonus time to invest cash in shorter-term assets that added a bit of extra yield. But this brought it into the shadow banking system. If Pimco's bucket of short-term assets had a problem—if, say, there was a run on the shadow banking system—that would be trouble. And in 2008, there was. Pimco's shadow bank was subject to the same ravaging fire as everyone else's.

Still, the fire was less severe than for its peers, as dire housing forecasts and visions of shadow banking had helped Pimco avoid the nastiest stuff. And externally, Pimco continued to look brilliant. Charlie Rose interviewed Mohamed El-Erian in July 2008. Rose lurched forward in his creepy-grandfather tilt, wanting to know how, how had Pimco seen the housing crisis coming?

Simple, El-Erian said. Stocks and bonds had been living in different worlds: In "2005, 2006, into 2007, the bond market, for example, was telling you, 'There's a major dislocation coming, be careful.' The equity market was telling you, 'It's Goldilocks; everything's perfect; the great moderation, nothing to worry about.'

"We figured out the market is trying to tell us that there's a major fundamental transformation going on, and the system is not ready for it."

Now, he told Rose, the unthinkable had become thinkable.

The following week, McCulley appeared on CNBC with Alan Greenspan, the former chair of the Federal Reserve, who was now consulting for Pimco. On *Closing Bell* with Maria Bartiromo, they unpacked what they thought the Fed needed to do with regard to a huge and growing problem: the "government-sponsored enterprises," or GSEs.

Fannie Mae and Freddie Mac bought mortgages from the firms that lent directly to consumers. In the fall of 2008, they owned or backed more than $5 trillion worth of mortgage debt, much of it crap. They funded this by issuing debt, which the market had treated as if it were as safe as Treasuries, U.S. government debt. But the U.S. government had never made clear just how "government-sponsored" Fannie and Freddie were, and now that question was urgent.

Gross and Pimco figured that if things worsened or stayed bad for Fannie and Freddie, the government would have their back. The two entities were too big and too important for the government to let them go bust. On that premise, Gross had put 60 percent of his Total Return fund into GSE-backed bonds, up from 20 percent in 2007. The problem was that bet was looking doubtful. The securities were losing money, and Pimco owned a ton of them. It was time to add a little muscle, in the public arena.

On CNBC, Greenspan and McCulley argued that Fannie and Freddie were inherently structurally unstable and that the Fed and maybe Treasury would need to pump money into them. Then Gross said much the same in his September *Investment Outlook*: The panic selling of crappy mortgages had leaked too far, bringing down the prices of bonds backed by the GSEs. The more prices fell, the more that counterparties demanded that trading partners put up more money, causing those partners to fire-sale their holdings, and on and on. "Unchecked," Gross wrote, this could "turn a campfire into a forest fire, a mild asset bear market into a destructive financial tsunami."

The panic wouldn't stop until buyers came in. Someone needed to step up. Someone with a greater interest, perhaps, in the public good. "Common sense can lead to no other conclusion: if we are to prevent a continuing asset and debt liquidation of near historic proportions, we will require policies that open up the balance sheet of the U.S. Treasury."

Bill Gross was telling the U.S. government, in no uncertain terms, that it had to buy. Fannie and Freddie were a few weeks away from the deadline to roll over $225 billion in short-term debt into fresh, new notes. Gross was warning that the market might not show up.

He elaborated on CNBC: Pimco and other market participants were "sitting on their hands," waiting for *some new, big buyer* to jump into the market. Somebody *else.* They were not going to buy Fannie and Freddie debt unless someone . . . hint, hint.

"You can say that I'm talking my book," Gross said on CNBC.

This didn't sit well with everyone. "Gross is begging the Treasury to support the assets on his books for the public good," wrote Michael Steinberg, an amateur investor and blogger at Seeking Alpha, in a column titled BILL GROSS POLITICKING FOR HIS OWN BAILOUT.

Another investor, Peter Cohan, told *Fortune* that the government needed Pimco's largesse to help fund its efforts to save the economy; it needed Pimco to buy its debt, and so couldn't "afford to let him walk away.

"This is a bilateral monopoly with one big seller and one big buyer," he said. "Gross, a famously good gambler, knows that winning in this type of market means threatening not to buy when the government needs to sell. Gross has the government in a weak negotiating position."

Soon after Gross published his line-in-the-sand *Investment Outlook* and underscored his point on CNBC, news leaked out in a report in *The Wall Street Journal*: Treasury was nearing finalizing a plan to bolster Fannie and Freddie. The government was doing exactly what Bill Gross had wanted, had asked for. His gamble would pay off.

Three days after his CNBC hit, on September 7, Treasury secretary Hank Paulson announced that the government would place Freddie and Fannie into conservatorship, and that the Treasury would inject billions to cover losses. Everyone with investments below Pimco in the capital structure got wiped out.

It was Total Return's best day ever: the fund surged 1.3 percent, for a gain of $1.7 billion, in one day.

The outrage went beyond the world of finance. On September 8, a *Washington Post* reader wrote in: "Journalists should flood the zone and investigate how Bill Gross and PIMCO loaded up on GSE debt, making the political bet that it would become the equivalent of Treasury bonds," the reader complained. "PIMCO shouldn't be allowed to use its sheer size and rhetoric to make a killing."

Another unthinkable, the worst yet, was brewing. Investment bank Lehman Brothers, from the same side of the aggression spectrum as Bear Stearns, was up to its eyeballs in mortgage shit and real estate holdings, and on Wednesday, September 10, Lehman posted a huge loss. The stock plummeted, and markets were gripped with panic. Lehman executives scrambled, looking for a lifeline, a rescue.

Pimco "had been preparing for catastrophe for a long time, but even so, there was a sense of apprehension," El-Erian later told *Fortune*. "Things were accelerating very, very quickly."

By Sunday afternoon, it was over. Lehman had failed to find a buyer. On Monday, it filed for Chapter 11 bankruptcy. The Dow Jones Industrial Average dropped more than 500 points.

It's rare that everyone feels a turning point at once. But Lehman's collapse was unmistakable. Before, things had seemed manageable. Even a week earlier, to call this dip a recession would have been considered un-American. The economy was in trouble, but it wouldn't fly off a cliff. Because it never really had before, at least not in anyone's memory. And surely someone would do *something*. Regulators had orchestrated and backstopped Bear's rescue and had saved Fannie and Freddie. *Something* would work.

But they *let Lehman fail*. Nothing was safe anymore. No trade, no trading partner. Everything was thrown into question. American institutions were crumbling, and suddenly the market grasped that there might not be anybody to stop it.

With this realization, things started moving fast. "Smart money" hedge funds were nursing bad losses, imploding, barring their clients from getting their money back. Everyone was suspicious of every counterparty and wanted more collateral, which created an escalating spiral of demands for cash that no one had. Billions of dollars hung in the balance. Pimco's traders were on a twenty-four-hour relay race of figuring out which counterparties didn't have too much exposure to Lehman. People were afraid.

Two or three days after Lehman fell, El-Erian asked his wife to go to the ATM, please, and take out as much cash as possible.

"Why?" she asked.

"Because I don't know whether there is a chance that banks might not open," he said.

American International Group, the insurance giant, was next to wobble, but having seen the destruction in Lehman's wake, the government wouldn't take the chance this time. On September 16, the Federal Reserve bailed AIG out, lending it $85 billion in exchange for 79.9 percent ownership of the company.

Even so, the fear and uncertainty continued to spiral, infecting every market, every asset class. Those eye twitches across Manhattan worsened; traders parked in front of blinking Bloomberg Terminals with an IV drip of Diet Coke and growing piles of emptied snack wrappers and takeout containers. Rumors raced around the Street: someone had punched Dick Fuld, the Lehman CEO, in the face while he was running on a treadmill, knocking him out cold. It wasn't true, but it was satisfying to imagine.

One Sunday night, Gross was at home with Sue, having a beer and watching the football game, trying to relax. He never had more than one beer at a time, but he was enjoying his one when Sue's cell phone rang. She picked it up and, after a moment, turned to Bill: "Somebody by the name of Geithner is on the phone?"

Gross choked. How had Tim Geithner, the president of the New York Fed, gotten Sue's number? Somebody must have told him it was the only way to reach Bill, given that Bill refused to get a cell phone. Gross was not prepared to talk, but he didn't have much choice. He took the call.

Geithner just wanted to know what Gross thought of the economy. Gross was sure Geithner didn't have much of a clue about the leverage, or about shadow banking. The guys at the Fed hadn't thought about it, didn't have enough experience to know, Gross says, because, "unfortunately, all of them were of the same mold, the Ph.D. consensual model": debate, ponder, discuss. No ultimate decider to shake out the best ideas, like Pimco had.

To be fair, the Fed calls many big investors to keep apprised of where the market's going and how participants are feeling, particularly in turbulent times. There's a committee. Even so, the fame Gross had worked so hard to earn, for Pimco and for himself, was about to pay new dividends.

By now, the spiral had reached beyond the insular world of finance, beyond the stock market: Lehman's failure had gummed up plumbing in the market where American companies fund some of their day-to-day functioning, the $1.97 trillion commercial paper market. The notes usually live just three months (at most, nine), and so are supposed to be supersafe: how much could go wrong in three months? If Dell or Kodak is going bust, you'll have more than three months' notice. Because of that perceived safety, the notes yield only a little more than U.S. government debt.

But now, Lehman. A huge money market fund, the Reserve Primary Fund, had bought almost $800 million in commercial paper from Lehman, which became worthless when Lehman failed. That's extraordinarily bad for any fund, but in a "money market fund," it's historic. In the $3.45 trillion money market industry, it's supposed to be a law of nature that $1 will always equal $1; clients must be able to get their $1 out, at any time. If the value of the fund's assets dips below $1 a share, which it never should, that's called "breaking the buck." When Lehman filed, the value of one Reserve Fund share fell to $0.97. It was the second buck ever broken. Investors rushed to pull their money from money market funds before the next guy could. In a matter of days, almost $200 billion evaporated.

To stop the panic in money markets, the government stepped in, promising to back these types of funds. One dollar would again be one dollar.

It almost worked. The pace of redemptions slowed, but stocks were careening, and money was pouring out of financial markets wherever it could find an opening. So, in October, the government tried again:

the Bush administration and Treasury's Hank Paulson introduced the Troubled Asset Relief Program, or TARP, to prop up American homeowners and America's banks. TARP could buy toxic mortgages off bank balance sheets, or the preferred shares of banks—almost whatever it needed to get the job done.

To head the program, Paulson tapped someone new. When Paulson was named treasury secretary in 2006, lowly Goldman Sachs tech banker Neel Kashkari cold-called him, asking to join; he wanted to learn how government worked. Ten days later, he was sworn in as Paulson's aide. In that job, Kashkari had helped draft an emergency plan, just in case the global economy melted down, a ten-page outline, "Break the Glass: Bank Recapitalization Plan." Now, two years later, "Break the Glass" was the de facto framework for TARP, and the thirty-five-year-old Kashkari the bailout czar. Over a weekend, Kashkari had to build seven teams, and also the entire program.

Slight problem: they had made the whole plan up. "Seven hundred billion was a number out of the air," Kashkari said. "It was a political calculus. I said, 'We don't know how much is enough. We need as much [from Congress] as we can get. What about a trillion?' 'No way,' Hank shook his head. I said, 'Okay, what about seven hundred billion?' We didn't know if it would work. We had to project confidence, hold up the world. We couldn't admit how scared we were, or how uncertain."

From its inception, taxpayers were suspicious of TARP, and Kashkari was met with snark and ridicule. "Critics described Paulson as a 'Dr. Evil' figure who brainwashed Congress into giving him unprecedented financial authority," Laura Blumenfeld wrote in *The Washington Post*, "so that Kashkari, his 'Mini-Me,' could distribute it to Wall Street friends."

Gawker's Hamilton Nolan called Kashkari "Our Favorite Asshole Banker," scorching him in a string of posts detailing his "egocentric, douchebag nature," or his pronounced stare, which, Nolan said, could "bore holes in a taxpayer's forehead, with only the power of his laser eyebeams."

Nolan did offer some mitigating context: "He's really just a front man, taking all the heat for Hank Paulson's decisions and the mistakes of a million greedy Wall Street traders before him. We feel more sympathy for him than any other Ferrari-loving overconfident Republican ski bum Wharton grad in America."

Meanwhile, with the commercial paper market still on fire, the government announced that it would buy commercial paper itself. That was October; by January, it would own more than a fifth of the market. The New York Fed set up the Commercial Paper Funding Facility, or CPFF, for an asset manager to oversee the $738 billion program to jolt the commercial paper market back to life.

It hired Pimco.

El-Erian went on CNBC in early 2009 to hype Pimco's progress in commercial paper. People weren't talking about it, he said, but there was a "healing process . . . going on"; the system was starting to "unclog." Pimco was now formally acting as an agent of the New York Fed, conducting buying on its behalf. The job was to buy up corporate notes, to stabilize and reinvigorate the market for short-term funding so that companies could begin functioning again. The firm got a fixed fee of $3 million per quarter for its trouble, plus 0.0025 percentage points per quarter on the assets in the program.

This program was too complex to get a lot of attention, so El-Erian's appearance on CNBC would pump some optimism into the mainstream. The CP market, the repo market, the money market, they were all coming back, he said. "That is the plumbing of the system. Without it, nothing else will come back." That process would be turbo-charged the next week, when the government facilities came online, he said.

Most everyone in money management was busy digging their way out of the craters in their portfolios; banks were putting out fires in their balance sheets; hedge funds were just trying to stay alive. Bill Gross and Pimco were among the few unscathed enough to concentrate on what to do next.

And that was: whatever the government was doing.

"When you lose half your 401(k), you care more about the return *of* your money than return *on* your money," Gross told *Forbes*. "The lack of animal spirits will influence investing for years to come. The government will have to play risk-taker of last resort."

Internally, Pimco called this the "umbrella." Assets like Fannie, Freddie, AIG, the big banks—they were all under the umbrella, the safe, dry protection of the U.S. government. The government would find a way to recoup its money, and Gross and Pimco figured they could hitch a ride to Get-paid-back-ville.

"In a way, we've partnered with the government," El-Erian told *Fortune*. He meant something far beyond Pimco's literal partnership with the Fed. "We looked for assets that we felt the government would eventually have to own or support." Finding what the government needed in the market, buying it first, and then selling it to the government.

This had become easier because the government was suddenly going to purchase everything. On November 25, 2008, the Fed announced a multipart plan to prop up the economy. In the new plan, one program would lend up to $200 billion to support new securities backed by everything from student loans to auto loans. Another would buy up to $100 billion in Fannie and Freddie debt, and up to $500 billion in securities that Fannie and Freddie backed.

The plan, inspired by the Japanese central bank's innovation in 2001 of buying government debt to give the system a cash infusion and to loosen lending relationships, became known as "quantitative easing." (Actually, QE1, because there would be more; it would take years to soothe the system.)

The $500 billion in Fannie- and Freddie-backed debt that the Fed intended to buy—it had never made such purchases on that scale. To do so, it could build its own team of traders, or outsource the job; it chose the latter.

Four asset managers won the honor of running the program: Goldman, BlackRock, Wellington, and Pimco. The potential benefits, in fees and prestige, were obvious, but it quickly became apparent that the

Fed would not be a passive partner: it imposed restrictions to limit self-dealing or insider trading. The asset managers had to create a barrier, a physical separation, between their Fed operations and the rest of their regular business, to ensure that no information leaked. Each firm had to certify all this in writing and undergo external and internal audits. "When Mohamed and I wanted to wish [traders] a Merry Christmas, we needed two lawyers and a special key to get in the door," Gross said.

Trading in the mortgage-backed securities started in January 2009. Every day, the four firms and the New York Fed got on the phone to talk through what to buy and when. Through the chaos, Pimco saw the Fed's programs for what they were: a get-out-of-debt-free card. The bonds the government was buying would also be as good as Treasuries. Maybe more than any of their competitors, Pimco understood and took the government at its word. Just months after sweating it out over whether the Treasury would back GSEs at all, the government was in farther than ever. If the Fed was going to buy bonds backed by Fannie and Freddie, Pimco would get there first and turn around and sell the bonds to the Fed.

So, while everyone else snapped up Treasuries and high-grade company debt in a panic, Pimco didn't. Supply of those would be too high, they figured. Instead, Gross bought more debt backed by Freddie and Fannie. "We tried to move ahead of the government," Gross told *Fortune*, "to purchase assets before we believe they will have to."

Gross and Pimco picked through the rubble for other things too precious to the U.S. economy to be allowed to fail. They found General Motors' finance unit: the auto industry was too important, especially now; the government wouldn't let a major American carmaker fail. Pimco started buying its debt.

But Pimco didn't sit back and let the government take over. GM's finance unit, GMAC, needed a capital infusion. If it converted into a bank holding company, it would get access to federal funds, like the troubled investment banks. But to do so, regulators insisted, GMAC had to raise money. It would need bondholders to swap their bonds for equity. Seventy-five percent of bondholders would have to agree, and time was short.

Pimco owned a huge chunk of those bonds. GMAC was offering sixty cents on the dollar—less than ideal, but more than what bondholders would get if the company declared bankruptcy. Pimco had seemed sympathetic, but now, at the moment it mattered, it wouldn't help; sixty cents wasn't good enough. It rejected the offer.

This left GMAC shy of its 75 percent threshold. Bankruptcy looked imminent.

Again, the government blinked: despite falling short of that one requirement, it would allow GMAC to convert anyway. Pimco had successfully called the government's bluff. GMAC bonds climbed, and Pimco got its money.

Gross also bulked up on preferred shares and senior debt of financial companies that, with so few buyers, were paying extraordinary rates. The government had already bailed them out with TARP, and now Gross could pick up basically the same things for twice the yield. He bought $100 billion worth of notes from Wachovia, Bank of America, Citigroup, and so on. "In for a nickel, in for a dime," he told *Forbes*.

These bank securities were Bill Gross's version of the proverbial twenty-dollar bill sitting on the sidewalk. No one snatches it up because they can't believe it's real. "It's the most incredible value I've ever seen," he said.

AIG, too. The way Gross saw it, the government had already poured hundreds of billions of dollars into AIG. It was going to let it fail; it wanted that money back. So, he bought bonds of AIG units, some yielding almost 40 percent—$10 million, $20 million a day.

"Pimco's view is simple: shake hands with the government," Gross wrote in an *Investment Outlook*. Sure, the United States had a "Ponzi-style economy" now, had become a "bailout nation," and that was troubling. But worry about that later. For now, he said, "Make them your partner by acknowledging that their checkbook represents the largest and most potent source of buying power in 2009 and beyond. Anticipate, then buy what they buy; only, do it first."

If the house always wins, become the house.

Whatever the government touched was becoming gold. So, whenever Pimco got visibility on what the government might need to buy, it could easily pick up the spread between not-gold and gold. This sometimes meant driving up the price of what the government was going to buy. Front-running the government's trades and pocketing a markup would cost U.S. taxpayers, but would benefit Pimco's clients. And what benefited Pimco's clients benefited its employees—ideally, in that order. And, delightfully, it was perfectly legal.

Where visibility was low, Gross exercised caution. To him, there was no safety in the stock market; by the end of 2008, he'd sold all his personal holdings of stock. Stocks would no longer be money-making growth instruments, he told *Forbes*; they would transform back into yield vehicles, as they had been in the 1930s and '40s, generating an annual 6 percent or 7 percent, "if we're lucky," he said.

At the end of 2008, there was no reason not to listen to him. That year, his Total Return Fund beat 82 percent of comparable funds, generating 2.5 percent on a ton of assets, more than $100 billion. A massive success. Not only were Pimco's clients safe from the terror outside, but they were also among the very few who'd been able to capitalize on it.

"The opportunities are just enormous," Gross said. "This is the Super Bowl for money managers." Nowhere was that truer than in Newport Beach. Pimco was the victor of the crisis, and everyone was watching. Gross was finally where he wanted to be.

5

Constructive Paranoia

On May 28, 2009, Gross was in Chicago to deliver the keynote address at the twenty-first-annual Morningstar Investment Conference. As he stepped up to the podium to face a roomful of beleaguered and besieged financial advisors, brokers, and investors, his tie uncharacteristically tied, his hair doing its thick-but-frazzled flop, Gross was bristling with the dark confidence of someone who knows he's seen the future. Hundreds of gatekeepers to the world of retail investors were stuffed in the ballroom of the sprawling, refrigerated McCormick Place Convention Center in Chicago. In the vast space outside the ballroom, salespeople crowded into temporary booths, advertising their platforms or technology or funds, handing out free branded paraphernalia. In good markets, it was a stuffed animal or a sturdy coffee mug; in bad markets, a pen or a bookmark.

This was a pen year. Attendees, who'd paid nearly eight hundred dollars to attend, were on edge: the market could make time away from their desks very expensive.

Against the background music of knives and forks scraping at conference chicken, Gross described the economic dreariness he foresaw. "Over the next several decades, the ability to make a fortune by using other people's money will be a lot harder," he said.

The audience listened solemnly as the finance industry's hottest celebrity painted his dire picture. He pulled the timeline back to the early 1970s, when President Nixon untethered the dollar from the fixed gold exchange rate, ushering in a new era of capitalism, of financialization and credit creation that would foster decades of prosperity. For more than twenty years, Americans had consumed what developing countries produced, with banks and shadow banks printing debt to pay for it. Why should they save when a second mortgage could cover their expenses? It had been mostly smooth sailing. But as Minsky had foretold, and Paul McCulley echoed, that calm created instability: U.S. consumers became over-indebted. The West owed a ton of money to China. The balances were due.

Consumer spending wasn't growing as fast as it had been. Savings rates were headed up. More regulation would dampen risk taking. Unless the Chinas and Brazils of the world started consuming like America had, the whole world would grow more slowly.

Investors had to adapt to what Gross called this "new normal," an expression he said El-Erian had coined, to describe a world of low interest rates, low risk taking, and muted economic activity. Investment returns would be predicated on injections from central banks, so investors should "shake hands with the government." They should expect considerably lower rates of return than the thirty-year rally they'd enjoyed.

Gross's worst news: lower returns probably meant they'd have to charge lower fees, a long-term double-whammy.

This settled heavily on Gross's audience, the exact crowd whose comfortable existence would bear the brunt of that shift. For years they'd been able to enjoy charging clients fat fees—not so fat relative to the rest of the asset management industry, of course, but fat enough to buy another big home for fun, maybe on the water; some exciting cars; fancy educations for their three-plus kids, all generally irrespective of how they actually performed, of what they actually managed to deliver for those clients funding their lifestyles. Now that would end. Lean times were coming.

On the bright side—at least for Pimco—these awful conditions happened to be ideal for bonds and their low, reliable returns. All anyone cared about now was safety. Slow and steady bonds were *cool*.

"Corporate bonds have the stock guys salivating," Morningstar's Russel Kinnel wrote, recapping the conference. And Pimco and Gross were at the indisputable top of the bond hill, just as Gross had dreamed of decades earlier. He often wished his "cold Canadian parents"—in particular, his mother—could see him now. Proving himself to Mother Goose Shirley had been another of his perennial motivators, an engine that drove him toward the extraordinary. "The Gross goslings were expected to perform at the peak of their capabilities, and when they did not, we would hear some very loud honks from Mother Goose," he wrote in an *Investment Outlook* in 2005.

"I can remember enduring her criticism even into my late 20s[,] when politely asking her to dance at a local dinner club," he wrote. "After only a few steps on the floor she counseled, 'Bill, you can do better than that.' She was right, but I had no intention of mimicking Arthur Murray, so we quickly sat down to our salads in order to control my frustration. I was her son who was going to do very, very well, but not so well, it seemed, that I couldn't 'do better than that.'"

It was Mother Goose Shirley who found Gross his first job; he was struggling to find one after business school when she spotted a newspaper ad for a securities analyst at Pacific Mutual. About a year in, his parents finally came to visit from Los Altos. Gross was excited to show his parents his new life; he and his wife, Pam, had stuffed their two kids into a new but small three-bedroom house in Mission Viejo, with green shag carpets and an avocado green refrigerator. He'd made the bookshelves in the family room himself—stacks of cinder blocks over which he'd pasted contact paper, to make the cement look like wood.

He sat with his parents in the family room, in three separate chairs at opposite ends of the room, while Pam busied herself in the kitchen. His parents swirled highballs as Bill sipped a Budweiser. He hadn't really talked to them about his job—he wasn't a caller or letter writer, so this was their first real catchup.

Gross wanted to tell them he wasn't just a securities analyst, as the ad had described; he was a "private placement loan officer," evaluating to whom to lend money. (He would evaluate a nice young man named Sam Walton in Arkansas, and Warren Buffett's Berkshire Hathaway.) But that had recently morphed, thanks to his own ingenuity.

Even so, Gross was proud of the life he and Pam were building, their little house and their avocado green fridge, the opportunity at work expanding before him. It was something he was randomly really good at, that suited his odd compulsions, his competitiveness, his obsessive mind. He tried to express this to his parents.

"With inflation, the prices of bonds are going down—they have to be actively managed," he said. So, now he had this small pile of Pac-Mutual's money to play with. "It's a huge opportunity!"

His parents sat silent, stirring their drinks.

"I'm going to be the best bond manager in the world!"

They were looking at him like he was on the moon. Finally, one of them asked what a bond was.

Gross knew what was running through their minds—that, to date, he had not proven he could be the best at anything. He could almost hear them thinking, *Didn't you just graduate Duke with a 2.9 GPA? Didn't you nearly lose your scholarship?*

Decades later, Gross visited the mausoleum where his parents rested. He sat in silence, addressing them in his mind. Addressing her. *You know, Mom*, he thought, *I can't do any better than this.* Surely, at some point, she'd have to agree: objectively, there wasn't room for any better. And yeah, maybe he'd wished for "a little more sugar in my childhood Kool-Aid," but maybe that would have blunted him. Without her silent disapproval, would he have pushed himself so hard, needed so badly to be so extraordinary? Like the time he ran a straight 125 miles, from San Francisco to Carmel, over six days, on a dare, the last five miles running with a ruptured kidney. *That* was extraordinary. Driving a brand-new market for trading bonds, when no one else was interested, or building Pimco in that unlikely, boring asset class; being the greatest bond trader who ever lived: *extraordinary*.

Now he was exceptional. Almost forty years after inventing active bond trading, almost forty years of outperforming the next guy, he'd irrefutably demonstrated it, was still demonstrating it. And here, onstage at the Morningstar conference, standing before his rapt subjects, the industry was recognizing him for it.

Another bright spot: Gross's depressing outlook in Chicago suited the global mood, and that pithy encapsulation caught on, better even than *shadow banking*. *New normal* was an instant classic, easily worming its way into mainstream finance vernacular, on CNBC and Bloomberg and in the *Journal*. Years later, after it was cemented in the lexicon, and as Gross and El-Erian began a passive-aggressive tug-of-war over the term's paternity, Gross would lament that Pimco had never trademarked it.

The "new normal" outlook made the case for bonds, and in turn for Pimco. Gross told AOL.com in February 2009 that stocks were dead: "Stocks will be more of a subordinated income vehicle as opposed to a 'stocks for the long run' growth vehicle," he said. "Risk-taking has been destroyed[,] and any animal spirits must come from Washington."

Despite this unequivocal statement, he was about to charge in the opposite direction, in concert with a new authority figure in his life; his own animal spirits, and Pimco's, were soaring.

As CEO, this was Mohamed El-Erian's mandate: find where Pimco could expand. He planned to bring the diversified-portfolio approach he'd overseen at Harvard Management Company to Pimco, by spreading money across products with different types of risks, the sum of which should have a lower overall risk profile than if all the investment eggs were in one basket. Pimco was definitionally heavy in the bond basket, which had just experienced an unprecedented run-up.

It was maybe the right moment for a new leader. Over his fifteen years, Bill Thompson had ushered Pimco from a hundred and twenty-five employees overseeing less than $50 billion to more than one thousand people with $1 trillion realistically on the horizon. But he'd "run out of gas," as he told *The Orange County Register*. Even with all the excitement of 2008, by the end of that year, he could see the outcome of every conversation, knew the conclusion of every meeting before sitting down, could soothe every Gross eruption. People in his position always stayed on too long, and he could feel he was at risk. Gross would miss him but Thompson was tired and needed an out. Plus, Gross was excited about El-Erian. Thompson would hang around through the beginning of the New Year, but he was in runoff.

El-Erian's leadership style was not all bubbly emails and optimistic PR spots, as his surface-level impression indicated. Within Pimco's walls, many thought he had less of a hand in smoothing the group's dispersive and jagged edges than in sharpening them.

Where Thompson had prized diligence, careful planning, El-Erian liked discomfort, uncertainty, what he called "constructive paranoia," feeling your competitor's hot breath on your neck. Constant, suspicious vigilance was how you remained in the lead. This dovetailed nicely with Gross's intensity and exactitude, which already fostered paranoia—as in the "shadow investment committee" Gross had formed to second-guess the decisions of the actual Investment Committee, to keep the latter on its toes, make sure they weren't missing anything important or blobbing into consensus thinking. El-Erian formalized the firm's natural paranoia further, politicized it. The transparency Thompson valued, thinking it encouraged partnership, El-Erian largely seemed to find unproductive. As on the biggest issue at Pimco: compensation. Every year, the partners published the percentage of profits they distributed among themselves. The practice stemmed from their early days of three partners, when they'd sit around a small table and write, in pencil, anonymously, what percentage each thought the others deserved. They'd compile the scraps of paper and take the average. This had to end when there got to be too many partners, but they kept disclosing the percentage, for both accountability and inspiration. El-Erian dissolved that disclosure, according to people familiar. (Through his lawyer, El-Erian says this change was "not made by Dr. El-Erian but was instead proposed by Mr. Gross and was endorsed by the Compensation Committee.")

In many ways, El-Erian's restless personality, his outsider mentality, was perfectly suited to Pimco. The son of a diplomat, he grew up changing countries, schools, languages, friends. He spent the first part of his career at the International Monetary Fund, when it didn't include many other people with roots in "developing" countries. He joined asset management late in his career, and from the public sector. He was always a little different, always reaching beyond what people thought he'd be able to do. Maybe a little insecure, anxious in ways he could brand as useful.

"Mohamed operated in a Machiavellian way," says former partner Bill Powers. "Mohamed operated behind the scenes, usually in unilateral conversations, where he would conspire to bring others into supporting his view that other people in the organization should not be given the responsibility they currently are, or compensation, or role. He was a champion underminer of people, in a stealth fashion."

El-Erian used email as enthusiastically as Gross, but with his own flair, in what Powers called "flame mail," "scorching emails," "where Bill [Gross] or Mohamed would kick back and destroy someone."

This was exacerbated by El-Erian's constant travel to see clients, Powers says. It gave the former the opportunity to check in on anyone, anywhere in the world, and send emails at hours disconcerting to those not being checked in on. "Mohamed would be in London and I would be in Newport Beach, and I'm evaluating a trade [and] next thing: I get this message from Mohamed cutting me to ribbons about something and everything, and when a phone call might have sufficed," says Powers, whose own C-suite ambitions were thwarted by El-Erian's ascent. Powers remembers notes saying, "I want this person fired," or "The end of the year is not gonna be pretty," which people took as a threat to their year-end bonuses. El-Erian's lawyer says he "did not make a practice of sending 'flame emails' and 'scorching emails' . . . [and] did not operate in a 'Machiavellian way' (or in any of the other [sic] pejorative manner)."

Of course, hiring and firing and visiting far-flung offices are normal parts of the CEO job. And Powers's analysis, while widespread,
was not universal. One former employee recalls that, when he arrived in California to visit Pimco as a prospective hire, El-Erian
picked him up at the airport personally. He was touched. And when
El-Erian told a colleague at HMC he was leaving to join Pimco, at the
end of the conversation El-Erian hugged the guy.

"Like, who does that," the guy says. "There are very few people in
the business world who treat relationships with the people they work
with at the level he does."

None of this mattered much to Gross, anyway. Whatever a people
manager did was probably fine, as long as *he* didn't have to do it. Plus,
he expected intensity; everyone should be operating at their most exceptional. The harder someone was pressed, the better they did (especially with a strategically administered allocation of praise). Gross's
own pressure on himself yielded his superhuman focus. It could work
for others. They had to perform, now maybe more than ever.

With investors rattled by terrifying stock drops, Pimco's "Authority on Bonds," as its longtime tagline had proclaimed, was catalyzing
the movement of billions of dollars. Every Bloomberg TV and CNBC
appearance, every new *Investment Outlook*, each new recommenda-
tion from the gatekeeping consultants, was helping to push a tide of
new client money through Pimco's doors.

So, now what? Pimco had always played a little in things other than
bonds—currencies, because buying international bonds meant it had
to. It had a smorgasbord of product offerings, different ways to deliver
mostly bond investments in different flavors, like the Pimco Income
Fund or the new Unconstrained Bond Fund, a trendy new strategy that
untethered managers from index comparisons. And, halfheartedly,
Pimco was considering an exchange-traded fund business, because
everyone seemed to have one. But what else?

The firm had run an internal survey for guidance, and reviewed the
results at that May 2008 offsite meeting. It had asked portfolio managers what new things Pimco could trade better than peers; it asked the

business side what new products made the most sense; and it sent the sales teams out to ask clients what new stuff they wanted from Pimco. They color coded the responses: green indicated something Pimco should get into, but wasn't doing yet; yellow meant something was complementary to what the firm already did but required additional resources. Red: don't do it.

Pimco put the returned matrices on top of one another for a color-coded "road map," El-Erian said. The road map would show them where to go, how to achieve that optimal "diversified portfolio," customized by Pimco's clients, for Pimco's clients. Green: asset-allocation funds, which invest across strategies, for diversification. Direct private equity investments were red. Equities were yellow: maybe do it.

Yes, sure, Gross had publicly slagged stocks over the decades. But it was usually for show, or an emotional response, the kind he still couldn't control in interviews even after all these years of speeches and TV appearances. He'd publicly said that stocks "stink," that earnings were "phonied up," that he'd sold out of them in his retirement account, that they were definitely overvalued; when asked, his brain's muscle memory reverted to that instinctive mistrust.

Upon reflection, he loved a good bargain more than he hated stocks. And there was money sitting on the sidewalk.

The stock market is huge. Smaller than the bond market by dollar amount, but for Pimco, mostly open runway. *Grow or die.* And right then, stocks were a fire sale, a vast market with weakened competitors. With all the trust Pimco had accrued by sidestepping the worst of the crisis, it might, maybe, actually be time to push into stocks. It had to be easier than raising private funds.

The project fell to Dick Weil. As COO, he explored whatever ideas Gross or El-Erian assigned. Though they had both highlighted stocks as a strategic path, neither believed strongly in stock picking or had much experience doing it. Weil was more or less on his own.

In early 2009, the thirty or so managing directors gathered in a conference room, and Weil got up to make a presentation about the stock-picking business's embryonic progress. One of Pimco's most polished, he didn't look or sound nervous. But as Weil spoke, Gross radiated anxiety and impatience from his seat. Everyone in the room was tuned to that vibration; it could mean the presentation's ending in grown-man tears.

Finally, Gross interrupted. Weil's efforts were insufficient, he hissed; this was not going fast enough. The moment was *now*; stocks were a fire sale *now*. Why was this at all difficult? It was easy to sell equities to people, he said; people fucking love equities. They gobble them up. It's like pepperoni pizza. Everybody eats pepperoni pizza. If the Pimco brand was so strong—which it was; everyone knew that—then why couldn't we sell equities? Every idiot can sell stocks. What are we doing? With the 2008 track record and influence, this should be easy.

As he spoke, his thin voice grew intense, pointed, reaching a small scream. Go find me equity people *now!* Gross whisper-yelled. "If we're going to do this, we should really *do* it." (Gross disputes that he would ever demand anything.)

The other managing directors looked on silently, praying for invisibility.

To them, his eruption wasn't so surprising. Nor was the contradiction with his public stance—Gross saying one thing in the press and doing the opposite had been strategic before. Maybe he wanted to disguise Pimco's intentions, divert attention from the firm's foray into equities, lest competitors realize who the incoming big buyer was and run ahead of them.

Angry as he was at Weil, Gross suspected he himself was partly to blame for the halfheartedness of Pimco's push. He knew his equity skepticism had strong gravity. He'd been Mr. Resistant for so long. It was an educated stance, from the many times they'd tried to add stocks before and failed. Even in the olden days, when they'd been in the same room with the stocks guys and Gross wasn't yet "Bill Gross," he could hardly help himself, looking down his nose at their foolhardiness, their brash optimism. He couldn't help it; it always came out.

Now he felt guilty for having stood in the way of Pimco's future. It needed to grow, and right now the way forward was screaming-cheap stocks. So, he would change. He would signal, in the best way he knew how, that he was putting the full force of his intensity on display in this meeting. *Grow or die*, same as always.

Other partners watched him scream at Weil to hurry the fuck up, or else he would find someone to put in his seat who *would* do it fast enough. El-Erian remained mostly silent during the onslaught. Weil was in a tough spot. El-Erian had counseled him privately *not* to find equity managers too fast, according to two former executives. Yes, Gross said he wanted equities, so they had to look like they were trying, but realistically, maybe it wasn't the right path. Even in their matrix it had just been a "yellow," not even a natural or easy next step, from a client perspective, and the clients' view should inform strategy. Client money drove the business. If Weil didn't hire anybody, if they held off, the idea might well fade from Gross's mind. ("Dr. El-Erian never counseled Mr. Weil to refrain from hiring equity managers," El-Erian's lawyer says.)

"Dick got hung out to dry," recalled one former high-ranking executive. No one ever really intervened in these attacks, though. It was customary to leave the victim for dead, let him get torn apart unaided. No one could afford inviting Gross's ire.

For El-Erian, silence was expedient. In Gross's eyes, equities were Weil's problem. By failing to back Weil, El-Erian cosigned on to that view, ensuring that any failure would bypass him and weaken his C-suite rival. The tirade also put Gross as the force behind the equities push, which meant El-Erian no longer had to decide how to execute this soggy idea. In Pimco's blame-seeking framework, Gross now owned the risk; it was his problem. Should it fail, unwritten Pimco code dictated that the blame would revert to Gross—which meant the blame would evaporate. El-Erian would stay clean.

Weil did as he was told. He hired headhunters to find equity managers. The search started the first week of March; the stock market hit its lowest point of the crisis on March 9, with the S&P down more than 50 percent from its 2007 peak. So, in some ways, Pimco again looked perfectly prescient, stepping out with a bold call on equities right at the bottom. Except that it wasn't buying stocks, but *stock managers*, adding a layer of accountability so everyone already in-house could outsource ownership of the project's risk.

Pimco interviewed stock market celebrities, but it felt like the market equivalent of touring a field hospital. Big-name fund managers were shaken, shell-shocked, bleeding out; they'd lost 45 percent year to date and were staring down the end of their careers, which in this business meant their identities. Every bite out of the market took a bite out of their performance, which took a bite out of them and their personal future cash flow. Their strategies had laid bare all their flaws—their overexposure to dumb risks, their inability to predict the future, their ability to lose money almost easily, their humiliating folly. Some were steadier, but none felt competent, confident; none presented strategies that made sense, that seemed like they would work. Pimco kept interviewing.

To get the message out about its beyond-bonds evolution, Pimco needed a new tagline, to graduate from "Pimco: The Authority on Bonds." They weren't boring men in bad suits at Bloomberg Terminals, watching prices rise and fall. Now they would be so much more. It was time to pivot, to a vast, all-encompassing Pimco that spotted tectonic shifts before the rest, that helped rescue even the strongest, most established governments in the world. The most powerful minds in economics and finance, the best thinkers, the sharpest suits, the cleanest presentations. Pimco: The Harvard of Asset Management. Pimco: The Final Word. Pimco: The Future.

Pimco's communications teams enlisted a branding firm in Orange County, HEILBrice, to create a new slogan. They analyzed competitors' taglines and positioning, compared Pimco's strengths, tried to determine what made Pimco *special*.

Finally, they had it solved: "Pimco: It's How We Think."

This new tagline shifted the focus from the products Pimco sold to its *process*, its thought leadership, its differentiated *vision*. They made mock-ups of the new tagline with a glossy design; they made a video. They filed an intent-to-use application with the U.S. Patent and Trademark Office.

The communications team "socialized" "It's How We Think" with more than two dozen managing directors, all of whom were on board: they said the tagline highlighted what made them so great: their *brains*. Pimco was seeding ideas like "new normal" and "shadow banking," and, in the years ahead, likely many pithier phrases and broader economic concepts distilled into digestible nuggets.

Gross decided he didn't like it. Maybe something instead, like: "Global Investment Authority." It was grand, but it retained the *authority* part, which was important. Someone suggested adding "Your."

Pimco introduced its new tagline at the end of the year: "Your Global Investment Authority"—YGIA, for short.

Pimco also needed a correspondingly attractive boldface name to helm its new push. The firm had a smattering of people famous in Fed/economist circles. But the partners wanted to aim even higher. Through their instrumental role in the crisis, they'd met some impressive leaders. A designer name from that roster would get attention.

Of all people, Gross had been impressed by Neel Kashkari, the wunderkind behind TARP. As the economy stabilized and it looked like the government efforts had been successful, the initial mockery had turned passively into respect. Kashkari was a brand-name crisis prodigy and had the flash Gross and El-Erian prized.

So, in December 2009, one day after *The Washington Post* published a long, glowing profile of Kashkari, detailing his post-TARP retreat from D.C. to the wilderness near the Truckee River in Northern California, not far from Lake Tahoe—he was chopping wood to build a house and to process the trauma of government work—Pimco announced that Kashkari was joining as a managing director and "Head of New Investment Initiatives."

The announcement was a surprise and a punch line. If Kashkari's time at Treasury had seemed to some a step beyond his abilities or experience, this new role was another step farther. He had never worked at an asset manager. He would lead building a new equities business without ever having managed an equities business or been an investor at all.

The hire entwined Pimco with the government further still. "The revolving door between Treasury and the giant investment funds and banks just never stops spinning," said Neil Barofsky, the special inspector general who oversaw deployment of the bailout money.

Kashkari's original job at Treasury, Reuters columnist Felix Salmon said, was to create a mechanism "to value precisely the kind of complex debt instruments that Pimco considers itself an expert in.

"It hardly matters whether or not they explicitly said at the time that they'd be interested in hiring him when he left government—Kashkari's a smart guy, and he knows how the revolving door works," Salmon wrote. "There's no shortage of jobs for the likes of Neel Kashkari, and yet he picked the one which conflicted most egregiously with his attempt to serve his country."

But the reception was largely positive; Pimco's cozy relationship with the government had so far garnered warm fuzzies. A *New York Times* article in June proclaimed TREASURY'S GOT BILL GROSS ON SPEED DIAL. It reported how the government leaned on Pimco, and Gross, for advice on the sales of troubled assets. The article was flattering—Gross was a civic-minded genius. Gross loved it. It was a milepost, a measure of his burgeoning reputation and influence. Pimco was so integral to the plumbing of the financial system that it had insinuated itself into the government.

Pimco's actual government partnerships, the commercial paper program and the mortgage-backed trading for the New York Fed, showed promise for future endeavors. Pimco had demonstrated its critical role in the economy in its strong hand with GM and in advising how to structure the bailouts.

"Gross was one of those guys, along with Warren Buffett, who were really interested in trying to give us ideas and be helpful in resolving the crisis," Robert F. Hoyt, Treasury's general counsel under Paulson, told *The New York Times* for a separate article. "They would send memos to Treasury. They weren't ideas we ended up implementing, but they were interesting."

Pimco's leaders had opened up a whole new business line for the firm: the business of helping governments, corporations, whoever needed it, in pricing things. The financial crisis had forced governments around the world into being buyers of last resort, which left them holding a bunch of stuff they had no idea what to do with. They needed to price assets, monitor markets, measure risk, and offload securities they never wanted to buy, and they were largely out of their depth.

Pimco's competitor, BlackRock, was now its most formidable by size and business lines, and it already had a help-a-government offering. BlackRock had leapfrogged Pimco in size in 2009 by acquiring a $1.5 trillion exchange-traded fund business, the world's biggest, from Barclays. But Gross and El-Erian were inspired by their rival's consulting business, BlackRock Solutions, which had been around in some form since the 1990s. Beginning in the depths of the crisis, it was the first call for a freaked-out government official—say, a Tim Geithner or a Hank Paulson.

Pimco saw no reason that *it* shouldn't get that call. It had strong relationships in quasi-government. Fed presidents ranging from Bill Dudley to Tim Geithner called the firm all the time. Alan Greenspan literally worked for Pimco, hired in 2007 as a consultant, his first gig after he stepped down as Fed chair. Why not "Pimco Solutions"?

To make their own consultancy a formal business, they needed someone with polish to run it. Someone who could credibly glad-hand and bullshit fluently, who could act normal. There was really only one candidate.

"Why don't you take it?" El-Erian asked Dick Weil, according to one executive's recollection. "I know you want to be left alone to do your own thing," he added pointedly.

Weil and El-Erian had been bickering frequently, according to former employees, and Weil felt stunted as COO. He had spent years as a potential Thompson replacement, so El-Erian had blocked his path. Here was a shot at success, runway, and relative independence to prove his abilities as a business leader, even under El-Erian's unwelcome foot. Weil had credentials to run an advisory business; he was a lawyer and had helmed other businesses within Pimco. It wouldn't be a promotion, but it wouldn't look like a demotion, either. That was appealing.

In May 2009, Pimco announced that Weil would take charge of the new Pimco Advisory.

Meanwhile, the crisis hero story was starting to grow stale, giving way to the beginnings of skepticism, questioning. *Fortune*'s Katie Benner asked Gross point-blank: was Pimco pursuing selfish goals under the guise of helping markets?

Gross paused. "If you're in a marriage," he answered, "each person has his or her own concept of what the argument is about. That's because they perceive reality differently, and not always because one is right and the other is wrong. The policy prescriptions I've proposed were a realistic attempt to assist the markets. In my eyes, they had nothing to do with bailing out our positions."

On Fannie and Freddie, economists and bankers had agreed with Pimco's view: allowing them to fail would have had extreme consequences, for asset-backed securities and for housing, which would have meant extreme consequences for Americans. Yes, Gross and others were ubiquitous on TV and radio, in newspapers and wire services, making self-serving arguments that the government should do as Pimco proposed and purchase Fannie and Freddie securities, from Pimco. And it should buy the toxic assets off the balance sheets of the struggling banks.

Yes, these opinions supported Pimco's book, Benner wrote. "But that doesn't make the views wrong," she said. "We seem to be in uncharted waters here. Rarely, if ever, has one firm occupied such a pivotal role in the nation's financial system; but rarely has the system been in such distress."

Indeed, one strategist told her, "If Pimco didn't exist, the government would have to create it. It needs an entity that can provide the market liquidity that Pimco can provide."

Gross didn't disagree. "Our role now is to make money for Pimco, but it is also much greater," he said. "We efficiently allocate capital around the U.S. and the world. We are in the business of capitalism." In the world of the markets, it was a truism that there was no greater cause, but now, too, within financially scarred America, there was no rebuttal.

Gross told Benner that Pimco's influence today was no guarantee for the future. "I do yoga to forestall the inevitable," he said. "I do what I do here at Pimco to forestall it, too. But even though I wish we did, no one has license to live forever."

6

New Normal

El-Erian had scoured Orange County for a bakery willing to deliver a cake at 4:45 A.M. It was no easy feat, but he finally found one that would do the job.*

As usual, the sun was not yet up by the time Gross got into the office on the morning of January 12, 2010. At about 5 A.M., he stepped onto the trade floor, expecting the luxurious predawn silence, mentally ticking through what economic releases were due that morning and what they might bring.

Pimco's traders erupted into a standing ovation.

Gross was stunned. The announcement was out: he was Morningstar's "Fixed Income Manager of the Decade." He'd delivered the best performance for Total Return clients, giving them an average of 7.7 percent a year for ten years.

In 2009 alone, Total Return had delivered 13.8 percent, more than twice the returns of its benchmark. Over the past three years, the fund had doubled to some $200 billion in the open mutual fund alone; adding on separately managed client accounts that tracked the same strategy put the total above $400 billion.

"It's been significant," Gross told Morningstar in December. But,

---

* "Dr. El-Erian placed an order consistent with the bakery's operating hours," his lawyer says.

he added, he wasn't a hero: he'd benefited from a long trend, a wind at his back.

There may have been some false modesty here. Ever since Gross was among the first out of the gate on trading bonds, he had been able to keep performance relatively steady with his market magic tricks. But those were mechanical; there were other ways he'd realized he could replicate his card-counting stint in Vegas, to an extent, trades in the markets that allowed him to "be the house," to help him keep a slim but consistent statistical advantage over fellow gamblers.

One easy innovation: early on, Gross bought riskier, higher-yielding debt, like mortgages or international bonds, when the benchmark index he was supposed to beat didn't include those things. That little extra fairy dust of risk meant a little extra fairy dust of return, which most of the time meant beating the index's returns.

The easiest trade was exploiting that difference between cash and "cash equivalents," holding higher-yielding short-dated corporate bonds where your competitors held actual cash.

Some of these moves became codified, like Pimco's "StocksPlus," an idea from 1986 that combined S&P 500 returns with extra juice from short-dated bonds.

One of Gross's favorites of these signature trades was "selling volatility," in which a trader sells derivative contracts to bet that prices will keep trading within a certain range. It was a finance equivalent of Gross's tightly calibrated blackjack bets. Using macroeconomic factors, the ten-year Treasury yield was likely to stay within a range; he would sell "strangles," a pair of options that draw boundaries around that range. He would reap a premium for guessing right. If the thing traded outside his range, he was on the hook. But, usually, it didn't.

Together, these and other reliable trades, like Lambda Cash, comprised what Gross called "structural alpha"—*alpha* meaning outperformance (whatever can be squeezed out of a market beyond the market's own rally, what every fund manager seeks), *structural* meaning replicable, persistent. Structural alpha trades were supposed to generate 0.5 percent, 1 percent in performance a year.

Such trades helped especially in those periods when a manager randomly lost his touch forecasting the direction of interest rates or picking the right credit over the wrong one. Which happened to everyone: it was unavoidable. So, when Gross was off, these structural trades helped provide a cushion to fall back on.

As far as Gross was concerned, these were the keys to the Pimco kingdom. He said as much in a 2003 IO and a 2005 article in the *Financial Analysts Journal*: Structural trades, he wrote, a portfolio's "genetic makeup," were one of two things that make a money manager successful over the course of a career. The other part was the "secular outlook," or the three- to five-year forecast. Setting that forecast, he said, "forces one to think long-term, and to avoid the destructive bile arising from the emotional whipsaws of fear and greed" that compel a trader "to do exactly the wrong thing"—just as he had witnessed in his fellow gamblers in Vegas.

Pimco had a tradition of an annual "secular outlook" firmwide meeting, carried over from Pacific Mutual, and that tradition's endurance helped it focus on the longer term, where there was less noise and less competition. It also helped inform Gross's Vegas sense, his ability to *feel* risk, to know when to follow and when to charge against the crowd.

Gross also found that just pushing harder than everyone else yielded more. Doing things that others weren't willing to do was a structural trade, too, a way to game the markets safely and legally, wringing out extra basis points wherever possible. One way was in his treatment of Wall Street sales coverage. Most traders view these relationships as long term and seek to invest in them. Gross saw them as utilitarian: they existed to get his trades done.

His first hire and protégé Chris Dialynas used to say, as one former portfolio manager remembers, "'If they hit your bid, you paid too much'—that if they agree to it, it must not be a good deal for us." This attitude was hardwired in at the firm's beginning. The Pimco (or Gross) view was that the banks ripped everyone off; why give them any basis point that should belong to clients?

This was an informed view, but it ran counter to how most everyone else conducted themselves. Normal behavior included attending the steak dinners, golf outings, and strip club visits hosted by the banks, which later resulted in getting the first look at a new batch of bonds. In exchange, investors were supposed to send their trading business to their favorite, most steakful and stripperful bank.

Not Pimco. Its skeptical, utilitarian view of the Street showed up in its daily interactions, in hissed phone calls and nasty emails. In the oppressive quiet of the open trade floor, some ducked under their desks to muffle their angry calls. If making noise couldn't be avoided, some made a show of yelling into their phones, insisting on a better deal, spewing anger.

One trader came up with a routine, arranged with a couple of trusted counterparties: as needed, he would message one of them "It's on," and the counterparty would reply "k," and then the Pimco trader would pick up the phone on his desk, in the middle of the trade floor, and call the counterparty, on a line accessible to anyone within Pimco, and he'd threaten and yell and scream at the top of his lungs, and all the counterparty would say was "I'm sorry, I'll do better, I'm sorry, I'll do better." This established the trader within Pimco as a hard-ass, with no cost to his actual relationships with counterparties.

If Pimco felt a bank had wronged them on a deal, it would refuse to participate in the deal. If the bank really messed up, Pimco would stop doing business with the bank altogether—putting them in the "penalty box"—until they repented.

Gross and Pimco knew they could get away with it, because Wall Street needed them. Gross believed that before it was true, before Pimco was big enough for this belief to make sense.

"Because [they] were so big and paid so much in revenue to these firms, people were forced to put up with [their] shit," says one former high-yield bond salesman. A lot of people tried to get away with bad behavior, but they couldn't; it caught up to them. Pimco could. "Because they did so much business, they had everyone in such tight competition against each other, they really could get away with squeezing that sixteenth, and they'd still get the next call."

Pimco happily abjured the unwritten ethics, the gentlemanly conduct that market participants expected from one another—like being nice to their counterparties at banks, or not capitalizing on the opacity of trading. From early on, one of Pimco's favorite tricks was to go to a Wall Street dealer and ask for a price on a set of bonds or derivatives—say, a block of $10 million. They'd agree on a price, and the dealer would buy, only to find that five other dealers had also bought $10 million of the same thing from Pimco and now the Street was flooded with supply, all the dealers bumping into one another holding the same thing, their hopes of selling at a reasonable price dashed. Had they known the true size of the trade, they would have paid less. This is considered at least in poor taste; many see it as shortsighted, a near-term savings in exchange for long-term mistrust from dealers.

Incidentally, this conduct had an added benefit for Pimco: anyone who worked there long enough and enacted the trademark scorched-earth trading attitude may find himself unemployable elsewhere, because everyone on Wall Street hated him. This helped reinforce a dependence on Pimco that kept miserable people in their jobs there.

Gross was, and Pimco was, always willing to be more aggressive on every front—more aggressive on risk taking and leverage, more aggressive at Wall Street sales in the name of better execution, more aggressive in the gray areas of terminology, mandates, regulations. Where other fund managers might avoid a gray area entirely, Gross, and Pimco, found it profitable to walk to the very edge of the gray, reap the extra yield, and wait until a regulator or client objected.

All these tools combined to build Total Return: the reliable "structural" trades, the "secular" view, the bond-by-bond selection by the analysts, the basis points wrung out of Wall Street dealers, the basis points wrung out of behavior that others called rude but that Pimco called "serving the clients." This was how Bill Gross had built Total Return's track record and why he was a three-time winner of Morningstar's Fixed-Income Manager of the Year title—a huge honor—and now Morningstar's Fixed-Income Manager of the *Decade*.

By now, Bill Gross had made his imprint on the bond market, his preferences woven into its walls, his personality embedded in its structure. His ascendance—and with it, his techniques—had inspired copycats across the industry. Gross and Pimco didn't invent pushing boundaries, but where they'd pushed, they'd created more room, and others filled in after them. Traits that, outside finance, might have seemed distasteful looked, in the cocoon of Pimco's power, admirable: the cult of celebrity, the willingness to stuff risk into portfolios through side doors, the cajoling of conservative clients, his brazen claims on TV that he saw no value in some security at the same moment that his trader was preparing to buy it from you, his bullying the government, functionally ranking himself, and the bond market, as a higher power, the highest.

Pimco was tight-lidded and Orange County insular, but half of this played out on television, and it all leaked out and spread. The twin arrogance of Gross and Pimco gave baby bond traders across the world permission to bully and say it was all in their clients' best interest. It was their job.

The narrow focus of that claim happily ignores what economists call "externalities" and what the rest of us call "unintended consequences." If pushing governments and companies is okay if it is done in service of the client, arguably people with money invested at private money managers outranked taxpayers. The public pays to serve capital holders. But this wasn't Pimco's problem. Its interests stopped with the client. The rest was society's concern.

The cake sat on the trade floor, ready for a celebration. As the applause subsided and the traders sat back down, Gross looked around the room, his face stretched into a smile that, without his attention, melted quickly into a grimace.

His idea of fun at work was structured, finite, something he could anticipate and control. That summer, he would decide that the trade floor was *too* quiet and abruptly institute an 8 A.M. conga line, which snaked around the trading desks in fitful, forced celebration. A few months later, he began a Song of the Day. Those on the floor could choose a song; Gross kicked things off with Cake's "Short Skirt/Long Jacket." Another day, someone requested "Turning Japanese," a reference to the debate among wonks and market watchers about whether the Fed's zero-interest-rate policy would yield a "lost decade" as in Japan. Another day: "Shape of My Heart" by Sting—Gross messaged that song's suggester that Gross himself had been about to recommend it.

Gross loved it. So, more must be better. Not long after, he instituted a Friday "closing bell" song when trading stopped at 1 P.M. Pacific time. That was a lot of classic rock, stuff beloved by white men in their forties raging against pudge. Popular on the trade floor: "modern alternative," what was sometimes on KIIS-FM or K-ROQ, like 3 Doors Down. Bill de Leon, the head of risk, enjoyed requesting somewhat harder rock than most everyone else, like Ozzy Osbourne, Sammy Hagar, Cheap Trick, the Who.

This was the *right* kind of fun, the kind where, after the conga line, everyone returned to their desks and sat in order, again silently staring at screens, the only sound the tapping on keyboards. Manageable fun.

This ambush was not. El-Erian later joked to Bloomberg News that a surprise party was "about the last thing [Gross] wanted, because then he had to say something." Gross was brief, thanking everyone for their support, before retreating to his desk and settling into the market. He grumbled that he didn't like to eat that much sugar so early in the morning.

"It only happens once a decade," El-Erian replied breezily, "so don't worry about it."

Aside from the demonstration, from all the eyes on him, the honor was exactly what Gross craved. He was a household name, at least in financial households. Bookers for financial and even mainstream television asked him to come on constantly, as did conference organizers in need of an impressive keynote speaker. Whatever he said was written up immediately. People cared.

He'd seen tremors of his own fame before, like in 2002, when he dashed off a quick, bearish *Investment Outlook* on General Electric before he hit the slopes. He returned to find the company's stock in a tailspin. And the bigger splash in 2008, for his calls on housing and the mortgage giants.

But now he knew he was getting *really* famous. He could just look to *The New York Times* for proof. Another sure sign was that even his stamp collection—a hobby first cultivated, by his own admission, to impress Mother Goose—was getting coverage. His was one of the greatest in the world, but stamps were still stamps. He had sort of forced that fame by giving $10 million and donating some of his treasures to create the William H. Gross Stamp Gallery at the Smithsonian's National Postal Museum in D.C. Closer to home, a $10 million donation yielded the Sue and Bill Gross Stem Cell Research Center, which would open with a local splash in 2010 at the University of California, Irvine.

His August 2009 purchase of a bayfront home on Harbor Island for $23 million (down from the list price of $26 million) showed up in headlines in *The Wall Street Journal* and in real estate blogs. Then came outrage when he tore down the 11,000-square-foot Georgian house to free up the double lot for some great masterpiece. Even though attention can feel a little dangerous, it was what he wanted; it was his destination.

He had stopped going to yoga religiously, and he was too busy to keep up the private lessons (with the same teacher, a Vietnam vet who'd taught Thompson and Muzzy, sparking a competitive frenzy over who could do an unassisted handstand first). But the practice proved durable as branding. In the press, Gross was eternally the yogi; his practice was mentioned in nearly every profile since a 2002 story in *Fortune*, for which he was photographed in Tree Pose, youngish and mustachioed, staring off into the distance.

Back on the trade floor, he shook off his annoyance over the cake and settled in for the day. In bonds, trading the "new normal" was humming along. The firm's muted optimism served to highlight an obvious trade in the Treasury yield curve. Before the crisis, the yield on short-term Treasuries had become basically the same as long-dated ones, which is an aberration: the more time in a promise, the more opportunity for things to go wrong, more risk. This should have meant more yield for long bonds. But then it got worse: The curve—more like a straight, flat line by then—flipped upside down. Short-dated ones paid more than long ones.

An inverted curve is a strong recession indicator, and it freaks people out every time. But as the crisis burned off, Pimco could see that things would revert to normal. Traders would again demand more yield for longer-term Treasuries. So Pimco put on a curve "steepener," buying the very short-term Treasuries and selling longer-dated ones, and it expressed it through interest rate swaps. Just as it predicted, as markets calmed, the curve recurved. Pimco raked in its profits.

Elsewhere, another pocket was humming along: Pimco Advisory, where Dick Weil was running the firm's consulting for public and private institutions, along with Sabrina Callin, a partner who'd helmed the Commercial Paper Funding Facility program.

Pimco Advisory had hit one snag, nothing serious; one program was less exciting than expected. Under the Public-Private Investment Program (PPIP), Treasury had planned to buy about $1 trillion in troubled assets from the banks. Pimco had said in March 2009 (two months before Weil formally took the helm) that it would help build and run the program. The *Times* called Gross "one of the most fervent supporters" of PPIP, having defended it against calls for nationalization, an outcome Gross said would be disastrous.

PPIP was turning out to be a case of "better on paper." Pimco was already getting scrutiny for being too close to the government, for exerting too much influence—and for what? For the privilege of participating in a program that was half marketing, half just good financing for leverage? Pimco had no problem borrowing for cheap, and in fact, the firm was already borrowing from the government, via the Term Asset-Backed Securities Loan Facility. Plus, things didn't look as dire later in the year as they had when conversations began. As the weeks passed, little green shoots of leverage and risk taking had started to spring up. Signs of healing and recovery, as El-Erian said. New client money was still flooding into Pimco, and borrowing was loosening up; what did they need the government for? The program was crowded; Pimco would be elbowing aside eight others for business, for a far-reduced opportunity.

In June 2009, Pimco withdrew its application from PPIP, citing "uncertainties regarding the design and implementation of the program." "The program has been dramatically scaled back, and is now expected to total around $40 billion," Morningstar's Katie Rushkewicz Reichart said in July 2009. "Having nine management firms in the mix—perhaps more than originally anticipated—and a smaller asset base could mean that Pimco would end up with a lower stake than it expected, making it not worth the hassle."

That dud aside, when Dick Weil went into his 2009 review late that year, he felt pretty good. Pimco Advisory was thriving. It had started out with the Fed mandate, and with some other, flourishing projects like a big mandate with a German *landesbank*, revenues were in the neighborhood of $35 million. Clearly they hadn't needed PPIP, and anyway, it hadn't been Weil's call to get involved. The operation was well respected and well positioned for growth; more mandates were sure to follow.

This success was no accident—it tracked the Pimco playbook of launching something new only when it was already fully viable. With the exception of the equities push, "starting" a new business was usually more a relabeling, admitting something was happening. Any new business was already walking by the time the firm sent out the birth announcement. By the time it offered a new fund to clients, that fund had actually existed for years as a building block, a "sleeve," used by other Pimco accounts. Total Return and others would buy a sleeve of the junk portfolio until it had a few years of performance, because a track record gives clients comfort to invest. This was Pimco's own history, too, starting as a shell within Pacific Mutual in the 1970s and gradually spinning out over the years.

Toward the end of 2009, Weil walked into the conference room where El-Erian, Gross, and the head of account management sat waiting for his annual review. Weil greeted them warmly and made some comment about the good year, the good prospects for growth.

Actually, El-Erian told him, the *firm* had won that Fed mandate, not Weil. That mandate was a substantial portion of those revenue figures, so without that . . . what had Weil really contributed? "I don't think you had a good year," El-Erian said.

Weil went nuclear. "Not one word you said is true," he yelled. "I don't respect your opinion."

"Whoa," Gross said, eyes wide. He didn't mind confrontations, but this was uncomfortable. He wanted no part of it. "You two guys have a problem."

"I guess we're done here," El-Erian said.

"Yep, we're done," Weil said and walked out.

A few weeks passed. On one of the first business days of 2010—just before Gross would receive his unwanted cake—Weil walked up to El-Erian. "Can I talk to you?"

They stepped into a nearby conference room.

"I'm sure it's not a surprise," Weil said, according to a person with knowledge of the conversation. "I'm leaving."

It was not a surprise. Indeed, it was helpful for Weil to bow out and leave El-Erian alone. But there was one small hitch. Bill Thompson had left a little over a year prior; losing Weil so soon after would look bad and would draw unnecessary attention to Pimco's management ranks, which might spark concern from investors, consultants, the press. It would give the appearance of turmoil at the top.

"Where are you going?"

"Janus." The stock-focused company had been the hottest money manager in the dot-com run-up of the late 1990s, with clients physically lining up around the block of its Denver, Colorado, headquarters, hoping to hand Janus their money to invest. When the dot-com bubble burst in 2000, Janus's funds crashed as spectacularly. Its assets cratered, from $330 billion to $145 billion in 2004.

And then came the financial crisis, which hit basically all stock investors hard.

Janus was struggling to recoup its lost glory. Weil would have plenty of room to conduct a turnaround.

El-Erian asked when he planned to depart.

"Two weeks."

"I need you to work the month of January."

"Will you pay me my pro-rated bonus?"

"Yep."

"Done."

Weil finished at Pimco on a Friday and immediately started to move to Denver, piece by piece. At forty-six, his wispy brown hair thinning and solidifying his senior-executive-or-senator look, Weil had to convince the Janus troops that, although untested as a CEO and without any investing experience, he could do more than look the part; that his background in bonds was transferable to stocks; that he could rejuvenate morale and company shares. He had to convince clients to return.

On the announcement that Weil would become CEO, Janus shares slipped 2 percent. It didn't matter; he was free.

Gross hardly noticed. Weil's utility had always seemed amorphous. He wasn't an investor, but he wasn't Thompson, either, yet he was always *around*. Everyone knew that, to Gross, people like that were suits, naysayers, pencil-pushing bureaucrats. Unjustifiably expensive and generally in the way. Gross was always looking to have fewer of them, so this was fine by him. If El-Erian was right, Pimco Advisory's business would grow without Dick Weil.

Pimco Advisory was not the favorite right now. Pimco was out making a big deal about the stocks push: Gross's grinning face graced the cover of *Bloomberg Markets* magazine, August 2010, with the headline WHY BILL GROSS LIKES STOCKS. A good joke, the Bond King's being into stocks; everyone got it. The beyond-bonds push was working and gaining attention.

Gross also made a big splash that January for saying that, as the

United Kingdom sold more and more debt, the market for it rested "on a bed of nitroglycerine." Later, he walked this back—he'd meant to say it about the *British pound*, and anyway, the government cut spending and shaped up, and he became less concerned.

This had been a contrarian call, and it would be proven right. Gross could wait—being contrarian was his style, and he was confident people would follow his lead. He was riding high after his victories in Fannie and Freddie debt and GM. He'd knocked out smaller ones more recently, too, like in November 2009, when he wrote in his *Investment Outlook* that stocks of utility companies were attractive, and immediately the Dow Jones Utility Average jumped; when he went on TV or radio and moved the market; and within the halls of Pimco, when he issued ordinances, a flurry of activity followed: "Buy Brazil!" (a perennial favorite). And suddenly, the guy in charge of emerging markets got a flood of requests from across the firm.

Gross had sweated before the recession, as the markets climbed and climbed despite his warnings; now everyone was listening.

As 2010 ended, he realized something about the most important asset class of all: "riskless" U.S. government debt. Gross's resulting call would shock everyone, bringing him more spotlights than ever.

7

Stinker

At the dawn of 1994, Mexico's prospects were bright. It had just signed the North American Free Trade Agreement, which went into effect January 1. Interest rates in the United States were low, so investors were hunting for somewhere more interesting to send their money. That plus NAFTA and Mexico's economic liberalization opened a spigot; investors were excited. International money poured into the country.

But as NAFTA flickered on, everything else went to hell. An indigenous army in Chiapas declared war on the government. The incumbent party's presidential candidate was assassinated at a public campaign rally in Tijuana. The U.S. Federal Reserve started raising interest rates, which always seems to spark an exodus from emerging markets. Then followed another assassination and kidnappings, and more chaos and violence reverberating from Chiapas. It was too much for skittish investors; they fled. The peso's peg against the dollar seemed increasingly fragile.

As the spiral picked up, the Mexican government tried to control rates by converting short-term debt it had issued in pesos into new debt denominated in U.S. dollars, known as *tesobonos*. It sort of worked, but the side effect was that those trades helped evaporate Mexico's international reserves.

Which helped fuel the spiral. Traders got too freaked to buy even the *tesobono*. An auction failed. Then another one. And another.

Four auctions total, unfilled. The government of Mexico was failing to fund itself. Yields on its existing debt kept climbing. Bad and getting worse, fast. "As they got higher, people got concerned that if they got too high, Mexico would say *no más*, we're going to abandon our currency peg and maybe default on our debt," recalls former Pimco partner Brynjo.

All the while, Pimco sat there with a moderate amount of Mexico's bonds. Not too big, but not insignificant. A modest but vested interest in the country not falling to pieces. With yields climbing, bond prices had dropped, so Pimco was looking at a "paper" loss on its books—a loss it would have to recognize if it sold the debt. That was one option—trying to sell its holdings and get out while/if it could. That would likely exacerbate the crisis. Or it could hold steady and let the chips fall. Or it could double down and extend credit where no one else would, pour money into a wildly uncertain situation.

As the calendar turned to 1995, another auction loomed—another $400 million. Pimco money managers had to make a decision.

A garbled rumor was making the rounds: that the U.S. Treasury was talking to Mexico about some kind of bailout, maybe through the Federal Reserve's Exchange Stabilization Fund. Nothing was certain. Few were willing to bet real money on that tenuous whisper.

Gross maybe saw something no one else did. He'd done it before. Like the time in 1981 when he and Muzzy could smell the mini-recession coming and, lo, as Gross recapped decades later, "yields turned down in September almost exactly as called for." And in 1992, when Gross predicted on *Wall Street Week* that short-dated rates wouldn't go lower, and they didn't. Gross trusted his ability to auger the future from market residue, to foresee shifts and weigh risk and get compensated appropriately. The odds that he'd win were always slight, 51 to 49—at best 55 to 45—but when they tilted in his favor, it was time to act. And, sometimes it's the vote of confidence that turns the tide, the act of betting that makes the bet money-good. Plus, at a certain point, yields get high enough that a gamble is worth it. Mexico was beginning to look like an opportunity.

At the next Investment Committee meeting, money manager Lee Thomas detailed an upcoming auction of Mexican government bonds. Yields were flirting with 20 percent, on one-year debt. That's an absurd amount of compensation for short-term government debt—especially if the United States or some other institution came to the rescue. If Mexico could survive twelve months, Pimco could reap 20 percent.

"Your problem is not going to be whether these bonds will mature," Thomas told the group, according to Brynjo's memory. "Your problem is going to be figuring out how you can ever replace twenty percent yield on four hundred million in your portfolio."

Despite the slight breeze of a rumor of a bailout, going into the next auction, few buyers were interested. So, if Pimco wanted to buy, now was the time. "We were pretty sure that we could buy as much as we wanted," Brynjo says.

Gross and his money managers put in a bid to buy the one-year bonds at a yield of 19.75 percent—a number carefully chosen, Brynjo says, even though they might have gotten even more. If the auction cleared with yields above 20 percent, there was some concern that Mexico wouldn't honor it. So, they got as close as they could—19.75 percent—without touching that wire, Brynjo says—and won "for all four hundred million."

With that, the auction succeeded, and market participants breathed a sigh of relief. MEXICO EASES CRISIS, SELLING ALL BONDS OFFERED, the New York Times headline blared. The rumor mill churned that, with so much firepower, whoever was buying must have known something—that a bailout was coming. Pimco didn't know anything more than anybody else, but the market didn't know it was the buyer, so Pimco traders kept mum and let the speculation run rampant, boosting bond prices all the while.

Not two weeks later, President Bill Clinton approved a $20 billion loan from the U.S. Treasury through the Exchange Stabilization Fund. Though its banks would remain in crisis for years, Mexico's debt markets emerged, depressed but stable, and the bonds paid off. Once again, it seemed like Gross had seen around the corner.

"Honestly, it was a little bit of a gamble," Brynjo says. "To me, it's not a positive reflection on Pimco's sustainability. Because it's doubling down." But he added that Gross's track record with doubling down was remarkably strong.

Whatever the components—recklessness, luck, heft, or a good nose for risk—that boldness, at times verging on hubris, would become a familiar groove for Gross. It defined him to others and to himself—the instinct to know when to take the big, high-risk, insistent bet. Bets that could work out almost by virtue of that insistence, a wish forced true. To traders across the industry, this looked like real power, the reward that might await them after years of eighty-hour workweeks and demeaning bosses and PowerPoint after PowerPoint. Gross proved that if he had the right factors, in the right environment, it was possible for one man to control the fates of governments, to bend markets and politicians to his will. What an inspiration.

Now, in March 2011, Gross made one of the most sensational calls of his career. He sold all of Total Return's U.S. Treasury holdings. He now held 0 percent in one of the biggest and most liquid markets in the world. Literally every comparable fund held some.

This announcement caused an immediate splash. *The Atlantic* and *The Washington Post* called, wanting exclusive interviews, offering profiles.

In his *Investment Outlook*, he explained his simple, clear logic: The yield on Treasuries was too low. He was not getting paid enough given the huge risk on the horizon, which was the imminent removal of the Federal Reserve as a buyer of $100 billion in Treasuries a month. The Fed said that, in June, it would stop the extraordinary stimulus measure that had it snapping up 70 percent of all debt Treasury issued every year. The government buying up the government's debt? Wasn't it obvious? It was a Ponzi scheme.

"The right hand is buying from the left," Gross told the *Post*.

"We've been supporting Treasuries almost one for one," he told

The Atlantic. "At 8 A.M., the Fed calls up and asks our Treasuries desk for offers to buy, and one hour later, the Fed's asking for bids to sell them." In doing so, the Fed was lowering rates across the spectrum, from safe savings accounts, money market funds, bonds that mutual funds could buy, and onward—"picking the pockets," in his view, of people who'd saved or invested their hard-earned money.

"God bless Ben Bernanke and Tim Geithner for what they're trying to do, but the net result of a lot of what they're doing is to take money out of the hands of savers." People with money sitting in bank accounts, not invested, not letting someone like Gross invest it for them for a better return. Maybe because many of these ordinary "savers" got burned in the recession by all those guys who had said they knew what they were doing with their money. Fed policy was rewarding risk takers, people who bought junk bonds and speculative real estate—people like Pimco and Gross, or worse.

So, when the "quantitative easing" government-buying-bonds program ended, who would step up to buy 70 percent of Treasuries? Gross suspected the Fed would leave a Fed-shaped void. Those artificially suppressed yields would jump back up—which would mean losses for bond investors.

At the same time, the thinking went, the government's spending had ballooned from financing bailouts and the stimulus act and everything after. So, to raise money, it was issuing tons of Treasuries. Pimco wouldn't tolerate such excessive borrowing from a company. Why excuse this borrower? Why would anyone want to buy something in a flood of supply? Government-suppressed interest rates also meant cheap-to-free money, which would inevitably translate into everyone spending more, Gross figured. And everyone spending, competing to buy goods, would mean higher prices. Inflation is bad for bondholders. Those fixed-interest payments, so enticing yesterday, are worth less in the future, as money loses value—which, for Gross, harkened back to his first days investing, when the 1970s inflation burned the value of those bonds in vaults and sparked active bond trading in the first place.

The first ten years he was in the business, bonds were called certificates of confiscation, he said. Now, in 2011, the fight was again to "preserve capital, preserve capital, preserve capital." In between, for basically thirty years, bond investors had been able to ride a falling-rate rally. "Investors got used to being on this magical journey, with bonds not only producing a nice yield, but some capital gains too," Gross said.

This was a worse new normal than in the crisis's immediate aftermath—the new normal minus the positive effects of government largesse. In September 2010, a full third of Total Return's holdings were U.S. government–related securities. By December, 22 percent; January, 12 percent. By March, zero. Instead, Total Return bulked up on mortgages, company bonds, emerging market debt, and 23 percent cash or in cash equivalents. "Everything you buy and hold must have value," El-Erian said, explaining the rationale. "In our estimation, there was better value elsewhere."

Zero Treasuries was bold. Investors benchmark Total Return's performance against an index, which always has a substantial slug of Treasuries. Any marginal deviation from the index weightings was a call, which clients tracked carefully. Total Return was disregarding an entire category, the most foundational one.

Gross ramped up his bet in April, adding positions in derivatives like interest rate swaps betting *against* Treasuries. Now he wasn't just at 0 percent Treasuries—these bets gave him essentially negative ownership of Treasuries. If Treasury prices fell, he would make even more money. He was in battle mode, and this was just another big contrarian call—the kind he was accustomed to getting right.

"Gross got out of Treasurys ahead of the crowd," *The Washington Post*'s Jennifer Rubin announced, and asked how long until other investors started to bail. Not to worry. Gross said it would take a while for investors to figure it out. If foreign governments, which held half of U.S. debt, sold out, too, he warned, it would be a "political tsunami."

Gross's execution gathered accolades: he'd repositioned the $240 billion Total Return gracefully, without disturbing markets much.

This took skill, said Reuters's Felix Salmon, and "showed that he's more than capable of repositioning his supertanker of a fund as easily and aggressively as if it were a hundredth of its size." Gross was "arguably the greatest bond trader the world has ever seen," Salmon wrote.

Not everyone was so positive. First, this was not entirely unprecedented. "He has been talking about some form of bear market in bonds for over 10 years now," investor Cullen Roche wrote on his blog, citing Gross's 2001 declaration that the bond bull market was "over" and a 2007 interview in which Gross called himself a "bear market manager." "In between these calls, he has consistently maintained a very healthy holding in fixed income and U.S. Treasury–correlated assets," Roche wrote.

Gross's logic also stumped Nobel Prize–winning economist Paul Krugman, who wasn't sure rates were low just because of QE. "If there were really a problem with the marketability of US debt, rates would be high regardless," Krugman wrote in his column in *The New York Times*. Plus, if it's so obvious, wouldn't the market have already moved? "You don't have to believe in efficient markets to believe that totally obvious gains or losses will be anticipated."

The criticism couldn't reach Gross. He'd learned as early as Vegas to press when the table was hot. He was right, and others would follow.

Plus, the firm was built for bold calls. Pimco had hired hundreds of people, doubling its ranks from the beginning of 2007 to over 2,000 by the end of 2011, as the newly very regulated sell-side banks slimmed down and as Pimco needed bodies to manage all the new money—but all these were subordinates. Traders grumbled that the Investment Committee meetings and forums, the deliberation and posturing—it was all theater, because in the end, they just traded what Gross already thought. The firm's broader structure, too, the separation of duties, the "three-legged stool" of Gross, Podlich, and Muzzy, was a little tilted. Anyone who touched the market outranked anyone who didn't. And Gross was the final word.

Especially since, by now, all his cofounders were gone. No one who could tamp him down was still around to do it. El-Erian was the only adult left in the room.

Many in the old guard felt that the old culture had been diluted by that flood of suits from the Street and MBA programs. It was harder and harder to recognize faces in meetings, much less in the halls, but their searching eyes as Gross walked past seemed to need something from him. He decided they could learn from him in the big meetings; he was giving them a platform, and they could distinguish themselves, at which time he would learn more about them, like maybe their names. But he did not owe that to them just because they were there.

Right when Gross announced his Treasury call, he looked smart: Treasury prices dropped, their yields climbing sharply. Was his prediction already manifesting? Or were folks just jumping on his bandwagon?

Either way, the game had begun.

Gross and Pimco weren't alone in their skepticism of the full faith and credit of the U.S. government. Many hedge funders and financial personalities made similar arguments, warning about inflation, insisting that the Fed was creating more money and that, invariably, the greater the supply of money, the less that money would be worth. This was the way it had always been.

A more immediate threat was brewing: blame for the financial crisis was still searching for a home. Homeowners blamed Wall Street; Wall Street blamed the government; the government blamed credit-default swaps. But almost everyone agreed that the credit rating firms had missed it. Blind to the risks, they had gamely competed when Wall Street banks went rating shopping for the highest-possible grade and had slapped perfect ratings on rotten CDOs. They started downgrading only when the money was already gone.

Aware of this credibility problem, the ratings companies sought to reassert themselves, to show they were on the ball. One saw an opening in the ugly politicking in D.C.

That summer, the government was approaching the "debt ceiling," the arbitrarily set upper limit of how much it allowed itself to borrow. Congress needed to approve any increase, and some congresspeople, reacting to Obama and his health care program, wanted to draw a line. They said the government was spending too much, that deficits were out of control. Their posturing threatened the certainty of the U.S. government's being able to fund itself. If the United States cracked the debt ceiling, Treasury would not be able to pay its bills.

Over the spring and summer of 2011, Standard & Poor's warned with increasing urgency that it might downgrade its rating on U.S. government debt due to the deficit and corresponding political gridlock. President Obama managed to get a law through that cut debt by $2.1 trillion and raised the debt ceiling. But it was too late. On Friday, August 5, 2011, S&P cut the government's credit grade, for the first time ever, from AAA to AA+. "Political brinkmanship" had made the government's ability to manage its finances "less stable, less effective, and less predictable," S&P said.

Downgrades normally push bond prices lower, as investors jump ship. Often investors are constrained by ratings—they have promised clients they will hold a proportion of bonds rated this or that and must trade around those promises. But at the moment of the U.S. downgrade, a few external factors were warping this normal chemistry.

Across the ocean, the financial crisis was still playing out. A new party had come into power in Greece, in late 2009, and discovered that the old powers had falsified the country's books. Greece had a budget deficit of 13.6 percent and debt that outweighed its output—demonstrating the dark side of bonds, fixed payments agreed to in sunnier times that became burdens when the future turned cloudy.

Greece's lenders saw no way to grow out of its debt, no way to improve the fiscal situation, other than a bailout. Yields spiked. Other eurozone countries were starting to look wobbly, further straining nerves. Because Greece was an EU member, the unified currency removed what would have been the easiest way to relieve fiscal pressure.

But that also meant its fortunes were intertwined with those of its richer neighbors, France and Germany.

Germany kept "supporting" Greece by saying coldly supportive things—"If the euro as a whole is in danger, it's in Germany's interest, and in every country's interest, to help"—but kept not cutting a check big enough to solve its problems. Without sufficient aid, the hole in Greece's finances kept growing. It threatened to swallow up the European Union, threatened to reach across the ocean—and at the same moment, U.S. economic data had started to look tenuous, soft. The mood was souring, fast.

A funny thing happens in financial markets in August. New York City gets so humid that walking feels like swimming. Skyscrapers and smog trap the heat. Everyone who can leaves, shifting the city's ownership to tourists and rats. The junior guys left manning the desks are excitable and overconfident. They get jumpy: they're not accustomed to responsibility, even if this responsibility is temporary and will be checked when the vacation ends. Trading slows, so volumes thin, which makes prices jumpier, too.

So, at the moment when S&P downgraded U.S. Treasuries, markets were skittish over Greece, fearful of sliding back into a recession, and sparsely populated Wall Street desks left more terrified child-traders in charge than perhaps was responsible. Stocks plummeted. Treasuries, that eternal safe haven, the safest thing anyone can buy, *rallied*, the opposite of what should have happened. Market muscle memory of a "flight to quality." Treasury prices surged. The yield on the ten-year Treasury had started at 3.7 percent on February 8. Now, in August, it dipped briefly below 2 percent, the lowest level since 1962.

Five months after he made it, Gross's bold call was publicly, exceptionally wrong.

In August, Total Return lost about 0.5 percent as its benchmark surged 1.5 percent. The fund's returns so far that year—slightly over 3 percent—put it at 157th out of the 179 funds in its category.

Gross was losing sleep. He'd been taking Ambien to help sleep since the crisis, but still, this kept him up. He told the *Journal* that his decisions—in February, to sell 100 percent of Total Return's Treasuries and, in March, to double down with derivatives bets—had been a "mistake." He was confessing because "we try to be very intellectually honest and honest with the public."

By October, Total Return had generated just 1.9 percent, compared with the index's 6.7 percent. Gross was trailing more than 90 percent of his peers.

Before the year was even over, he sent out a literal "MEA CULPA."

"Let me begin by stating this," he said in the opening of his October *Investment Outlook*. "There is no 'quit' in me or anyone else on the Pimco premises. The early morning and even midnight hours have gone up, not down, to match the increasing complexity of the global financial markets. The competitive fire burns even hotter. I/ we respect our competition but we want to squash them each and every day.

"I'm just having a bad year," he wrote. "This year is a stinker. Pimco's centerfielder has lost a few fly balls in the sun."

Apologies, in finance, are almost unheard of. *Business Insider*'s Joe Weisenthal analyzed why Gross felt compelled to apologize: volatile equity markets made people more emotionally reliant on bond portfolios as an "anchor of stability, smoothing out volatility and canceling out losses in any climate." Total Return had been anything but an anchor; over a rolling twelve months, it had actually *lost* money. New client money had stopped pouring in. Hence the apology.

Meanwhile, Gross swore to the investors in his fund, and to the public, that he hadn't lost his touch. He was still "showing up early every day at the ballpark." He would bounce back!

People had stuck with him before, as in the run-up to the crisis, in 2006, when he was too early (which is another way of saying "wrong") forecasting lower rates. He'd said then that it was a "big mistake," and later on clients had been richly rewarded when he bounced back. They knew this; they'd remember. In the meantime, he made an aggressive U-turn. In September, the Fed announced it would buy longer-term

U.S. Treasuries and sell the same amount of shorter-term securities, a move everyone called "Operation Twist," for how it twisted the yield curve. Gross flipped from bear to bull, guiding the Total Return supertanker toward a huge bet that the program would work and that long-term rates would fall.

It helped, a little. By the end of the year, Total Return had managed to generate 4.2 percent. But it still lagged 87 percent of peers, who returned an average 6.3 percent. If an investor had bought thirty-year Treasuries at the start of the year, they'd have made, incredibly, more than 30 percent. If they'd bought ten-years, north of 15 percent.

Two thousand eleven was a big change for Pimco's track record. Until that moment, it had trounced 97 percent of peers over ten years. Such longer-term performance did earn Gross patience from clients; most of them stuck with him. But even the most loyal had to consider withdrawing, as they were, in turn, accountable to their own clients.

They'd seen a glimmer that, maybe, Pimco wouldn't always deliver.

In September 2011, Pimco threw itself a fortieth-anniversary party. In attendance, against his better judgment, was Ben Trosky, the wild-eyed, cowlick-haired founder of Pimco's high-yield business. It would be one of the last Pimco alumni events he went to after leaving almost ten years earlier, and he didn't know anyone anymore. He watched from across the room as El-Erian basked in the glow of being the favored child. When Trosky spotted Gross, he wanted to say something; he walked over.

"Hey," he said. "Any of the hedge fund luminaries took a swing like that at the ball, you'd see [the fund] down twenty [percent]." But Gross's big, bodacious bet hadn't blown up the firm or even the fund; he should take a bow. "No one lost any money; you ended up just lagging the universe, and they were all riding with the duration of the index."

"Well, thank you," Gross said, as Trosky remembers it. "Unfortunately, you're the only person besides me who sees it that way."

Trosky knew Gross too well to buy this; he knew that if Gross really saw it that way, he would defend it. Unless clients were that pissed.

For the twelve months through November 2011, clients had pulled more than $10 billion, leaving a little over $240 billion in the Total Return mutual fund, right as Gross's competitors raked in billions.

The misstep, and the public apology, were firsts for Gross. He was still "the Bond King," within Pimco and without. But the U.S. government had finally proven it wasn't totally beholden to Pimco, wasn't completely subject to its whims as Mexico had been decades earlier. And Gross was no longer infallible.

8

Edge

Gross wouldn't spend time licking his wounds. He needed to move on to whatever thing needed conquering, and right then the thing was exchange-traded funds.

Gross introduced the new offering with a populist spin, hanging the product launch on an old injustice that he said still gnawed at him.

Here was the pitch: Many years before, Gross's mother had tried to buy shares of her son's pride and joy, the Pimco Total Return Fund, but she was barred by the high minimums at brokerage firms at the time: you had to have $1 million to invest in it, or you couldn't ride. Size limitations had long precluded small clients from buying into such funds, which, to Gross, was an outrage, because it meant they missed out on the great returns that would've turned their small pile of money into a larger pile. (Of course various Pimco funds including Total Return had accepted piles of client money as tiny as $1,000 for a couple of decades.)

Gross told his mother's story to Bloomberg News to hype the "exchange-traded" version of the Total Return Fund. An exchange-traded fund (ETF) is a mutual fund that trades like a stock, letting investors buy and sell shares at the market price throughout the day on a stock exchange. ETFs had become very popular since they were invented in the 1990s, though in the world of bonds, they were still pretty new. ETFs usually have lower trading costs and taxes than traditional mutual funds, and many passively track an index (and barely charge fees at all), which appeals to investors who are suspicious of active mutual fund managers.

Pimco would roll out its Total Return ETF on March 1, 2012, buying similar stuff in approximately the same strategy as the world's biggest bond fund, which had reliably delivered returns for institutional clients since the 1970s.

The new vehicle meant that clients like Gross's late mother could easily buy shares for just a few hundred dollars. Yes, the new product might cannibalize the slightly more expensive flagship, the mutual fund; at least that was the conventional assumption. But conventional assumptions weren't always right: everyone thought Starbucks would cannibalize its own business by opening a second Starbucks across the street from the first; instead, it ended up amplifying sales. For further proof that this was a good idea, Pimco had only to look at BlackRock's runaway success with their massive and growing iShares ETF business. Plus, Gross underscored to Bloomberg, it was the right thing to do. For decades individuals had been functionally shut out of the market except through pooled mutual funds, missing out on decades of extra money on top of extra money, or they were charged too-high fees for the privilege. Now, with Treasury yields at all-time lows, not having an expert working for them would smart even more: "small investors don't always have access to active management, with a higher yield and a higher total return."

"We are hoping 'mom and pop' can do a little bit better than the bond market," Gross said, "at a time of historically low yields."

This problem for mom and pop wasn't an accident; the finance industry wasn't built for them. It's not economical to cater to individuals. It's a lot of trouble for folks who definitionally aren't going to have as much to invest. Pimco figured out it was more expedient to target those giant institutional clients. Until now, the firm hadn't really been playing directly with the savings of people who couldn't afford to lose them, because it hadn't paid much attention to those people at all.

Despite this institutional focus, Gross had long had a bit of a populist streak. In his 1997 book, *Everything You've Heard About Invest-*

ing Is Wrong!, he emphasizes the importance of avoiding hefty fees. Firms "charge exorbitant fees for very little, if any, value added," he wrote. If the reader discovered their manager was charging too much, they should "think seriously about a replacement." He went so far as to recommend low-fee index fund provider Vanguard, to the horror of Pimco employees. Where normally a company's salespeople avidly push a founder's book, Pimco salespeople refused to sell clients Gross's.

In the old days, investors could buy a Treasury bond yielding more than 10 percent; now, post–financial crisis, that was about 2 percent. Which meant high fees mattered more than ever. Gross argued that, with rates so low and the forecast for returns correspondingly pitiful, investors needed to find the cheapest funds possible. A 1 percent fee that was a rounding error a few decades ago now took a huge bite out of meager returns.

The firm's new ETF was not materially cheaper than the mutual fund. For Pimco, it was reasonably priced: total expenses came to 0.55 percent of the money put in. This compared with 0.85 percent for Total Return at the time, depending on the share class and not including a steep "front-end load" fee charged at the outset. The discount was relative: retail investors in Total Return paid up to eighty-five dollars in fees for each ten thousand dollars invested, so fifty-five dollars for the ETF seemed like a steal. Institutional share classes of the mutual fund, gated by that steep minimum, charged forty-six dollars.

And a competitor's ETF, tracking the index that Total Return aimed to beat, charged ten dollars.

The Total Return ETF did charge more than most ETFs. But *actively* managed ETFs, with a human being at the helm, were only a small sliver of the market. And none of the others had Bill Gross. "The challenge is obvious," Gross said.

"We could fall flat on our face, or we could roar like a lion in a year or two or three and become the largest ETF."

The reception was huge. This was in part because moms and pops were no doubt thrilled about investing with "the Bond King," and they were also a slower audience, less informed and less responsive to every single call Gross nailed or didn't. They cared less about one misstep than they did about who he was, the promise he offered: He was a financial-world celebrity they'd heard about for years, whenever they turned the television to the finance channels. He was smart; you could trust him. Now they had access.

"This is a watershed event," said Todd Rosenbluth, an ETF analyst with Standard & Poor's Capital IQ, in a story titled ALL EYES ON PIMCO ETF LAUNCH. "There's a cachet behind this," Rosenbluth said. "Smartphones come out on a regular basis, but they don't get the same buzz as when a new iPhone comes out."

The launch did bring a new complication: actively managed ETFs disclose their holdings daily, instead of each quarter like regular mutual funds. So, with the new daily window of this ETF, anyone could see what Gross did, every day. Some traders chattered about the possibility of copying the market master, ripping off his trading, for free.

This wasn't too troubling to Gross. No one could foresee his strategy shifts, the shaded nuance of his positions. No one could rip off his trading because no one could trade like him. Most important, even he couldn't replicate Total Return in its twin ETF, because under current SEC rules, the new product couldn't use derivatives nearly as much. The ETF gave ordinary investors access to Bill Gross, but it didn't give them the full range of his magic or fully capture what he did in Total Return.

The excitement around the launch was a huge relief. It didn't erase the ugly effect of 2011; Total Return would lug around that performance for years, until it rolled off the critical three- and five-year metrics, ages from now. Luckily, the very long-term track record still looked fantastic, and performance was bouncing back. The new ETF helped rekindle excitement around the brand, and showed that Pimco could play in ETFs just fine.

The ETF was introduced under the stock ticker "TRXT," but that wasn't memorable, so it soon switched to "BOND." Even with the dud ticker, the ETF gathered $180 million in its first few weeks and $1.7 billion by June 30—a massive start for an ETF.

Gross had his confirmation that he was still a household favorite. But now these actual moms and pops had put their savings on the line. They were betting on him, and if he wanted to keep them happy and also invested in his funds, he would need to prove they'd made the right choice.

There was that one added challenge: he couldn't use his derivative superpowers to their full capacity.

Then, Pimco's head of structured products, who oversaw some of the securities the ETF would buy, delivered more bad news. Another of Gross's favorite tools would have to be off-limits. Gross, and Pimco, loved an exemption to the 1940 law that had birthed mutual funds. The rule, 17a-7, allowed for cross-trading among a family of funds, provided they move the security at the market price. Determining that price requires independent data. Therefore 17a-7 is helpful in chucking bonds into a new fund as it launches. But also, normally, if clients demand their money back, a fund has to sell assets to raise the money to hand over. This exemption means the firm could avoid selling into the open market, which otherwise might get word of its "forced selling" and move ahead of it, giving it bad prices. The fund manager could just shift its favorite bonds to other funds it managed. It's always better to keep the good bonds if possible. It was an incredibly handy tool.

But there were too many eyes on the new product. "Compliance [is] especially sensitive given visibility of this ETF launch and likely focus by bloggers and/or regulators," the structured products guy wrote to Gross. So "17a-7-ing" bonds into the Total Return ETF would be off-limits.

Well, if not that loophole, there would be another. It was just a matter of reading the documents closely enough, seeing what exactly was permitted and what wasn't explicitly ruled out. This persistent prodding for weakness worked to identify job candidates, market opportunities, and weird trades that no one else could or would come up with. And even if they could see the trade, they wouldn't have the gall to actually do it. Pimco did.

Pimco prided itself on finding a way; on its history of burrowing into the particulars, arguably too far sometimes, and coming out with profits no one else thought were in there. Pimco had put itself on the map in the 1980s with a feat that was so complicated, so elegant, so comprehensively and forcefully effective that it felt like it had to be a miracle. That one trade established its reputation on the Street as an intimidating trading partner, someone who might rip your face off more than the average counterparty without your knowing it had removed your face until long after.

In 1983, the little band of traders orchestrated a perfectly legal stunt in the mortgage futures market. The business was beginning to catch traction, but the brilliance of this one trade established a reputation for Pimco as shrewd, meticulous, and with a stomach for very high risk.

That summer, on a sunny, warm day, two of Pimco's six most critical employees landed in Chicago. Dean Meiling, in charge of client services after Jim Muzzy, and Pat Fisher, the head of the back office and operations, were there to execute carefully a high-stakes mission that almost no one else understood.

They met up with armed guards to accompany them to the Chicago Board of Trade, the country's largest futures and options exchange. Meiling straightened his suit jacket and tie and Fisher quickly brushed her poofy pageboy bob into cooperation as they walked in. She had already talked with someone at CBOT by phone, negotiating the logistics of their proposed transaction, though she had envisioned meeting in something a bit grander than the dim, old building they were walking into. "You've got this big thing in your mind, like *wow, this is where it's all happening*," she says. "It was kind of dumpy."

CBOT thought these Pimco folks were from another planet. Nobody had ever tried to pull off something like this. "So they didn't know how it was going to transpire," Fisher says. She basically had to teach them.

Chris Dialynas had warned Fisher that this would be difficult. She would need to prepare, he told her: they were buying up as much as they could of this one type of contract, and the play was to demand physical delivery.

The idea had arisen when Dialynas returned from his regular rounds visiting select Wall Street dealers and trade associations for good ideas. Back in Newport Beach and bursting with excitement, he gathered a group including Gross, Muzzy, and Podlich in the portfolio manager's room. He'd heard of a trade idea almost too good to be true—too complicated, too precise, too aggressive for most money managers, so Pimco might have it substantially to themselves. It was also too Chicago, home of Dialynas's alma mater (the University of Chicago), land of mathematical perfection and eternal market efficiency, birthplace of modern-day derivatives. It was just right for Pimco.

The trick of it arose from how poorly understood a new mortgage future was. The contract, which allowed bets on future prices, first debuted in 1975 with a series of unwieldy names: Government National Mortgage Association (aka GNMA, known affectionately in markets as "Ginnie Mae") collateralized depository receipt (CDR). The market for trading them was still developing.

Each contract expires on a set date, at which time the buyer can settle in cash—accepting money if they were right about the price, handing over money if not—or the buyer can "roll" into a new, fresh contract with an updated expiration. There was another option, one people hadn't paid attention to: the buyer could take delivery of the underlying security; they could demand that the seller hand over the thing they were betting on.

Here, the thing they were betting on was a Ginnie Mae mortgage-backed security, a bundle of home mortgages. People borrowed money to buy houses, and banks packaged thousands of those mortgages together into mortgage bonds and sold them to investors. The homeowners paid interest and principal on their loans, and the payments were passed through to the investors. Different Ginnie Mae securities had different interest rates—in the 1980s, some as high as 17 percent—based on the interest rates that homeowners agreed to pay on their mortgages.

Usually, the higher the coupon on a bond, the more it was worth. This becomes truer as interest rates fall—high-coupon bonds become even more valuable, because if new bonds today get you only 8 percent, you'll pay more for an old bond that yields 16 percent. But mortgage bonds are different, because homeowners can prepay their mortgages, and often do. When interest rates fall, homeowners with expensive 16 percent mortgages will refinance, taking out new loans at lower rates and repaying their old ones, killing the payment stream on the old bond. Investors receive the principal, but lose out on all the future years of valuable high interest payments. So, investors who own mortgage bonds with high interest rates don't get the full benefit when interest rates fall.

The Ginnie Mae CDR futures were tied to any Ginnie Mae mortgage bond. When a CDR buyer demanded delivery of the underlying security, the seller could choose what bond to deliver. There was a formula for normal futures delivery: deliver fewer high-coupon bonds (which were normally worth more) or more low-coupon bonds (which were normally worth less). The formula didn't account for that unique problem of mortgage prepayment: that high-coupon mortgage bonds were less valuable than, say, a standard twenty-year bond that didn't pre-pay and kept that steady stream of payments for twenty years. Because of this flaw, in practice, it would always be much cheaper for a seller to deliver high-coupon Ginnie Maes: the futures formula treated them as more valuable than they were and, so, required sellers to deliver fewer of them.

The market was aware of this. Futures traders generally assume that they'll get the "cheapest-to-deliver" security, and the Ginnie Mae CDR futures were priced as though they were futures on the highest-coupon bonds.

But there were only so many of the highest-coupon Ginnie Maes in the world. Rates had been sky-high, which meant they were clipping new bundles of high-coupon Ginnie Maes. But rates had begun to turn in 1982, so the sun was setting on future supply of those high-coupon bundles, the cheapest to deliver. They were going to be more scarce.

"The pricing of the contracts was always following the cheapest to deliver, and that migrated so far from what existed," Meiling recalls. "The high-coupon bonds were small fractions [of the universe of securities], but the traders kept using that algorithm for their pricing. We stood back, and our thought was, *You shouldn't be using that, because not enough exists. If you want to play the game that way, we'll jump in.*"

The market didn't yet realize their mistake, that it was pricing the futures as though there was an unlimited supply of high-coupon, cheapest-to-deliver bonds.

In finance, there is not really a mechanism to say, "Excuse me, but you have made a mistake in your model," other than to exploit the mistake for all it's worth. That's basically the theory that markets are efficient: some asshole in New York or Chicago or Tokyo or Orange County will correct your mistake, albeit at great cost to you and your clients.

There was another strange wrinkle to the contract. It also gave the choice of converting the CDR into a perpetual security, locking in a set coupon payment of 8 percent for the rest of its life. This became particularly powerful if rates declined.

At Pimco, Chris Dialynas and Gross "discussed and realized that it was an option-loaded contract," Gross says. "If interest rates went down, and the [Ginnie Mae] mortgages prepaid in a very short period of time, the holder could choose an option that allowed him/her to collect a perpetual 8 percent coupon paid by the seller. If interest rates went up, the holder could keep the collateral, which would likely outperform twenty- to thirty-year Treasuries."

No one else seemed to register the contract's multiple levers or to have done the math. "We were focused on the nuances," Meiling recalls, "and the fact that we could probably get enough of a position, it would overwhelm the pricing rules that were being used commonly by the traders."

What was absurd was that this opportunity was just sitting there. "Until you open people's eyes to the possibility, they can go along that path" for a long time, Meiling says.

Carefully and as slowly as possible, so as not to show their hand, Dialynas and Gross canvassed the Street, asking anyone who knew about the contracts, to confirm that the Pimco men weren't, in their excitement, imagining things or missing something crucial—the contracts were totally different from what the market had seen before, but they were trading them like the other things they'd seen before.

"We must have spent at least a month trying to figure out: why was this feature in the mortgage in the CDRs that the Street wasn't seeing?" Muzzy recalls. "We finally figured out that it was totally being mispriced."

This made every trader the market equivalent of a wounded animal, unable to outrun Pimco—and they didn't even know it yet. These futures were the perfect investment: a forever bond, if they wanted; or a short bond, if they wanted. It was as close to no risk as Gross had ever seen. "A once-in-a-lifetime situation," he called it at a conference in 1984. "That's a whale of a statement, but I do think . . . I will not see this opportunity in my investment lifetime again. It is truly unique.

"It was not a question of being smart; it was simply a question of being first."

Pimco needed to go big, to enlist as many clients as possible. It started with the biggest ones. The trade obviously required the use of futures, for which the Department of Labor had recently cleared the way in pension funds in late 1982, and most clients hadn't approved them yet. To pitch clients on using them, Pimco had to register as a "commodity trading advisor." So, all its investment professionals had to pass an exam, and then they had to go get client buy-in.

"We flew in a guy from Chicago that did Chicago Board of Trade classes," Muzzy says, "and we spent a weekend, just a really concentrated, intensive weekend," of all the investment professionals taking the class. Then they all took a test. If they passed, they would become "CTAs," commodity trading advisors, certified futures traders.

Given Pimco's rabid competitiveness, "it wasn't a question of passing, but what score did you get?" Muzzy remembers. "Passing was expected . . . You don't fail. But: *I got a ninety-eight. I got one hundred percent. I got a ninety-six.*"

Everyone passed. So, next, they had to go out to their conservative clients, who had money allocated to bond managers like Pimco because they wanted the lower risk profile, and coax them into allowing this upstart West Coast manager to use scary new derivatives. "We created some graphs to describe the option, characteristics of the situation, and how the pricing had been predicated" on flawed assumptions, Meiling recalls. "Quite a few of the big pension clients went along with it."

In Chicago, New York, and Newport Beach, the firm hosted as many clients as would come, maybe half its clients in total, to extol the virtues of the use of futures, this partner says. "They were totally blown away," Muzzy says. In the end, some dozen clients signed up, he says.

And good for them: it was a killer trade.

With permissions and certifications in hand, Dialynas and Gross started buying up Ginnie Mae futures, as many as they could. The market took notice of this insatiable appetite and tried to keep up, feeding it as fast as possible, not realizing it was digging itself into a hole.

"They kept selling them to us, it was crazy," Muzzy says.

Even as they were buying, they wondered whether they could get away with it, Meiling remembers. "We were worried we were doing something that might be perceived as so disruptive that the commodity boards in Chicago might put a stop to what we were going to do."

They did not want to be stopped. Meiling remembers Dialynas telling him, "We really have got to be careful. We can probably do this once, and then . . ."

So, they were meticulous, building the position over months. They would "roll" into the new contracts when it was time, growing and growing, a snowball of futures.

"We kept getting a bigger and bigger position," Meiling recalls.

"We basically cornered the market," Gross says.

Counterparties began to get wise. "Finally, it dawned on somebody that was making a market in these that there's something wrong here," Muzzy says. Even if they didn't know exactly what was up, those on the other side refused to sell more contracts. "The people that were making the market in this, creating these futures, just pulled . . . and disappeared."

In the end, Gross told *The New York Times*, the traders on the other side, who had been selling Pimco the contracts, started waving their hankies in mock surrender to Pimco's brokers.

By the time the buying spree ended, Pimco had amassed some $2 billion in notional exposure. That was about the same as its entire assets under management at the time, an incredibly high-risk gamble—or, it would have been if it weren't such a slam dunk of a trade.

By then, interest rates were falling. Meiling remembers, "We said, 'Okay, the music's stopping; everybody find a chair.'" Pimco told the Street it would like to exercise its right for delivery now, please. So suddenly everyone took a closer look at the contracts. "Most didn't seem to know [about the options], but word quickly spread, and the price of the CDR skyrocketed," Gross says.

To settle the trade, Meiling and Fisher flew on that summer day to Chicago, where derivatives come from and where, in this case, they could die, too.

Practically speaking, it was Fisher's attention to detail that made this trade possible, her precision that gave Pimco the agility in accounting and trade settlement so it could take on complicated trades like derivatives, like the Ginnie Mae CDR, like investing gnarly pools of mortgages.

Fisher thought, out of an abundance of caution, that Pimco should use a neutral bank, one that housed none of its clients, to keep the operation clear of conflicting duties. Using her contacts—Fisher knew all the banks—she tracked down one in Chicago that could take the deliveries.

Having confirmed the deal at the Chicago Board of Trade, the firm now swung by the bank to finalize what they'd agreed to by phone: that the bank would collect the money from the individual servicers and then relay the paydowns to Pimco.

This next part doesn't exist in Fisher's memory. But Dean Meiling recalls it very clearly: The team pulled up outside another bank and spilled out, their armed guards standing at attention behind them, they greeted the bank clerk, who politely received them. They produced their credentials and paperwork to prove who they were and to dictate what they were there to collect.

The clerk checked through the documents. "Gee, we've got a big delivery on these Ginnie Maes, and we're short," the clerk muttered to another employee. "Go into the vault and find some Ginnie Maes and deliver."

They escorted Meiling and Fisher down into the vault. While they walked, Fisher went over the details of the whole process, carefully enumerating each component, emphasizing that she needed to be kept up to date on every development.

The bank clerk plunked the duffel bags down on their reinforced leather bottoms and piled a bundle of certificates into them. The bags were zipped up, stacked onto a wheelie cart, and rolled to the truck waiting outside.

Clean, efficient. They were out in half an hour, forty-five minutes, tops.

"They knew we were coming," Meiling says.

He remembers stopping at three or four financial institutions that day, spending about forty-five minutes at each. They'd show their documentation and wait, watching people wheel big dollies out with towers of certificates and then thumb through the stacks, counting them, before plonking them into the duffel bags.

"We got lots of lower-coupon Ginnie Maes delivered to us, which were just like gold," Meiling recalls. "They might have been worth twenty percent more than a high-coupon Ginnie Mae. Just made all sorts of money for the clients." He wasn't very afraid or nervous about the trade working. "Maybe I was naive, but I knew the papers we had, they weren't negotiable bonds," he says. And despite the security, he didn't get the sense they would be robbed of bags of confusing mortgage documents. Those documents were gold to Pimco, but inscrutable to everyday people.

The cumbersome, complicated trade was in hand, and now Fisher closely tracked the incoming payments, to make sure each dollar got routed correctly. She kept stacks of the trade's computer runs, two feet high, around the entire outside perimeter of her glass-walled office, she says, "so I could double-check and make sure that every account got exactly what they were due."

Pimco held the certificates for months. Every month, each contract earned $635.

Only Gross remembers this part: he says that finishing up the trade required a bit of discretion. "We eventually met with Salomon Brothers," Gross says, "at an LA airport guest room—to negotiate an exit for us and for them—at a great price, without having to face [regulators] about a 'squeeze.'" (Pimco disputes that this happened.)

Pimco's big trade ruined the product. Ginnie Mae CDRs had been a huge hit right off the bat, surging past 2.3 million contracts traded annually by 1980. But by 1985, as the market for similar products bloomed, that number had dropped to under ninety thousand contracts; and to below ten thousand contracts in 1987—effectively dead.

"People realized" the contracts "had serious flaws," Meiling says.

Pimco hadn't set out to "corner" the market, as Meiling remembers it, or at least its employees didn't talk about it in those terms. It meant only to exploit the product's flaws. "Cornering the market" wasn't the goal; it just happened to be the means to executing the trade.

"Maybe if you were somebody like the Hunt brothers, when they were trying to corner the silver market, or some of these people who've tried to corner other markets, [you] might have been able to imagine something like this," Meiling says. "But we were dealing in markets where nickels and dimes made all the sense to us. And I think other people who try to corner markets are looking for a moonshot kind of strategy. Well, we weren't thinking along those lines. We were going to be quite happy to make some money for our clients."

In the end, the trade generated an estimated $70 million for clients. While that wouldn't move the needle for Pimco today, at the time, that figure was huge. It remains probably the biggest trade by relative value in Pimco's history. For the brave clients who participated, the trade added some two hundred basis points to that year's performance.

Perhaps even more valuable was the precedent: Pimco had now paved the way for its own strong embrace of derivatives. "It was really important, because it was the vehicle through which we were able to enlist our clients into futures, because we had a very compelling story to tell them about a special trade," one partner says. "It was a very tough sell, because it required pension plans to legally re-rewrite their pension documents, and that required legal help," which Pimco got from the attorney at Pacific Mutual. Introducing these new, sophisticated derivatives into pension plans had worked out beautifully for this once-in-a-lifetime stunt.

Much of Pimco's early-day outperformance was largely a function of getting into the details of derivatives before anybody else, this partner says, and the firm could do that because the Ginnie Mae contract had been so compelling that it was able to get approvals and documentation to enable trading of futures contracts. Future futures would reap less per contract than the Ginnie Mae CDRs did, but few trades ever were that great, and these structurally clever trades were budding constantly across the market, providing an ongoing source of extra profit. And futures would underwrite Pimco's future. Driven by Gross and Dialynas, Pimco was very often first to a new contract, and its willingness to get into the tiny technicalities of each new contract would generate profits for decades.

The Ginnie Mae trade also changed Pimco's reputation around Wall Street. It had been building a good track record, but now it was a scary-smart investor. Now it was shrewd, notorious. One Chicago trader had been "carried out," lost all his money, they said, and then his wife left him, too. The trade demonstrated, to people who had never heard of the firm, that Pimco "could pull it off," Meiling says, that "we really did have an insight that other people weren't capable of."

It demonstrated Pimco's mortgage expertise, something few others had then: the market wasn't well understood, and it would remain that way for years. Pimco had a fortuitous inheritance from its parent, Pacific Life: Because it sprouted from that insurance company, it already had accrual accounting methods, which translated perfectly to buying mortgage securities. "It was an incredible benefit, because we could track the income stream and principal stream," Muzzy says.

Back then, Muzzy remembers, other asset managers mostly relied on the banks to tally the interest and principal payments, but the banks often did it wrong. "So, we'd buy mortgages in the client portfolio, and the banks weren't giving clients the interest and, primarily, the principal when it got paid down . . . so we'd go back to the banks and claim the principal payment—and require them to pay interest on that. So, we were able to get a lot of structural value from an administrative standpoint as well as from an investment standpoint."

That, again, was Pat Fisher. The efficient systems that could handle complex accounting, the perfect trade execution—her operations facilitated the differentiated trading that made the stellar track records.

She used a bank-ranking system she'd invented, a scale from one to five to track which performed best on different metrics—accuracy, responsiveness to Pimco's at-times absurdly demanding requests, and so on—which of course meant that when the banks learned of her rating system, they jockeyed to be the best. It was Fisher's practical solution to an ongoing structural problem: you're only as strong as your weakest link, she felt, and if you piss off the mail girl because you look down on her, you're going to get your mail last. So, Fisher had started telling the banks about her rating system, and they all wanted to be on the top, and suddenly the service Pimco got improved tremendously, on accuracy and timeliness and willingness to be helpful. Her rankings helped keep the banks in line and competitive, despite the abuse they took from elsewhere in Pimco.

This precise administrative work paved the way for an enduring and rewarding overweight to mortgages: Pimco simply bought more mortgages than its peers, which was a big reason it beat those peers. Pimco was proficient in trading mortgages, which enabled it to start big: by 1984, the firm owned a huge proportion of the mortgage bond market. Because the securities were so poorly understood, it took decades for others to get comfortable, which meant decades of an easy premium for Pimco.

Which is how it spotted trouble before the financial crisis. Pimco had helped to build and fuel the machines that propagated the mortgage-backed world and its derivatives, provided much of the demand for the products over decades. So, it was uniquely attuned to malformations. Pimco started the party, but famously, and to its great profit, it was first to leave.

Pimco's advantages were structural, too: Technically, anyone could spot flawed assumptions and sniff out potential profit, and indeed, some others did. But normal banks and investment companies were often more constrained by mandates and rules, or took those constraints more literally. And they weren't always interested in dancing on the edge of a futures contract knife.

Pimco was. It was more than happy to corner a market and would absolutely stop when any authority told it to stop. It was happy to approach the end of that thin border between acceptable and illegal if it served the mission of making more money for clients.

Gross knew what was good for the client—outperformance—and he would do what it took to get that, as one former partner says. If regulations were perfect, the former partner muses, everything that was good for the client would also be legal. But that wasn't the case. Gross would seem frustrated by any arbitrary rule that limited his ability to perform his magic, so where he could, he would push. The rules he pushed against were often poorly constructed or ill-defined. But that also meant Pimco's compliance people had to buckle up for unpleasant calls to the trading room. Should an investment manager *not* surreptitiously corner a market, exploit a contract so much that it broke? Maybe to some it was in poor taste, but clients were richer for it.

To many within Pimco, especially the old guard, this was Pimco's value proposition: it pushed clients a little outside their comfort zone, where there were more profits. Yet it rarely got into trouble with regulators—it had a multi-decade run with no pink slips from the teacher, no "Wells Notices" from the SEC, declaring impending action. In part, that's due to discreet phone calls, some former employees say: someone would get a call, and afterward, some risky-feeling, gray-area trade would relax, evaporate, retreat back to the bright lines.

When Pimco's brand-new must-succeed mom-and-pop Bond ETF was rolling out in 2012, and Bill Gross was going to have his derivative-trading hand tied behind his back, he was in the market for good ideas. If their usual magic tricks were muted, they would find other loopholes, other ways—securities in the market with embedded leverage, or language in the documents that didn't explicitly rule out something.

The structured products guy had a suggestion: "We can find you several odd lot positions in the coming days that trade well below round lot levels," he wrote.

This meant exploiting a fluke in the bond world's pricing systems. Big institutional investors like to buy bonds in large chunks, of at least $1 million. But as mortgages get paid down over time, the structures they populate shrink accordingly, so little pieces float around the market, unloved and largely forgotten: "odd lots" were oddly shaped, not nice "round lots," that is, standard-size chunks that trade easily. Most investors think these little fragments are more trouble than they're worth, so they trade at a discount.

Pimco saw a game it could play. It had to report the value of the portfolio to customers and the market every day. Unlike stocks, which trade on the stock exchange and have an official closing price each day, many bonds, particularly mortgage-backed securities, trade infrequently and don't have an easily available market price. So, asset managers rely on outside pricing services to estimate the value of each bond each day, using a mixture of things like old trading prices, hypothetical prices at which banks say they'd transact, and comparisons to similar bonds. The prices generated by these services are what firms like Pimco report to their customers.

But pricing services generally account only for round lots. This meant that a clever bond expert could buy a bunch of "odd lots" for cheap, slot them into the pricing system, and watch as they were rounded up to the full-size lot price. Instant profit. It wasn't illegal, though it was maybe not something to advertise. It happened when managers brought in a new haul of bonds and divvied them up between the many accounts; funds can't hold too high a concentration of one thing, so, for little funds, odd lots can just happen.

This pricing fluke "will help with performance out of the gate," wrote the structured products guy.

On March 2, Gross sent a handwritten note to the trading desks with instructions in his characteristically stilted cadence, a bond market Emily Dickinson. "Today—ASAP—within the next 2 hours—find 1–2 million bonds in your area that are 2 points or more cheap to how they would be marked by pricing services at close tonight."

The desks did as they were told.

On March 9, Pimco bought an odd lot at $64.9999 and plopped it into the system, where it was valued at $82.7459. A tidy instant gain of 27 percent, for zero work. The ETF's "net asset value" (the cumulative value of everything it held) jumped by almost $0.02 per share in one day, thanks to that trade alone. And that was one odd lot, among many.

This price jump caught the attention of Pimco's internal pricing group, which ran around policing trades, making sure things weren't out of whack enough to cause snarls with trading partners or, God forbid, regulators. The group got automatic notifications whenever the difference between a purchase price and the pricing vendor's mark was too great, and each time, they had to ask the relevant trader if he wanted to "challenge" the vendor's mark, if he had evidence as to why he was right and the vendor was wrong. If the trader didn't reply, the vendor's mark was automatically challenged.

The $17.75 difference got flagged immediately. On March 12, an employee from the pricing group emailed the mortgage-backed securities trader, noting that the trades "potentially" impacted the net asset value of the ETF. "No need to challenge," the trader replied, noting that a bigger chunk of the same bond issue "is likely to trade at low 80s," where this smaller chunk was now generously marked.

Gross sent another handwritten note on March 23, asking the mortgage-backed securities traders to look for more nonagency MBS, "cheap odd lots preferred."

He offered an incentive: He gave traders "gold stars" to reward good behavior, good ideas; each star translated to a one-thousand-dollar cash reward (and conversely they'd get Communication Demerits for poor communication). At this moment, any trader who dug up significantly discounted odd lots for the Bond ETF would get a gold star.

After one month, it was working: the Bond ETF was outperforming even its supposed twin. In March, the Total Return ETF gained 1.6 percent, while the Total Return mutual fund eked out 0.04 percent. The benchmark Barclays Capital Aggregate Bond Index lost 0.6 percent.

They kept up the strategy: in the ETF's first four months, Pimco bought $37 million worth of odd lots, more than 150 bundles in total. This would be a drop in the bucket for the Total Return Fund, or for Pimco as a whole, but in the still-small ETF, it made all the difference.

By the end of June, the divergence was gaping: the Bond ETF had generated 6.3 percent since its birth, while the Total Return mutual fund it was supposed to track had managed to generate just 2.8 percent.

Internally, there was no problem. The compliance department, which polices trades to ensure legality, was aware that much of Bond's outperformance was thanks to the odd-lot trick and noted that the pricing group had signed off on it. Externally, no one knew about the pricing fluke or Pimco's exploitation of it, which meant that the growing gap with the mutual fund was becoming awkward, difficult to explain to clients and the press. Maybe they had overdone it; people were starting to ask questions. The *Journal*'s Kirsten Grind wrote that Gross had "pulled off an unusual feat: He beat his own performance."

The product management team conjured up a way to talk about it. In early April, the group sent around "internal only" updates for the sales force that had to explain to clients this strange and growing performance discrepancy.

"The Total Return ETF has benefited from the overweight to mortgages that were executed at particularly favorable levels. Well-publicized inefficiencies in the non-agency market offer opportunities for an active manager to add value."

True, sort of! The "value" they were "adding" looked suspiciously like buying bonds at one price and then reporting them at a higher price. (Years later, Pimco was in fact able to sell many of those odd lots near the reported values.) But now there was an answer to any question, and that was all that was necessary.

The *Journal* article quoted experts chalking up the ETF's uncomfortable outperformance to its agility due to its small size relative to the cumbersome mutual fund. The ETF has "certainly exceeded our expectations," Gross told Grind, using his trademark performed modesty for some trademark hype.

Pimco's ETF strategist told the *Financial Times* that feedback had been "very good": "People have been pleased with the performance, pleased with the liquidity and trading volume. Our general sense is that we are reaching people where we haven't been able to reach before."

To Pimco, that was what mattered: Performance and scale. *Grow or die.*

9

Grow or Die

Being ginormous had its perks.

For years now, the bond market had been where everybody wanted to be. Money that flooded into the asset class, seeking safety after the terror of the stock market's 2008–2009 drops, had created a strong tidal effect: every bond had gone up in price. At first it felt improbable, like a fluke, but by 2013, it was in full swing: Investors elbowed one another aside to snap up new debt when companies came to market, which meant those companies had to pay less and less for their new money. Yields on corporate bonds were lower than anyone had ever seen, even before the crisis. Every new deal was a food fight. Newly issued bonds popped in price in "gray market" trading before they were formally issued.

The new postcrisis regulations rendered the banks much less able to hold on to bonds to trade for profit, as they often whined. The "sell side" simply had to sell. This shifted the balance of power to the buy side: the cool, big-kids-only hedge funds that could slither into any market and the "eight-hundred-pound gorilla" asset managers: Black-Rock, T. Rowe Price, Wellington. And Pimco.

The downside to regulations hobbling the banks was that trading overall had slowed substantially. Suddenly everyone fretted about "bond market liquidity": When the markets started dropping, who would buy if the banks wouldn't do it anymore? Who would "catch a falling knife"? This narrative was driven largely by the banks, complaining so regulators would unchain them. But friendly buy-siders and journalists, as conduits, helped propagate it.

This had an effect for Pimco, too: Once it grew to a certain level of assets under management, wouldn't it be unwieldy? Had Pimco's growth outpaced that of the growth in active bond trading? With so much money rushing in the door, insisting on buying something, wouldn't the manager, at some point, have to buy whatever he could find, almost irrespective of what a good investment it might be? What if the market turned, the now-four-decade bond rally ended, and bond prices actually fell? What would happen to the behemoth that held all those bonds?

By the end of 2012, Pimco's assets under management had almost reached $2 trillion. Clients, competitors, the press all chattered: was Pimco too big to function? Gross had gotten the question for years. In *Risk* magazine in 2003; *Fortune* in 2009; *The Wall Street Journal*, 2010. Clients had asked, too—he could remember hearing this concern as far back as the 1980s.

He always insisted that Pimco could keep performing thanks to its "structural" approach: its three- to five-year view; its machine of small-but-effective trades; its carefully but consistently taking more risk than everybody else, pressing every dollar for an extra penny, pressing every dealer for an extra basis point, converting minutes into money.

"Like the casino's edge at the craps or blackjack table, it is what gives us the odds at winning," Gross said in one speech in 2003 addressing this question. In that speech, he veered into a tangent: every successful firm had to watch for "susceptibility to the disease of size and success," ego inflation and too much money. To gauge "hegemonic decay at Pimco," he said, watch for deviation from prioritizing clients, any "impulse to conserve and protect instead of grow—or conversely an obsessive concern for—the bottom line."

"It will not be size itself that brings down this firm," Gross said. "It will be the accoutrements and trappings of size. It will be the assumed privileges of the rank and station of belonging to one of the best and most successful money management firms this country has ever known. Pimco is less likely to explode externally from the ingestion of too many assets than it is to implode internally from a self-induced ulcer."

Pimco had been at over $300 billion then, in 2003. Even after growing sixfold in a decade, it still wasn't the biggest: BlackRock had shot past $4 trillion, much of that expansion fueled by low-fee ETFs. Measured against its competitors—which is, to some, the only measure— Pimco had plenty of room to grow. Ideally, more profitably.

But it was in the same camp as BlackRock: able to strong-arm the bond market, more powerful when aligned. Where banks had once ruled, BlackRock and Pimco's representatives in the group that governed derivatives and swaps functionally set the terms in that world.

They could no longer sidestep the question of how big was too big, with its vast and expensive potential repercussions. Regulators and politicians were still talking about who might be "too big to fail": which firms were so important that, if they took too much risk and threatened the system (again), they'd have to be bailed out (again). The Financial Stability Oversight Council (FSOC), created in the 2010 Dodd-Frank Wall Street Reform and Consumer Protection Act, sought out these liabilities and had updated their canvass of inquiry from banks to add a broader category, "systemically important financial institutions," or SIFIs.

Banks with more than $50 billion in assets were automatically considered SIFIs. In July 2013, FSOC voted that AIG was, too, and also GE Capital. The threat that it would add more names hung in D.C.'s swampy summer air. The FSOC started with insurers and moved down the list. A Treasury Department research paper gestured at adding asset managers.

This would be a disaster, according to Blackrock and Pimco. To be labeled "systemically important" was to be ensnared in a horrible tangle of regulations, just as the banks had been, which would mean hiring expensive lawyers and constricting profitable activities. It might mean limits on risk taking; it might derail Pimco's carefully constructed "structural alpha" machines in their pursuit of scraping profits from the underbelly of financial markets.

Pimco sent lobbyists to Washington to meet with the Federal Reserve Board alongside the asset management industry's trade group. They argued that Pimco and BlackRock didn't *own* the assets; they *invested* them on behalf of clients. They would never need a bailout because asset prices would just go up or down, and that was how capital markets worked. It was fine. Plus, they pointed out, many of their clients were just people, individuals. How could simple pools of small people's money be dangerous?

The SIFI threat was intensifying at just the wrong time.

Firmwide profit growth had surged in the years after the crisis, as the flood of new client money poured into Pimco's traditional products, its fixed-income mutual funds. While Pimco had high hopes for its new ETF, it would never be great for margin expansion. And what wasn't great for-profit growth was correspondingly bad for individual compensation.

Compensation was Pimco's devil's bargain. It was also largely how the firm expressed affection. Why else would anyone tolerate such a scorching office climate? Why else would anyone relocate families from New York to the barren strip-mall desert of Orange County for a job everyone knew was miserable? Never seeing your family again, watching as their interests withered to surfing or real estate or plastic surgery or barre class, to combat the moneyed boredom. The pitch-black early mornings, the politicking, the disrespect, the never-ending emails from Gross and El-Erian and on down the line. The extreme unpleasantness was the cost of fatter paychecks than almost anywhere else, at least at the top—and beneath: the hope of those future paychecks.

The hitch: much of that compensation was predicated on profit growth.

Pimco employees got a base salary and a bonus based on performance, as usual in finance. On top of that, the partners got a cut of a pooled portion of the firm's annual profits—about 30 percent. Of that, Gross received a fixed proportion, which had been 26 percent, but he volunteered to lower that figure in the 2000s as the numbers got increasingly unseemly, and now he took home just 20 percent. Though that was a substantial slice, internally there was little friction over it. Gross had invented the company, invented the strategies, invented the market. He was the last of the founders and the face of the company; he determined strategy, determined everything. If anyone thought about it, 20 percent was pretty reasonable.

All employees deemed "key" enough (senior vice presidents, executive vice presidents, partners) also got "shadow equity," small slivers of ownership in the company. Originally, this was "B units," or B shares from the profit-sharing agreement in the original Allianz deal. This had yielded a flood of personal wealth for holders: *B is for Billionaire.*

But anyone who joined after the Allianz deal missed out on the fat B shares. Pimco management told Allianz it needed incentives for the younger generation. The line Gross remembers using was "Hey, maybe we've gotta stick around with the B shares, but all these other people, they're the future of the company—you've got to equitize them with M shares and L-TIPs," or otherwise, "the company is just going to walk across the street, and nothin' we can do about it."

"Wasn't gonna happen, but they bought it," he says, laughing. "They never could figure it out, that everybody was so rich over here that nobody woulda left anyway."

The negotiations resulted in "M units" or "M shares" for newer employees. (The *M* wasn't explicitly for *Millionaire*, but it worked.) These shares were nonvoting shares of Pimco, like the B shares, but even more keyed to profit growth. A good deal, as long as growth reigned.

Except, things were changing. Client money was still flowing in, but the pace had slowed. Two thousand eleven had hurt, and the new ETF product was never built to be a profit center. Now would be a particularly perilous time for new regulations and fancy lawyers—useless bureaucrats, as Gross might say, from behind a desk on which sat a mug that read, YOU CAN ALWAYS TELL A GERMAN—BUT YOU CAN'T

TELL HIM MUCH (a gift from the Germans at Allianz, as a joke). As long as Pimco was translating the firm's success into individual success, Gross figured the next generation would stick with him.

Back in 2003, a few months after Gross warned about "the disease of size and success," he'd taken everyone on a cruise to Alaska, an extravagant twelve-day affair for basically the whole firm, over a thousand employees. Pimco executives estimated it cost $10 million or more, which Gross paid himself. The cruise featured extensive and stressful poker games on deck, allowances for on-shore activities, and shows including a popular stand-up comedian and a ventriloquist. Gross said it was the kind of thing he liked to do only every ten years or so. Manageable, contained fun. But here, ten years later, with the company incomparably bigger and under incomparably more pressure, no such celebration was scheduled.

That change, that cadence wasn't easy to intuit, not least because it was governed by Gross's mood. It could be hard to get the rhythm of Pimco's culture.

Especially for someone like Neel Kashkari. He came from investment banking, which is driven by personal relationships, and then D.C., which, obviously. He was formal, respectful, well dressed, good-looking. He was unflappable, as evidenced in a heated cross-examination before Congress when he led TARP. His shaved bald head was shiny, those bugged-out eyes still shooting lasers of intensity.

All this was pitch-perfect Pimco—the intimidation, the polish, the intensity. But somehow everything that had served him at Goldman and then Treasury had ceased to work once he got to Newport Beach. He stood out in myriad small, daily wrinkles. For starters, he was of South Asian descent. When he started in December 2009, Pimco's leader, El-Erian, was also not white, and there were folks of East and South Asian descent visible at senior levels. Still, Kashkari was one of only a smattering of people of color throughout the firm.

He was also kind of famous. This had helped him negotiate his way into partner status—the first non-CEO to achieve that status without rising through the ranks, *Pensions and Investments* reported. But fame externally didn't translate to respect internally.

Most problematic was Kashkari's warmth, his diplomacy. He was polite to the point of kindness. He made eye contact with Bill Gross, daily. He spoke to the assistants, even. For one former Pimco executive, a single moment captured it: When walking up to the building, a more junior person always held the door for more senior people, to allow them to walk frictionless and first into the capacious lobby. The senior people took this as expected, a function of the natural order; usually they'd pass without a nod or other acknowledgment.

Not Kashkari. One day, this lower-ranking executive recalls seeing Kashkari approach the building behind him, and the man of lower rank held the door as expected. Kashkari sped up and, upon walking in, turned his head and made eye contact.

He said, "Thanks."

The executive froze in shock. *This guy will never make it here*, he thought.

There were other ominous clouds at the outset. Like the ambiguity of Kashkari's assignment—basically, "build stuff." Pimco wanted Kashkari to find new engines to power it forward. Stocks were the one that had caught Gross's imagination and, thus, had become the most pressing. But Kashkari was supposed to find *more* than one. The low, lousy returns predicted in a new normal framework meant managers should diversify, scraping wherever possible. What else had he built?

Then there was the matter of his never having done any of this before. Never having bought or sold a stock. That wasn't supposed to have been a problem: "I'm not a stockpicker," he told *Bloomberg Businessweek*. "I hired the stockpickers."

But those stockpickers, in turn, were not doing great. They'd launched six mutual funds that, in 2012, lagged their benchmarks. Kashkari said that was no problem: the funds were built for downside protection, to limit losses when the market plummeted, so gaining less when the market was climbing was considered functioning properly. Still, by the start of 2013, those six funds had gathered only $1.3 billion, less than 0.1 percent of Pimco's total assets.

This wasn't totally on Kashkari: that Pimco had gotten any new client money in 2012 was a feat, given that investors were moving away from such actively managed stock funds. But the outlook wasn't good; the funds were reaching their three-year mark, and with subpar performance, they were likely to get a low rank from Morningstar, one star instead of the four or five needed to attract client money. A strong start determines everything. The game was already over.

Compounding matters, Gross felt compelled to say in his August 2012 *Investment Outlook* that "the cult of equity is dying," that investors wouldn't get the returns of yore, that the inflation-adjusted 6.6 percent average annual gain over the past one hundred years was a "historical freak." Not new for Gross, but this turn back to pessimism fit the doomed cycle of Pimco and equity.

This was Pimco's third try at stocks—once in the 1980s, which ended in the few stockpickers getting overwhelmed by the bond traders in strategy meetings, enough that they quit after two years; again in the late 1990s, when Pimco's then-parent company launched a separate equity unit, "Pimco Equity Advisors," into the dot-com bubble and then the dot-com crash. That exercise in stocks had ended in legal disaster: Pimco got swept up in the "mutual fund market timing" scandal, a hobby horse of Eliot Spitzer, then the New York State attorney general, which snowballed into SEC accusations that several fund companies had allowed clients to hop in and out as they liked, multiple times a month, a week, a day, to exploit market inefficiencies. In the end, Pimco Equity Advisors was dissolved, and it paid fines and repayments to settle suits against it, without admitting or denying wrongdoing, and the two Pimco Equity Advisors executives most involved were banned from the industry.

That whole thing had sat poorly with Gross. He'd worked for decades to build this respected, client-first brand, and these reckless jokers in New York had threatened to destroy it. He wrote a public letter, signed by him and Thompson, vehemently drawing a line between Pimco and Pimco Equity Advisors. "Is Pimco—the bond manager—really down there at the bottom of the barrel?" he wrote. "We shout an emphatic 'NO!'"

This was the messy legacy Kashkari had inherited.

Gross's latest comments ignited a firestorm externally; and internally, they proved awkward. "We believe returns across asset classes, including both stocks and bonds, will be lower in the future than we've been used to," Kashkari said in response to the kerfuffle, delicately forecasting equity returns "in the 3.5 percent range" rather than the historic 6.6 percent. How could anyone win in that environment?

"No one should be surprised that Pimco equity funds are a step-child," Josh Brown, a Pimco investor as the vice president of investment for Fusion Analytics Investment Partners, told Bloomberg. "What they have against them," he said, is "dislike for equities and the fact that it's a bond shop in everyone's mind."

Add this to the residue of El-Erian and Weil's war, their explosive meeting in 2009 that had cemented itself in institutional memory: *Find me equity managers, or I'll find someone who will.* Kashkari was never set up to succeed.

Anyway, he had bigger plans. He went down to Texas and met with his former boss, former president George W. Bush. He asked Bush if he should run for governor of California. Bush didn't say no.

On January 23, 2013, Kashkari wrote to colleagues and the press that, after three "terrific" years, he would leave "to explore returning to public service": "Leaving is not an easy decision because our equity business is off to a great start and we've assembled a wonderful team. Nonetheless, my passion lies in public service."

So, Kashkari would go from building an equities business in a bond shop to exploring running for public office as a Republican in a place where every statewide office was occupied by a Democrat. He wasn't one to shy from a challenge.

To replace Kashkari, at least for now, Pimco named Marc Seidner, a former fixed-income portfolio manager at Harvard's endowment. A

Mohamed person. The change was not met with much protestation within Pimco. Kashkari had been in over his head, the chatter went. Some snickered that governor of California seemed like a better fit.

Kashkari's departure was hardly a bellwether for company retention, but it was noteworthy in one way: it represented a public step away from Pimco's once-cozy relationship with Washington. Just a few years earlier, Pimco had touted these relationships to clients: presentations cited as advisors or employees Kashkari, Alan Greenspan, and Joshua Bolten, White House chief of staff for George W. Bush during the crisis. Rich Clarida, the top Treasury economist in 2002 and 2003, was then a global strategic advisor at Pimco in New York. Rumors crested periodically that Paul McCulley (now an alum, having decamped to an economic think tank) was about to be tapped for a Fed seat.

It was a robust list of connections, which had at first telegraphed that Pimco was optimally positioned to navigate the postcrisis regulation-heavy world—that, of anyone, it had the right babysitters. Plus, there were its myriad federal partnerships, advising and executing crisis-related programs, the expanding businesses of Pimco Advisory predicated on helping the United States and other governments. All this proximity to Washington was something to be advertised . . . until maybe it wasn't anymore.

Media skepticism existed at a simmer for a while, as in 2010, when *The New York Times* highlighted "the all-too-close relationships between our largest financial institutions and the people who acted as their regulators," quoting Joshua Rosner, of research consultancy firm Graham, Fisher. "The 'too big to fail' concept is not just about assets. It's also about relationships."

Three years later, those words seemed like a warning. Not only was Pimco's relationship with its regulators not quite as close, but it was becoming adversarial, even dangerous. Profitability was on the line.

There was new hope. Dan Ivascyn, who in 2005 had toured homes to sniff out the rot in the mortgage market, had been quietly toiling away in the asset-backed market, building profitable products, striking gold but not making a fuss about it. It was good to have good performance, even the best performance, but it was also good not to draw too much attention to yourself.

He and Pimco had started a series of funds to capitalize on the holes left by the financial crisis. In 2010, he'd started the Bank Recapitalization and Value Opportunities fund, fondly called BRaVO. Regulation-bound banks had needed to raise money, more than $550 billion, to shore up their balance sheets in the United States and Europe. BRaVO would buy up distressed assets from banks that could no longer hold them. Prices had plummeted in the crisis, and Pimco would scoop them up from forced sellers (the best kind) at a steep discount.

Ivascyn and the team raised $2.4 billion for BRaVO, with maximum flexibility—it could buy commercial, residential, consumer, and financial assets, nearly a go-anywhere mandate. The fund wasn't as predicated on trading as some of Pimco's earlier funds had been; this was buying long-term stakes in things, investing in shopping malls in Spain, owning the assets, collecting the cash flow. No trying to surf the intraday waves of mark-to-market risk.

Ivascyn had been quiet, private about the beginnings of BRaVO and the other similarly structured private equity–style funds, but his profile was on the rise. He was rarely interviewed, rarely cited before 2012, but all of a sudden, people began to take notice.

In part this was a function of money flowing into the public mutual fund he managed, the Pimco Income Fund. He and his co-manager, Alfred Murata, were trouncing their peers, topping all the relevant metrics, attracting attention from consultants, investors, and the media.

The fund started in March 2007, as the cracks in the financial system became canyons. It was not auspicious timing, but it survived.

Then, in the depths of the crisis, Ivascyn got the cue correct: buy risk. As home prices stopped dropping and started to stabilize, he amassed a huge bet, buying up mortgages not backed by the government agencies—the stuff that was *really* obliterated in the crisis.

Indiscriminate selling means bargain-basement prices, so Pimco Income snapped up bonds from panicked sellers. The timing was perfect. Prices for those mortgages climbed 32 percent in 2009 and 21 percent in 2010, according to estimates from a competitor. Home prices across the United States started to climb again in 2012, surging 28 percent that year and 10 percent the next. Improving prices were helping to calm the frequency of defaults. Fewer defaults mean more cash for investors.

This helped spur Ivascyn's fund to returns of 19 percent in 2009, 20 percent in 2010, and 6 percent in 2011. "We didn't die on the way in, and we made a ton of money on the way out," said Scott Simon. "And a large part was due to Dan."

By 2012, Ivascyn's area of specialty was in a good spot: mortgage-backed securities were recovering. If you had the time, patience, and reading comprehension to dig into the often staggeringly boring documents, you could separate the good assets from the bad. By mid-2012, almost a quarter of Pimco Income comprised agency mortgage-backed securities, another 19 percent in nonagency.

A spate of news articles heralded Ivascyn's great performance in 2012, in *Barron's* and Bloomberg. GROSS DETHRONED AS PIMCO BOND KING, yelled the Bloomberg article. "Bill Gross is the biggest and best-known bond picker at Pacific Investment Management Co. He isn't the top performer."

Ivascyn was careful in the accompanying interview. His returns shouldn't be matched against Gross's, he said, because the funds had different mandates, different goals. The Income fund was supposed to give investors a stream of income, while Gross was focused on providing Total Return, price appreciation on *top* of income.

Externally, consultants extolled how great Ivascyn was. He was young, promising—he still had a head of wavy brown hair, which indicated healthy years of future profit—and he demonstrated none of Gross's more extreme quirks that, had Gross not been a proven entity, might have set off alarms in risk management. Internally, the response was even better: Ivascyn's compatriots and subordinates in that squat white office building were excited about his work, for the only reason anyone cares about anything: it was getting them paid.

Yet Ivascyn's caution was warranted: it was common knowledge that Gross didn't like to see other stars rising, particularly not anyone he had not hand-selected. A glowing interview in the press was the fastest way into his bad graces.

Ivascyn kept his head down in Pimco's halls, did his work and stayed out of Gross's way. But he wasn't exactly stealthy. His first boss, Scott Simon, had always made a lot of noise on the trade floor and, occasionally, got excommunicated to Siberia, his seat moved as far from Gross as the trade floor would allow. ("He'd be stationed right next to my desk, just to the left, in the mortgage area, but he's a very social guy, talks talks talks, hooooo! He has a deep, masculine voice, and even when I'd go, 'Scott, keep it down,' it would go on all afternoon.") Gross would message others sitting nearby, so *they* could tell Simon to pipe down. But despite his noise, Simon knew his performance gave him an impenetrable force field. "You couldn't deny Simon his ability to outperform the market, so I always respected that," Gross says. "I would never suggest he leave, I just suggested he shut up."

Under the safety of Simon's umbrella, Ivascyn made noise, too. He talked and he laughed, loudly. He was one of the few high up at Pimco who were ostensibly "normal" or "fun." He wore cargo shorts on the weekends, and flip-flops. After Taco Bell introduced its Doritos Locos Taco, Ivascyn ordered a batch for the mortgage desk. He used to gather some friends from the mortgage desk to blow off steam at one of his extra houses, which some started to call "the Playpen." But he was also serious about the job—one day, he left work early, which was unusual. He'd left to get married. He'd planned to come back a few hours later, but Simon told him to take the rest of the day off.

In early 2013, Scott Simon announced he was retiring, to focus on "my life and my wife"—to travel, fly planes, do philanthropy, and otherwise delight in being rich. He was too mentally healthy to stay confined within Pimco when the best of the world beckoned.

With that, the mortgage kingdom was Ivascyn's.

As the outside world adjusted to Pimco and its peers throwing off the old power balance, inside Pimco, things were feeling a little upside down, too. The home truths that had held the place together felt increasingly threadbare: that aligning with the government was an unquestionable good; that Pimco was an infallible risk-taker too smart to play in the stock market. Even the firm's central hierarchy, from which everything else flowed—with Gross as the core, Gross as king—was starting to feel a little wobbly.

10

Ratfucked

Back in 2000, Jason Williams hadn't seemed like he was going to be a problem. A lowly trade assistant in the high-yield group, Williams started out normal, if a little rough around the edges. He was funny, salty; he liked beer and football. But over the years, Williams's sales counterparties on Wall Street watched as the Pimco atmosphere soured him, corroded something in him. He became surly, mean—past Pimco's usual style. Outside of work he still seemed fine, affable, a good time. But on the field, he was utterly horrible.

It wasn't strictly unusual for people to rot inside Pimco—Frank Rabinovitch, the Stanford-math-nerd-turned-trader who wrote much of Pimco's early coding after hours, had turned into something unrecognizable in the 1990s, overwhelmed by the constant bullying on the trade floor. He recommitted his life to Jesus in 1995 and founded the Blue Letter Bible—the Bible, but online and searchable. He started shortening his hours at Pimco to work on it, and eventually just retired. He recouped some of his lost self; he was much happier.

The high-yield group, in particular, always seemed to be in chaos. Ben Trosky had fought to create the product in the 1990s, convincing clients to buy corporate bonds rated below investment grade. These were a little tarnished after the market's inventor and "Junk Bond King," Mike Milken, got in trouble for fraud, but it was a growing market where real research could lead to higher profits. Trosky was tall and imposing and plainspoken; he often didn't wear shoes, only socks, but he was a good trader who could match Gross's intensity. All the desks had their own personalities—the hair-trigger nerves of the cash-trading desk, the circus freaks Scott Simon hired to analyze mortgages—but ever since Trosky left, in 2002, the credit team had always seemed on the brink.

To ease the transition, Pimco tried out Andrea Feingold and Ian O'Keeffe. They started with a great résumé, and seemed smart, promising.

They were there for less than a year. (Immediately after leaving Pimco, they cofounded their own credit shop, which they sold almost fifteen years later at $2.3 billion under management.) After that, Pimco elevated Trosky's loyal subordinate, Ray Kennedy.

Trosky had protected the people under him from Gross's glare, standing up to the latter's more unreasonable requests where possible. He called Gross "Smiley" because he wasn't, but their relationship was respectful in its own way, manageable. His departure was destabilizing.

Kennedy was gentler. He didn't have Trosky's wildness, or Bill Powers's specific social skills, or Scott Simon's mental escape hatch that he didn't need this shit, anyway. He was smart but didn't have the quant brilliance that would have given them protection from Gross's ire. He had no special armor; he was a regular smart guy trying to do the job, with a family who depended on him.

Without Trosky's buffer, Kennedy and the team were in for more misery than maybe they'd realized. For years after Trosky left, they took it, but it wore on them; eventually, breathing that acrid Pimco air every day became too much. After the financial crisis, he prepared to quit, along with the portfolio manager for loans, Jason Rosiak, who'd come up through the ranks from operations. They would start their own risk analytics firm. Rosiak would go first.

Rosiak, a compact, powerful guy, had tried to train himself out of smiling at Pimco—it wasn't helping him fit in—but it wasn't natural for him to be so angry all the time. One day in 2005, mustering his best stone face, he prepared to chat with a tippy-top executive. They stepped into a conference room. Rosiak explained that it was time for him to go, thanks so much, and there wasn't much Pimco could do to change his mind.

The executive made all the right noises about how valuable Rosiak was, how he should think about it for another day or so. Was it money? Could they give him more money? The executive offered to leave Rosiak in the conference room for as long as he needed with two blank pieces of paper, one to write a dream number on, and one to write the job description that would make him happy. They'd figure out a way to make it happen.

It wasn't money, Rosiak said. He was just done. They shook hands and left the conference room. Rosiak felt a wave of relief, a lightness. He had clawed his way out.

Rosiak packed his things and went home. But then he didn't hear anything from Kennedy; he heard nothing. He had started working on things, but Kennedy's silence made him uneasy. He phoned; Kennedy didn't answer, didn't call back. He waited.

Eventually, he heard through the grapevine: Kennedy wasn't leaving. Rosiak called Kennedy at work: "What the fuck?" Very quietly, Kennedy apologized. He couldn't walk away from the money. He had a family.

Rosiak mentioned the existence of his own family, which somehow had not precluded his sticking to his word.

Word raced around the desk: Rosiak had gotten ratfucked, they said. Kennedy stuck around for longer than a year, trapped in his shining golden handcuffs. When he finally left in 2007, Pimco noted that Kennedy was leaving to be a math teacher. His subordinate, Mark Hudoff, took over the high-yield fund in April 2007.

In late 2008, Kennedy joined another investment manager, Hotchkis and Wiley. In May, Hudoff left Pimco, which to Morningstar analysts did "raise eyebrows" and also the "question of why such top-notch folks haven't wanted, or been able, to stick around longer." In July, Hudoff joined Kennedy at Hotchkis and Wiley.

Gross took over the high-yield fund until they could find someone to manage it full time. By November 2009, they'd hired a guy, Andrew Jessop, from Goldman Sachs.

Jason Williams had outlasted all that turnover, all those personalities. But now, in 2012, he was sinking. And in March of that year, he was let go.

Gross always distrusted high-yield credit as an asset class, even when Trosky ran it. He loved risk, but only risk he felt confident he understood. In high yield, it always felt like he was getting ripped off. The whole junk bond market felt scammy—volumes were thinner, which meant less reliability that prices would hold still when you traded, and also meant a wider distance between where a bank would buy or sell, which incidentally translated to profits for the banks. Gross's respect for Trosky mitigated that distrust, but with soft jokers like Kennedy and Hudoff running the book, his vitriol increased. His strong conviction that he was getting ripped off meant he applied intense diligence to ensure he wouldn't be; he insisted, even more than with regular old investment-grade corporate bonds, on extracting discounts from the Street, buying bonds cheaper than anyone wanted to sell them.

Everyone wanted cheap bonds, of course, but Gross demanded maximal pressure in high yield to wring more basis points out of the Street. Executing this fell to Williams: whenever Bill Gross wanted high-yield bonds, Williams had to go out and get them, which meant Williams had to go on a suicide mission to the banks and badger them, again and again, demanding discounts he knew were unreasonable. This soured them toward him, and soured him.

Which was why, after he was fired in March 2012, he was fucked. Couldn't get a job anywhere. He interviewed at some of the worst credit shops, bottom-of-the-barrel places, and even they wouldn't hire him. He knew why. Every potential employer called Wall Street sales guys and asked, *Hey, do you know this guy? What do you think of him?* Their view of many Pimco people was poor, but Jason Williams in particular? *Fuck that guy.*

Outside the heat-retaining walls of Pimco, if the Street didn't like a trader, it meant poor allocations on new bond issuance, it meant not getting a "look" at a deliciously fat bond issue coming down the pike, it meant not getting good information. "You become a persona non grata," one former employee says. No one wanted to hire a pariah who could never get allocations.

For many employees of Pimco, this meant their power derived from being an agent of Pimco; they couldn't accumulate goodwill or even credibility. Gross's impression that people stayed for the money was perhaps willfully overoptimistic: they were also, to some extent, stuck. They could take nothing with them when, if, they left. This was reinforced by Pimco's closed-circuit culture of "constructive paranoia": Without Pimco, you were nothing. Traders were fungible, easily replaceable tools.

So, Williams's next move shouldn't have been entirely unexpected. On March 5, 2013, the deputy clerk in the Superior Court of California, County of Orange, filed Jason Williams's complaint against Pimco and twenty-five unnamed "Does," for wrongful termination in violation of public policy and violation of labor code.

It was a bombshell. Packed with details from his almost twelve years there, the allegations included insider trading, market manipulation, and breach of fiduciary duty. Williams claimed that Pimco had manipulated the price of its ETF; that a senior manager had directed him to "arbitrarily" boost a bond rating, so that a fund with ratings restrictions could buy it; that "senior management" had transferred thinly traded securities internally from the hedge fund to other Pimco funds, "to the detriment of the holders of the receiving funds"; that another manager had talked up Bank of America bonds on TV while Pimco was "simultaneously aggressively selling" Bank of America securities; that yet another—anonymous in the complaint, but speculated to be Gross—had moved a security away from one Pimco client to his own fund after the thing had jumped 10 percent.

Williams said in his complaint that he'd objected to some of the egregious behavior he witnessed and been forced to execute. In response, he said, his manager had cut his compensation. And "subjected him to verbal abuse." Which, to many finance people with at least passing Pimco familiarity, sounded at least credible.

Williams claimed that in December 2011, he reported the conduct to three agents of the U.S. Department of the Treasury's Office of the Special Inspector General for the Troubled Asset Relief Program (SIGTARP). Then he waited. He did not hear back.

He then told Pimco's human resources department what he'd told SIGTARP, and he told Pimco's counsel that he had talked to federal agents. Less than three weeks later, according to his lawsuit, he was abruptly terminated for "'performance reasons,' even though his work performance had been satisfactory." These actions against Williams were "despicable, oppressive, fraudulent, malicious, deliberate, egregious, and inexcusable," his suit read. The firm was trying to make an example of him.

When the lawsuit hit the wires, a shudder went through the Pimco trade floor. This was terrifying. Williams was alleging the most damning sins an asset manager could commit.

Pimco didn't respond to the specific charges; a spokesman said only that "as a matter of policy, we do not comment on legal matters." But, he added, Pimco always conducted an "appropriate review" anytime an employee complained or voiced a concern.

Credit markets lit up. Rumors swirled that Williams had a whole bunch more allegations that he hadn't included in his lawsuit, and evidence.

A few of the allegations were familiar and unsurprising, like the charge about talking up securities while selling them. Pimco had gotten that accusation for decades; it came with the territory of being on TV. But it had also occurred to regulators and government officials over the years. One former Treasury official recalls Bill Gross appearing on CNBC five minutes before 1 P.M. one day in the early aughts, talking about how he saw no value in U.S. Treasury inflation-protected securities, known as TIPS—and then, at 1 P.M., Pimco entered a huge bid in the TIPS auction.

The way this official saw it, Gross was intending to manipulate the market to Pimco's benefit. The official phoned some compatriots. Can someone do that? Is it OK to use your CNBC interview to try to influence an auction? But the department's lawyers didn't want to pursue it, he remembers, and he didn't push it. Pimco snapped up the very securities Bill Gross had maybe just made cheap.

Pimco's managers knew that talking on TV, done artfully and within parameters, was legal. It was simply sharing opinions—or, at least, that could be argued in court. They could also take some comfort from the fact that market manipulation and insider trading were hard to prove—at that moment, prosecutors for the Southern District of New York were trying to pin insider trading on Steve Cohen's SAC Capital, but they were having a hell of a time.

The allegations about manipulating the Total Return ETF, however, were concerning. As were the ones about internal share transfers, that 17a-7 exemption in the 1940 Act. This exemption was a legal loophole. Pimco was liberal in its practice of it and knew it 17a-7-ed far more than other asset managers. Even the lower-down guys knew it, but they generally assumed it had been cleared, that Pimco's conduct was approved, kosher. The rule was a black-and-white legal exemption, and Pimco was not one to avoid a useful profit-generating tool out of fussiness or anxiety.

The 17a-7-ing had ramped up even before the crisis. It was a strategic decision, in the memory of one former employee: a little while after El-Erian returned, Wall Street banks' record trading profits, quarter after quarter, "irritated the lights out of Gross," the former employee says.

Gross convened a special meeting for anybody involved in trading, in the big conference room. Zhu Changhong, a derivatives specialist and a favorite of Gross's, ran it. *This is unacceptable*, he told the gathered crowd, according to the recollection of the former employee. *The Street is making too much money. Which means you guys are not doing your job. You need to pound the lights out, you need to squeeze more basis points.*

The traders looked at each other. *We don't do that already?*

Gross had long expressed frustration about paying the Street a commission when he was just selling bonds out of one fund that another fund might have wanted. It was a costly round trip when he could have passed the bonds from right hand to left. To this employee, it seemed like Gross realized they were underutilizing 17a-7. Pimco was a massive warehouse for bonds; they were stuffed in different closets with different labels ("Income," "Total Return," "Global Multi-Asset") to delineate the different styles. But their strategies overlapped, so trading among them was allowed. And if it was allowed, Pimco would do it to the hilt.

Which is why Jason Williams's cross-trading allegation was so uncomfortable. The discomfort stemmed from one of Pimco's few true panics during the financial crisis, when Zhu was running the Pimco Absolute Return Strategy (PARS) hedge fund.

Williams's complaint alleged that "between or around late 2008 and early 2009, senior management directed the internal transfer of illiquid securities, securities that had been arbitrarily overvalued, from the PIMCO PARS hedge fund to other PIMCO funds, to the detriment of the holders of the receiving funds." At the time Williams outlined, new client cash had begun to pour into the Total Return Fund. So, if needed, Total Return could easily buy illiquid securities for, say, another fund that was hurting. And over several months in 2008, one PARS hedge fund had declined 26 percent, and a similar one 42 percent.

Compounding matters, Williams's allegations hit on that trader, Zhu, who'd already figured in a troublesome class action lawsuit against Pimco.

Gross adored Zhu. He was brilliant, utilitarian, and hyper-focused on markets—right up Gross's alley. Few others found Zhu very friendly: he could be short with execution traders and back-office people, and, like Gross, he did not seem to appreciate the utility of niceties. Gross would occasionally tell the firm that he and Zhu could run the whole place, every dollar, the two of them. Zhu was fierce, as in his constant wrangling with Chris Dialynas over China—traders and analysts recall Dialynas questioning China's reported economic data or fore-casting the end of the world, be it through a war with China or China's selling Treasuries. Zhu would light up to defend his Motherland. But Zhu's grasp of fancy math, and Gross's auspices, had always rendered him untouchable.

In the spring of 2005, Zhu found himself mired in a market dislocation. The federal government had reduced the supply of some new Treasuries coming to market, creating a violent scarcity. This scarcity had a ripple effect on futures contracts, derivatives that commit a purchaser to obtain Treasuries at an agreed-upon price on a future date, in the hope that the price will have risen, yielding a profit. The number of futures began to dwarf the supply of the actual bonds underlying them.

This created a problem in settling trades for expiring contracts: a trader could either deliver actual Treasuries or roll into a new futures contract. Rolling into a new futures contract was the normal way; only about 3 percent of all Treasury futures resulted in physical delivery. To roll, a trader would sell the contract, evaporating the trade like candies in a game of Candy Crush Saga, and then buy a new contract with an updated expiration date.

But physical delivery was always an option, just as in Pimco's famous 1983 Ginnie Mae CDR trade. All Treasury futures follow the fluctuating price of actual Treasuries. The exchange that houses the trades determines the pool of notes eligible for delivery, and the market then prices those notes based on the cheapest one in that pool.

By the end of March 2005, Zhu had amassed an oversize long position in futures contracts expiring that June, bullish bets on U.S. Treasuries. Pimco—again an echo of its CDR trade—held $14 billion of that June contract, a pile that itself exceeded the supply of the cheapest-to-deliver Treasury (which in this case was, by far, the ten-year note maturing in February 2012).

Futures are bilateral: Anytime someone buys a long future on something, there is necessarily someone on the other side who is "short" that thing, positioned against it. (This is often a bank, who can then go sell the position to someone else, like a hedge fund, or it can hold the trade itself.) By virtue of their buying, Pimco created a wildly large bet, which required a matching wildly large bet against Treasuries.

But the scarcity of the cheapest-to-deliver Treasury was freaking traders out: fewer Treasuries meant a mad dash for the cheapest-to-deliver notes, driving up their prices and terrifying those with short bets. By the spring, Pimco was already pricing in the scarce supply of deliverable February 12 notes. Traders figured that everyone would have to roll into the September contract, so the price of those contracts surged.

With the September futures contracts skyrocketing and eligible Treasuries to settle the June contracts nearly impossible to find, both possible choices for settlement were mangled. The shorts were screwed.

And there was Pimco, sitting on a pile of those cheapest-to-deliver Treasuries. In addition to amassing a monstrous position in the futures contract, Pimco had bought up as many of the underlying February 12 notes as it could. It was such a war chest, across Pimco funds, that the firm owned almost half of all the February 12s in existence. Maybe as much as $13.3 billion, which would have been 75 percent of the deliverable supply. Pimco was forcibly constraining the already-constrained supply.

The Treasury market was becoming a desert, filled with frantic, thirsty traders. In late May, billions of dollars in trades started failing, every day. A cumulative $200 billion in futures needed those February 12 Treasuries that no one could find (because Pimco was sitting on around half of the already thin supply). Traders weren't sure who was doing it, but whoever it was wasn't lending the February 12s out, as would have been normal. The shorts were getting increasingly desperate, and in the frenzy, prices soared.

As the market panicked, Bill Powers took his annual vacation. Every year he flew to Nantucket, heading to the East Coast to reap some of the benefits of his intense California life. Like a salmon.

The way Powers remembers it, a Treasury official stood on the beach, looking out at the water. The official happened to vacation near Powers there, and over the years, given their similar interests (markets), they had forged an easy friendship.

Powers joined him on the beach. They stood together, watching their kids.

"So," the official started. "What do I need to know about Pimco cornering the market on the Feb. twelves?"

Powers didn't let his face move, didn't register surprise. He continued staring at the ocean and held perfectly still, like an animal hoping its predator won't spot it. His eyes ticked back and forth at the placid horizon.

Water's deep, he thought, laughing to himself. He managed to dodge the official's inquiries—at a certain point, any real conversation became disclosures—and the official let the matter drop. (This Treasury official does remember talking to Powers on the beach in Nantucket, but remembers specific conversations about this issue with other senior Pimco executives.)

As the clock ticked closer to the futures' June 22 expiry date, the number of contracts wasn't dropping as it should: 152,000 contracts were still open on June 21. Holders of more than 142,000 contracts took delivery, almost double the previous record.

Much of this was Pimco: instead of peacefully rolling, Pimco demanded physical settlement delivery of the bonds that no one could find, bonds that were MIA largely because Pimco was hoarding them. Many traders saw the move as financial market chicken: Pimco had decided against playing nice.

All $14 billion worth of June futures settled by delivery used the February 12s. But it was costly.

Zhu wasn't alone in the trade, but he led this war. To people like him and Gross, anybody who got the better of them in a trade was stealing from them. And it was their job to make sure that didn't happen. People who worked with and around him at the time remember this mentality: what he was doing was aggressive, rude, but he wasn't paid to make friends. His job was trading; it did not encompass regulatory problems or reputational optics. That was for compliance and legal, someone else's job entirely. Zhu's job was to get every basis point he could, which meant not letting hedge funds steal from him. If it wasn't explicitly codified that bullying hedge funds was illegal, then it wasn't illegal. And if it made money for clients, wasn't it Pimco's *imperative* to do it and not to be too terribly sorry if it hurt competitors or Wall Street banks?

According to the aggrieved shorts, Pimco made over $1 billion off the trade.

Markets were far looser then, before the crisis, so the risk of some government body objecting was low. One person close to the process recalls being startled at how poorly regulators, led by the Commodity Futures Trading Commission, understood the underpinning of the Treasury futures delivery process, the market mechanics. The market's babysitters were mostly clueless.

The Chicago Board of Trade intervened. On June 29, 2005, it added new limits to how much a trader could buy or sell in a given security in the last ten days before the futures contract expired. Traders would be limited to only fifty thousand contracts tied to the ten-year Treasury. (Fifty thousand is slightly under one third of what Pimco held of those June futures.)

The CBOT wouldn't say why it had felt compelled to take this action, except that it wanted to underscore its "commitment to protecting the integrity of these contracts": "We established position limits precisely for the purpose of reducing the potential threat of market manipulation, congestion or price distortions," its CEO and its chairman wrote in August 2005.

The rule change caused the price of the September contracts to plummet.

Investors on the short side were pissed. It was like they'd been bullied out of their money. In August, some investors filed a class action lawsuit: they said that Pimco had pushed up the price of the June 2005 futures contract, building up a $10 billion position in the contracts, alongside a position of billions of dollars in the cheapest-to-deliver Treasuries, so when time ran out on the contracts and the shorts had to deliver the Treasury notes, they were forced to pay artificially high prices. Pimco had sat on the outstanding supply the shorts needed in order to settle futures contracts with Pimco.

Gross explained at the time that it had been simply an economically rational decision: Pimco held all those June contracts and had watched carefully as the price of the September contracts ticked higher. Eventually rolling them became prohibitively expensive—that "was the original problem in this whole process," he said on Bloomberg Television. And then everyone just *assumed* they were going to force physical delivery. Pimco, too, was a victim here.

The class action suit, filed by the wronged purchasers of the June 2005 ten-year Treasury note futures contract, alleged that shorts had lost more than $600 million by being forced to pay Pimco's manipulated higher prices: Pimco had cornered the market. That was an act of monopolization, in violation of the Commodity Exchange Act.

Pimco denied misconduct. "The plaintiffs are a purported class of investors who took speculative 'short' positions and tried to profit from what turned out to be a bad bet," said Pimco spokesman Dan Tarman. The federal regulators and the CBOT had found no manipulation by Pimco, he added.

Gross said it was just haters piling on because Pimco had gotten so big and successful. "There wasn't any squeeze," he said. "When you're this size and this big, you're a target of class-action legal maneuvering. . . . Like an elephant, you have to watch where you step, knowing there are people out there who are willing to make accusations."

A managing director at Morningstar corroborated his view: "Everybody is watching [Pimco's] every move. . . . Just whispers that Bill Gross is doing something in the market can cause people to dramatically alter their own investment strategies. In an industry where good ideas are at a premium, your ability to execute can be limited if you're the most visible player in the marketplace."

This dominance, of course, was also what could make cornering possible.

Pimco argued that many of those alleged victims had counterbalancing long bets, which made *more* money than they lost on the shorts. How can you sue for having lost money on one isolated trade when you made money on a pair? Pimco tried to have the suit dismissed, appealing all the way up to the Supreme Court, but in February 2010, the court kicked it back down, saying the suit could proceed.

In late 2010, Pimco agreed to settle with the aggrieved short sellers, denying any liability but agreeing to pay $92 million to resolve the suit, in addition to around $20 million in fees to a fleet of lawyers.

Pimco maintained that it had acted in the best interest of its customers: "All such trades were properly designed to secure best execution for its clients," the company said. "By lending cheapest-to-deliver notes back into the market, it eliminated any concerns; and that all parties making delivery did so using cheapest-to-deliver notes. Thus, the parties strongly disagreed about whether PIMCO was entitled to protect its clients to the extent that it did."

If Pimco sinned, it was only because it put its clients *too* first.

Whether this seemed a formidable demonstration of trading prowess or the behavior of a bully using its size and influence to coerce other market participants depended on which side of the transaction an observer fell—Pimco traders and clients or their counterparties.

"We settled the case with a decent amount of money, and again, I don't think we did any wrong," Gross says. "Because we were so big, you could always mess with things if you didn't like the pricing or the final pricing.

"I can see both sides," he says. "That's what the SEC is there for, is to regulate, and to tame the Wild West. We were sort of Wild West, in a way, because we're an innovator, and we're big. We were the fastest gun in the west."

The "fastest gun" reputation was exactly what made Jason Williams's 2013 lawsuit so disconcerting. The suit retread ground from the class action lawsuit in 2005 and then seemed to confirm every suspicion everyone had about Pimco and its tactics. The Street paid attention; everyone in the credit markets read the complaint. Williams had already found himself to be unemployable, so he was gambling on a settlement that would set him up for life.

Three days later, Williams filed a request to withdraw the suit; his lawyers and Pimco had entered into negotiations. The financial press paid only a passing notice.

After protracted, and private, negotiations, Williams settled for an undisclosed sum. After legal fees, he ended up with enough to buy a bar in Troy, Montana, right near Bull Lake. He fixed up the Halfway House Bar and Grill and refurbished the menu to serve mini corn dogs for $5.50 and Grandpa Ed's Irish Nachos for $5.50. The area out back, ideal for camping, hosts live music at the annual Big Sky Rendezvous every summer. Pimco people don't hear much from Williams anymore.

Pimco had dodged his damning accusations and somehow managed to keep the situation relatively buttoned up. The press barely had time to digest the complaint before it disappeared. Williams had given no interviews, nor had his lawyer. Pimco's behavior—pressing the outer boundaries of definitions, swapping bonds in-house—continued without pause.

But regulators were getting smarter and tougher, the Wild West losing its wild. More formal rules meant fewer gray areas; loopholes would get stitched up, which meant less room to maneuver.

11

Taper Tantrum

Bill Gross stared at Bill Gross in a gold-framed mirror. In a banker's shirt (white collar, blue stripes) with his yellow Hermès tie draped around his neck, untied as usual, he cocked his head slightly to one side, and addressed himself.

This was the illustration Gross chose to accompany his April 2013 *Investment Outlook* to clients and the world. He titled it A MAN IN THE MIRROR, and captioned his self-face-off with Michael Jackson lyrics: "I'm starting with the man in the mirror / I'm asking him to change his ways . . ."

He was feeling pensive again. Here he was, turning sixty-nine, still king of the bond hill, still presiding over this strange empire he'd built over forty years in an unlikely pocket of Southern California. There had never been more money in Total Return: $293 billion in the mutual fund and some $200 billion more in "separately managed accounts," pools of money for big clients that ran the same strategy alongside the public fund.

But that sense of satisfaction coexisted as always with its twin, paranoia, nipping at the edges of any moment of respite, threatening to overtake him. He knew from experience that introspection in client notes performed well, got people's attention. He could use this insecurity constructively: he shared the question that had been gnawing at him.

"Am I a great investor?" he wrote to start the April *Investment Outlook*. "No, not yet."

He went on: "When looking in the mirror, the average human sees a six-plus or a seven reflection on a scale of one to ten," he began. "The big nose or weak chin is masked by brighter eyes or near picture perfect teeth. And when the public is consulted, the vocal compliments as opposed to the near silent/whispered critiques are taken as a super-majority vote for good looks.

"So it is with investing, or any career that is exposed to the public eye," he wrote. "The brickbats come via the blogs and ambitious competitors, but the roses dominate one's mental and even physical scrapbook. In addition to hope, it is how we survive day-to-day. We look at the man or woman in the mirror and see an image that is as distorted from reality as the one in a circus fun zone." He didn't write about the other half of what was reflected back: the corrosive insecurity that didn't make it into any scrapbook. He had an image to maintain.

"The longer and longer you keep at it in this business, the more and more time you have to expose your Achilles heel," Gross wrote. He recalled Peter Lynch, the famed stock picker who had an incredible run at Fidelity's Magellan mutual fund, racking up thirteen years with total return topping 2,500 percent, before stepping down in 1990. Lynch was brilliant "in one respect," Gross wrote: "he knew to get out when the gettin' was good."

This was an evolution from his feeling in 2002, when he'd told *Fortune* that Lynch's exit was "a chicken-shit way out." Back then, Gross said he could never see quitting. "My desire isn't to make money. I have more money than I know what to do with. My desire is to win—and win forever."

Now, eleven years and vastly more money later, he was wondering: Had he won? Even after forty "rather successful" years, Gross wrote that he couldn't say for sure. Part of any success is luck and timing; sometimes the difference is indiscernible, as when an investor captures a cycle just right, loading up on cash or stocks or bonds at exactly the right moment. If the investor proves they can maneuver money to profit through markets good and bad, they must be capable, not just lucky, right?

"Then a confirmation or coronation should take place shortly thereafter!" he wrote. "First a market maven, then a wizard, and finally a King. Oh, to be a King.

"But let me admit something. There is not a Bond King or a Stock King or an Investor Sovereign alive that can claim title to a throne. All of us, even the old guys like [Warren] Buffett, [George] Soros, [Dan] Fuss, yeah—me too, have cut our teeth during perhaps a most advantageous period of time, the most attractive epoch, that an investor could experience."

Simply taking risk had made money, he knew. From the early 1970s, when the dollar was untethered from the fixed exchange rate to gold and kicked off the boom in credit creation, taking risk smartly, adding leverage and avoiding a few sinkholes, made money—which meant investing "greatness."

As usual, he'd been here before. He wrote in November 2008 that "we" were "all bull market children," trained to buy when the market dipped; from the year of his own birth (coincidentally!) onward, "credit continued to be the mighty lubricant of capitalism's engine, allowing its pistons to accelerate at an increasing pace as financial innovation mixed with our own animal spirits produced more and more profits, more and more jobs, more and more everything."

He didn't much examine the costs of more everything. And back then, in the thick of the crisis, it had been more urgent to find a self-effacing way to say that he'd called it, that he and Pimco had seen the risk in the system before it bucked up. Now, he sounded closer to humble.

"Perhaps, however, it was the epoch that made the man as opposed to the man that made the epoch," Gross said.

What if that fortuitous era was over? If the next phase was better for risk avoiders than risk takers like Pimco? If climate change or the aging populations reversed the credit expansion of those recent decades? Or if the world broke out into war over scarce food, water, oil?

"What if there is a future that demands that an investor—a seemingly great investor—change course, or at least learn new tricks?" he wrote. "Ah, now, that would be a test of greatness: the ability to adapt to a new epoch."

But, he wrote, the would-be greats of this epoch, himself included, would probably be dead by the time a new one rolled around. Rationally, he knew he would have to step back at some point, given that he would one day die. It would be wise to figure out "succession," who would carry things on, before that day. That would be good for the firm. Clients always asked for "succession plans."

Gross knew this. Executing it was another thing. He expressed it to Pimco's top management, sporadically, beginning around 2013—that maybe he could delegate responsibilities more, especially the managerial duties he hated, and just focus on the markets. No rush, though. They could focus on it, actually think about the particulars, tomorrow.

For all his rumination, Gross missed that the sands had already begun to shift. His April 2013 *Investment Outlook* was published into a placid credit landscape: yields on high-risk bonds were grinding to new record lows as happy investors demanded the least-ever compensation for risk. As they "reached for yield," stretching farther down to the bottom of the risk spectrum on the assumption that nothing bad was looming, the worst-rated corporate bonds outperformed better ones. An index of leveraged loan prices climbed to the highest level since July 2007.

Pimco's annual three-day Secular Forum, at the start of May, ended with the conclusion that although the U.S. economy was healing, it had not managed to "reach escape velocity," as El-Erian put it in the firm's official recap. The United States would "maintain a cruising-growth speed": not much more than 2 percent on average, with a lot of angst and fretting that it might sink lower.

The angst was immediately greater than forecast. By the end of May, markets had descended into chaos, and it seemed like the thirty-year bond rally was finally, maybe, over.

This time, the catalyst was singular: it was the Fed.

It started when chair Ben Bernanke began to forecast the future path of the Federal Reserve's asset-purchase program, a holdover from the crisis-dig-out efforts. Years of ultra-low interest rates had stimulated the economy by encouraging risk taking; the Fed's extraordinary measures had reassured markets, as hoped. In what he presented as good news about the economy's stability, Bernanke said the asset-purchase program would become less necessary as a recovery took hold.

Which, paradoxically, spooked the market. The stock market's mood now seemed to hinge on the reliability of that support, the promise of it, as if no one would remember an economy that did not flatter its participants by juicing profits and buffering potential losses. So, the market had begun to perseverate on every word out of the Fed, searching for hints that the support would be removed, ready to panic at the first sign. Hamstrung, the Fed faced a choice: cut support short and risk the country sinking back into a recession, or continue it too long and prepare to be blamed for new asset price bubbles. There was also the fear that the Fed had used up all its tools to fix the last crisis, leaving nothing to combat inevitable future problems when they arose. Some at the Fed wanted faster "normalization."

At one of the Fed's congressional checkups, on May 22, 2013, Bernanke gently tried to communicate that the economy was healthy enough to take the patient off the medicine. The Fed could, later in the year, should the economic conditions continue to be strong, perhaps begin to moderate the pace of its bond purchases. And then—maybe one day in the future, next year?—cease those purchases. Depending on the data!

The markets did not hear all his qualifiers and modifiers, did not hear his careful framing and conditional tenses. Jittery traders heard only that the supportive measures were going away. This brought rushing back all the memories of panicked weekends, emergency meetings, cardboard boxes carried out into Times Square, the freefall, Dick Fuld punched on a treadmill. Europe still felt like it was on the brink, even now. The only message traders heard was that the good times were over; the Fed might "taper" its support, slowly reduce and eventually end its quantitative easing programs, and maybe, one day—God forbid—raise rates.

They panicked.

The violent bond market sell-off that followed immediately became known as the "Taper Tantrum." The yield on the ten-year Treasury jumped from 1.61 percent on May 1 to 2.75 percent on July 8. An unbelievable surge.

That was it, then: rates were headed up. It was the end of that thirty-year bond rally. Which meant Total Return strategies would also be over. After May 22, 2013, no one could escape fast enough from the asset class they'd flocked to in 2009. Investors pulled their money out of bond funds and would not stop.

A few weeks earlier, Gross had boosted Total Return's holdings of Treasuries to 39 percent of the fund. Just before Treasuries got clobbered. Also in the first half of the year, he'd bet on U.S. inflation-indexed securities, some of his personal favorite securities. Pimco's enthusiasm for TIPS had long helped sustain that market, but they were never really winners. Now, in early 2013, Gross had thought they really would be: betting that global money printing would result in higher prices, he loaded up on TIPS.

The Taper Tantrum increased yields but not inflation expectations. Inflation-hedged debt, TIPS, lost money. In May and June, Total Return fell 4.7 percent. Over half of that—2.6 percent—was in June alone. It was Total Return's worst month since 2008. Every bond fund was taking a beating, but this time, Pimco was standout bad.

That month, investors in Total Return pulled $9.6 billion—the most on record.

"One-to-two month performance numbers are a blip on a 40-year performance history," Gross tweeted on July 7, in a bid to stop the rush out of the fund. "Pimco marches on a long-term path."

But the Taper Tantrum wasn't done yet. Gross was getting "hosed," as they say. So periodically, he would order a trading freeze: the Investment Committee told employees to limit "nonessential" trading. Gross took it one step further: don't touch Treasuries. With everyone watching, Gross could not risk a headline of some Pimco trader deviating.

So, on and off throughout the summer, they would suddenly have to stop what they were doing and wait. More anxiety than normal permeated the trade floor. Its usual silence turned tense. Gross slammed desk drawers. Any quiet, rare laughter evaporated immediately.

The traders in the options group felt it the worst, according to one former partner: Because options are built on time, they must be constantly maintained to account for the passing days and market changes. Traders must tend to their hedges, trimming here and there, just to hold them constant. With the trading freeze, some of the traders were confused—could they hedge? Rates moved, markets changed, time passed, and they watched the market anxiously as their positions threatened to grow unruly, wild.

With the outflows and sinking performance, the traffic between Pimco's funds reversed course. For years, Total Return had been a net purchaser of securities from other Pimco funds, using that 17a-7 exemption that allowed movement between funds under the same umbrella. For the five years through March 2013, Total Return bought about $37.6 billion from fund family members and sold about $14 billion. Amid the tantrum, this changed: in mid-2013, Total Return sold about $12 billion in securities to its cousin funds and bought less than $5 billion.

Beneath all this was a potentially bigger problem. Many of Gross's structural alpha trades, his secrets for wringing extra performance out of the markets, were built in a world where rates were falling. There'd been short blips in the other direction, with dips and corrections, but mostly, for the duration of thirty-plus years, always falling. If rates had truly stopped their grind lower, it was no longer clear that longer-dated corporate bonds were always underpriced, offering extra yield for less risk than everyone else perceived; it wasn't clear that buying short-dated corporates instead of holding cash would always yield more; it was no longer clear that Gross could neatly predict trading ranges and sell options around that range. The structural trades that had built the firm were suddenly, a little, possibly, in doubt.

Likewise, Gross was beginning to see how far the firm had grown beyond where he'd started it. He'd always wanted Pimco's growth. He'd encouraged it, fostered it. *Grow or die.* But this was so much. At times, these days, Pimco's trades seemed outside things he understood, markets whose rhythms were familiar to him. Facing this would take more than looking at himself in the mirror.

In April 2013, a group convened to hear the commercial real estate team present a trade, one involving a pool of securities backed by commercial mortgage loans in the United Kingdom, sliced into different prices and risk. Nothing too extreme or unexpected. The team had worked on the deal for a couple of months with JPMorgan and Starwood. This wasn't really a trade pitch—this trade was raw real estate loans, backed by physical buildings, which meant, if the loan went south, the owner might end up with a literal building somewhere five thousand miles away. Mutual funds like Total Return weren't allowed to buy these types of loans. So today's meeting was more an informative *hey, what are the private-side folks up to?* And, if there was interest, maybe they could think about ways to structure things like this so more funds could partake.

Gross was certainly interested. He pressed the team on the details, questioning the valuations. That wasn't unusual: Gross always pushed everyone in these meetings, testing the trade but also the presenter's grit. No one jumped in to help anyone else; you were always 100 percent on your own, standing in front of a wispy-voiced one-man firing squad. Infractions could be as small as page numbers. Proud grown men had been brought to tears.

So, these things always had some sting. But today was different.

Gross kept pushing. But they didn't have some of the answers, because they hadn't done the deal yet. It was an ongoing negotiation. This was not a bond deal, conducted over a phone call or by email, where a dealer gives you a price, you wrangle and snort, and then you agree, and you're done. This was an auction. Pimco and its partners on the deal, JPMorgan and Starwood, had already been bidding, were about to submit their "best and final" offers. No one would know the final numbers until someone won. How could he know the price before it was priced? This was by no means the first time Gross had encountered an auction. Why was this confusing to him?

The explanations weren't good enough for Gross, king of the

secondary market, of liquid Treasuries and interest rate swaps, where things were priced in an instant.

Finally, others including Ivascyn did interject, trying to slow Gross's growing aggression at the team. *These aren't for you,* they tried to say. *You're being unfair.*

Which just turned his attention toward them. On to Ivascyn.

"So, you're buying stuff you don't know how to value?" Gross asked, getting agitated, tilting forward in his seat. Had Ivascyn worked with JPMorgan to screw him over? Was Ivascyn going to keep the fattest, most profitable parts for his own portfolio, depriving Gross, putting Gross at a disadvantage? Quickly it came down to a binary: Either Ivascyn didn't know what he was doing, or he was fucking Gross over!

Which made no sense. Ivascyn tried to point this out: "Bill, you can't buy buildings."

Things spiraled from there, getting nastier. Gross attacked Ivascyn as a person, not just as an investor: he was a scumbag, a piece of shit.

Those in the meeting were taken aback. Not because Gross was being a jerk; that was normal. This was new territory, inappropriate and disorienting. First off, there were plenty of scummy people at Pimco, but Ivascyn was not one of them. Second, Ivascyn couldn't possibly be disadvantaging Gross. How could Gross think Ivascyn was depriving him of unrated whole real estate loans that Total Return couldn't even buy? Gross had missed something, misunderstood something, and had jumped to unwarranted conclusions. And rage.

Ivascyn was bringing in some of the most spectacular returns in the firm, and new client money, which meant fees. His Pimco Income mutual fund was performing great and growing; the locked-up private-equity-style structures were raking in profits. Everyone knew that if it weren't for him, profits wouldn't have grown much over the last three years—which translated directly to their individual compensation. Ivascyn was the reason their M unit options would convert to money-minting units. One meeting attendee recalls thinking in disgust, *Without Dan Ivascyn, no one would get paid.*

They watched Ivascyn, the engine of new growth and the future, get belittled by Gross, the aging king, his weird mop of hair quivering as he shook with rage. That stuck with them. They were repulsed by this hollow, vindictive abuse of power, unusual even for Gross. And it achieved nothing.

Pimco pulled out of the mortgage loan deal. This surprised executives at JPMorgan and Starwood, who had to find someone else to buy the components that would have been Pimco's. This didn't breach any contracts, but it was poor form. Act like that, and you won't find anyone to deal with in the future.

Ivascyn seemed embarrassed. He apologized to his partners at JP-Morgan.

The episode didn't stick with Gross. He went back to his desk and immersed himself in the market, filling his line of sight with blinking amber numbers and flashing red headlines. There was still plenty to do. Wrangling in the now-less-Wild West was still, to some extent, possible. In the beginning it had been wide-open possibilities, thanks to their ingenuity, their intensity, their aggression. They still had all that, but the field was more crowded, and now their biggest advantage was size. The threat of SIFI designation was still out there but less imminent, as the giant asset managers' lobbying seemed to be working.

The Fed had softened its tapering stance since May and looked scared to move too fast and upset the market. So, policy changes appeared on hold—which meant Bill Gross, and the bond market, still had time.

The corporate bond market couldn't fully bring itself to trust the omens and was caught between panicking over a "taper" and fighting over new bonds as companies rushed to lock in the lowest rates the modern U.S. capital markets had ever seen. Just a few months after Apple conducted a record $17 billion debt sale in April, the record was about to be broken: that spring, Verizon needed to fund a big purchase, so it approached a group of banks to sell around $50 billion of debt.

The bonds needed a particularly juicy yield to entice investors because the deal was so huge, but also because the "new-issue window" was maybe closing—if the thirty-year bond rally was over, rates would rise, ending a golden era for companies to sell new bonds dirt cheap. Verizon's bankers knew they had to line up the most crucial buyers first, to secure an "anchor" for the deal that would coax other investors. They asked Pimco and BlackRock if they were interested in buying. They were.

Verizon priced the bonds very sweet; the deal was a total frenzy. Verizon ended up with about $100 billion in interest for $49 billion in debt. After the chaos cleared, Pimco had taken home about $8 billion of the deal, and BlackRock about $5 billion.

The bonds surged immediately, handing those two firms profits on a massive scale.

With the Fed still on hold, Gross had more time to take it at its word. He built a huge bet in credit default swaps, wagers on the future health of company credit, by selling the CDS index (CDX), a basket of contracts on corporate issuers. Gross got paid a premium in exchange for taking on the risk that one or some of the 125 companies in the index might fail to meet its debt obligations. If that didn't happen—if nobody defaulted—his bet would make money.

By late fall, that bet had grown to as much as $30 billion. Plus another $2.5 billion in emerging market CDX. Gross was betting, big, that the Fed would extend its stimulus into the next year.

The size was something, but the structure wasn't unusual. Pimco had built CDX trades before, as when it sold $11 billion in 2011, or bought $12 billion in 2012. Pimco had a good track record of making money on trades like this. The indexes are a blunt instrument to take a view on a broad category of credit without the complication of interest rates, but with the precision of a liquid standard contract.

That monster trade made money, giving Gross a needed boost. Yet it couldn't reverse the damage from his bad call on Treasuries earlier that year. With that, Gross had messed up in his own market, where he grew up, where his skill and influence were best known. By his own admission, he was facing the first real test of his mettle in an unfriendly market—and so far, he was blowing it.

His Treasury miss this time was worse than in 2011, too, in one important way: he *lost* money. Everyone did, but Gross lost worse. Total Return underperformed 64 percent of peers. It lost 1.9 percent in 2013, compared with a loss of 0.9 percent for comparable funds, and a loss of 2 percent for the benchmark Barclays Aggregate Bond Index.

Gross hadn't lost any money since 1999; this was his worst loss since 1994.

This time, clients weren't going to wait around for him to get back on track. They'd come to Gross—to Pimco, to bond funds—for safety, to put their money in the care of someone who had presciently dodged the big crisis. Here, with the first hint of trouble, his strategy fell apart. The safety was a mirage.

In May 2013, Pimco Total Return clients started to pull their money, and they would continue redeeming every month for years. By October, Pimco Total Return had lost the title of world's largest mutual fund, an honor it had held for five years. By the end of the year, clients had withdrawn more than $41 billion.

Market missteps make traders wounded animals in the halls of Pimco, and this was true even for Gross. He was as hard on himself as he was on anyone, though his self-flagellation was less about public humiliation, more internal.

Gross wasn't alone in his shame. The Global Multi-Asset Fund was also "stinking up the place," in Pimco parlance. Pimco tried changing the benchmark for the fund's products, from a balance of two indexes to 5 percent over the floating rate benchmark LIBOR, but it didn't go unnoticed. A Morningstar analyst said the move "smack[ed] a little of moving the goalposts" mid-game.

Bad performance happens to everyone. But to Gross, the fund was El-Erian's problem, and he wasn't upholding his end of the management. "Performance was stinky, and that was really the only account Mohamed really had," Gross says. "That was his baby. It was stinking up the joint really badly."

The fund wasn't just El-Erian's; he was a co-manager on it, with three others including Saumil Parikh, a Pimco golden child. Parikh was lead manager, which gave him a greater share of responsibility.* Parikh ran the important and formal thrice-annual agenda-setting Cyclical Forums, moderating in his beautiful suits with his precisely landscaped beard. He incited some envy: He was so young and had risen so fast, making partner in his early thirties. McCulley loved him, Gross loved him.

Parikh presented on the Global Material and Asset Fund (GMAF) to the Investment Committee in one of its near-daily meetings in the spring of 2013. It went badly. The fund wasn't doing well. In Gross's memory, El-Erian interrupted, saying something along the lines of *Damnit, Saumil, you gotta fix it, you gotta fix it!*

His railing on Parikh felt, to Gross, gratuitous, even unfair. El-Erian deserved at least some responsibility for the fund. Gross intervened to this effect.

It was not appreciated.

"GROSS!" El-Erian shouted, as Gross recalls. "You've got Saumil under your wing!"

"Nobody is under my wing!" Gross said in reply. But he was taken

---

* El-Erian's lawyer says, "In the beginning of 2013, the lead portfolio management of this fund was changed from Dr. El-Erian to Mr. Saumil Parikh. Mr. Gross made this call, while repeatedly ignoring the misgivings expressed by Dr. El-Erian and others. Because of this decision, Mr. Parikh was ultimately responsible for the decision-making for this fund throughout most of 2013. Mr. Gross also decided that Mr. Parikh would be 'PM-1' (lead PM) on other accounts, including unconstrained bond accounts. All of these accounts performed terribly that year. By the end of the year, Mr. Parikh was relieved of responsibility for the GMAF, as well as some other accounts. A November 2013 article from Bloomberg correctly notes that it was only at the end of 2013 that Dr. El-Erian increased his role on the GMAF, after Mr. Parikh was removed from a leadership position."

aback; El-Erian rarely lost his cool, certainly not in public, in Investment Committee. There was something here Gross hadn't felt before, a chasm he hadn't noticed before and didn't know how to bridge. Even as, in some ways, the firm's future rested on the stability of their partnership, it had never really been Gross's job to babysit the relationship; that always fell to the other party.

Gross didn't realize it then, but later he would suspect this exchange wounded El-Erian. That he'd felt betrayed, that Gross hadn't stuck up for him enough.

GMAF continued to sag. That November, El-Erian finally stepped up, formally taking a larger role by jettisoning Parikh from the fund's management. By then, GMAF had fallen 8 percent for 2013, lagging 99 percent of peers.

No matter whom he might try to pin it on, El-Erian had to know the rules; he was wounded, too. For a time, this was shirkable, thanks to his rank. At his level, the accountability was a little diluted, and the responsibility could be ignored, at least temporarily—which might give him long enough to fix it, either through skill or through the luck of a market reversal.

Not that either he or Gross would hurt too badly, personally. El-Erian would take home a bonus of about $230 million that year,* and Gross almost $300 million.

Gross had been a billionaire for years now—already, his personal wealth was about $2 billion and was throwing off $150 million per year in interest—but his rich-person habits had stopped developing. He had a private jet and liked to golf. Pretty normal. He had an expensive real estate habit, but that was also to some extent in pursuit of returns. He and Sue mocked the frothy art market together: Sue liked to copy famous

---

* Through his lawyer, El-Erian says references to his compensation are inaccurate but offered no correction. The figures have been previously published elsewhere.

paintings, using an overhead projector to get the outlines right. "Why spend $20 million?" she'd say, "I can paint that one for $75." They hung her fake Picasso over the fireplace in their bedroom. Bill Gross liked stamps. He liked to get tacos and a beer on Friday nights with Sue and her family. That was more or less it.

In late 2013, though, that perspective began to shift. He got in a scrape that October that showed him a new, pressing need for some of his money.

Shareholder activism was bubbling up all around, and it was annoying, appalling: stock investors were pressuring companies to issue bonds only to give the money back to the stock investors! A totally unproductive use of money, especially given that many of those activists ran hedge funds that were open only to sophisticated investors, so they were bullying companies to funnel profits to the already rich. Something about that didn't sit right.

One day in late October, as the notoriously pugnacious activist Carl Icahn was loudly pushing Apple to buy back stock, which would inflate the price of shares he held, Gross snapped. "Icahn should leave #Apple alone & spend more time like Bill Gates," Gross tweeted on October 24. "If #Icahn's so smart, use it to help people not yourself."

Icahn took the bait. "To Bill Gross @PIMCO," he tweeted on October 28, "If you really want to do good, why not join givingpledge.org like Gates, I and many others have?" Icahn and Gates had both committed to the Giving Pledge, promising to give away more than half of their wealth by the end of their lives.

Two days later, Gross went on CNBC. He and Sue would give away all their money before they died, he said, in what he referred to as an "Andrew Carnegie" pledge. "Sue and I are well on our way," Gross said. Already they'd put almost $300 million in a family foundation, but to date, they'd been quiet about their other modest giving. In 2005, they gave $20 million to Hoag Memorial Hospital Presbyterian, for what Hoag told the press was maybe the biggest donation ever to an Orange County hospital. (An accidental but happy by-product of this gift: Bill Gross's first wife worked at Hoag, so in the mornings on her way in, she had to walk past an enormous portrait of Bill and Sue.) And that $10 million to the University of California, Irvine, for stem cell research. More recently, in 2012, they gave another $20 million to Cedars-Sinai Medical Center for the Sue and Bill Gross Surgery and Procedure Center. They'd just donated $20 million to Mercy Ships, a Texas-based nonprofit that operates floating hospitals that bring medical aid to patients in coastal countries. Those local donations had gotten some local attention.

In 2012, the Grosses had started an anonymous donation tradition, writing $10,000, $15,000 checks to people they considered in need. They'd watched an episode of *60 Minutes* about workers struggling after losing their jobs when the space shuttle program shut down, and they were moved to act.

No one knew they had done this. Gross had pondered how best to do it—how to make sure the money got to the right people, and also how to do it anonymously. He'd thought of a show he and his childhood best friend Jerry used to watch, *The Millionaire*, a fictional drama in which a benefactor named Tipton randomly gave a person $1 million. The show depicted how the wealth changed the winners' lives, in ways good and bad. Gross and Jerry didn't know any millionaires, so they'd watch the program and ask each other, *What would you do with a million dollars?*

One day, out of the blue, Gross emailed Jerry, subject line: "Proposition." Could they create their own Tipton Trust?

Jerry had watched Gross transform into a billionaire. A retired schoolteacher, he did not care at all about Gross's wealth, Gross knew. He didn't want any of it. Jerry wasn't threatening to Gross.

Over the years, Jerry had heard about the constant onslaught of calls and emails Gross got, from people wanting him to send them money, to invest in their vision. It was exhausting. "It doesn't matter if he changes his phone number; they'll be finding out and calling him asking for money, and he just doesn't want to bother with it," Jerry says.

But conducting something like this anonymously—"for somebody of his wealth and notoriety, for good or bad, that's an almost impossible thing to do," Jerry says. "He didn't want to be walking down the streets of Hollywood handing out checks for fifteen thousand, twenty thousand, or whatever." Gross needed help figuring out who should get the money, vetting all the stories of different lives. Jerry had worked in underserved communities and had more exposure to this stuff, and he had more time than Gross to devote to it.

Jerry agreed to help, to source people and vet them and then compile their stories for Gross to review. Gross figured out how much he could give tax free—over ten, but generally under fifteen thousand.

"The only stipulation he wanted to put into it was—this was the idea, that this influx of unexpected resources would enable the person or the family—that it would be transformative," Jerry says. "It wasn't just a handout. It had to move them beyond; to do something to be able to get their lives together that were crumbling or problematic. So, it wasn't meant to be temporary in that sense; it was meant to be transformative."

This giving mitigated some of Gross's weird feeling of being too rich. He had been uncomfortable, or at least had voiced discomfort, for years: he'd opened a 2002 *Investment Outlook* with a quote attributed to Balzac: "Behind every great fortune, there is a crime." It bothered him how many capitalists were criminals—Enron and its Wall Street partners "participat[ing] in the implicit bilking of the American public." Gross knew that he, like other filthy-rich people, had been lucky, lucky at someone else's expense. What could, or should, he do? He certainly couldn't stop accumulating—at a certain point, the money compounds on its own, throwing off dividends and interest and yield, growing and growing.

But now the issue of inequality had abruptly become pressing. Occupy Wall Street hadn't really touched Pimco, but in October 2013, Gross had had an unpleasant experience at what should have been a happy homecoming.

Earlier that month, in October 2013, UCLA's business school had sponsored a talk with two of its most successful alumni, Gross and fellow bond world titan Larry Fink, moderated by CNBC's Brian Sullivan at the Beverly Hilton in LA. The conversation turned to markets, as it always does—how Gross and Fink viewed the financial market recovery, where they saw opportunities.

Pimco and BlackRock were, at that moment, tussling over one area that recovery had not yet reached. Many residents of Richmond, California, were still underwater on their home loans, their houses now worth less than what they paid. The city had proposed a radical use of "eminent domain," the government's power to seize private property. Usually this is exercised to seize land the government needs to build a highway or a park, and it has to pay the market price for whatever it seizes. Richmond proposed using that power to seize *mortgages*, to buy more than six hundred home loans from the bondholders and banks that now held them. The mortgages were underwater, so buying them at their fair market value would mean reducing the loan. Homeowners would owe less— and the lenders and investors would recoup less. Naturally, investors including Pimco and BlackRock had sued the city to block the plan.

They had reason to believe they would prevail: The U.S. mortgage market rests on a steady but unconventional agreement between the government and investors. Mortgages in the United States are not a product of a free market; it's a little sandbox where the government supervises play, promising money if any mortgage investor gets hurt. That promise is why homeowners in the United States and nowhere else can borrow money at a fixed rate for thirty years with a free option to refinance, anytime. The government makes this promise so that people can get cheap mortgages, so they can buy homes and build wealth. This guarantee was only implicit until Pimco pressed in the crisis, forcing the government to say it out loud. And Pimco strongly suspected that the government wouldn't renege for a handful of underwater homeowners in Richmond, California.

These mortgages in question were not backed by any government entity, but that agreement still extended to them: if Richmond was allowed to go forward with its radical plan, it would scare lenders, the investors argued; they'd be less willing to lend to hopeful homebuyers if now those loans could be eminent-domainly reduced at some unknowable time in the future. Richmond's plan would undermine confidence in the market for mortgage-backed securities, they said, and "by extension, the national housing market and national economy." (The plan was also discriminatory and unconstitutional, among other problems, according to the complaint.)

At the Beverly Hilton, Gross was debating the merits of investing in physical assets in a world of artificially suppressed yields when suddenly he was interrupted. Two protestors stood up in the audience, shouting, asking why Gross and Fink were refusing to negotiate with homeowners.

Fink shook his head. The audience groaned in protest.

"Thank you for your comment, sir," Sullivan said, putting a hand out for peace. "Guys, it's fine, he's got a valid point."

"Throw the bum out!" someone in the audience shouted.

"Why are you suing the city of Richmond instead of negotiating?" one of the protestors shouted as the audience hissed. Already security guards were moving toward them. "Negotiate, don't litigate!" Scuffling. "Your day of reckoning is coming! Don't push me."

The audience laughed.

Gross looked at Sullivan for guidance. "Should I answer?"

"I want to actually follow up on their points," Sullivan said after the protestors had been escorted out. "The anger at Wall Street is palpable. And rightfully so, in a lot of cases. People have felt hoodwinked . . . I worry this lack of confidence in the financial system by millions of Americans, by many, many people, who probably have a damn good right to be angry about a lot of things—how do we fix that? How do we make people trust the system? Should we?"

Fink cited a lack of job creation since the crisis, and wage compression, without offering suggestions, and then evangelized about how the Richmond lawsuit actually was a righteous fight for BlackRock's clients (pensioners, retirees), as was his duty as a fiduciary.

"Good one," Gross said, to laughter, of Fink's rhetorical pirouette. Since its advent as an occupation, the widows-and-orphans line had been the defense in any fight for the honor of the money management business. Gross picked up the inequality baton: "Wages have gone down," while corporate profits have expanded, he said. "What Wall Street and corporations have gained, Main Street has lost. And ultimately Main Street is the customer."

Main Street, normal people, "moms and pops"—they were the ones who bought the stuff that funded the revenues of the companies that issued bonds that paid the interest payments to Pimco. Their purchasing power made up some 70 percent of the U.S. economy. And yet, as the crisis receded, somehow they seemed more and more to bear the brunt of the lopsided "recovery."

The UCLA talk settled back into more standard-issue finance topics and talking points. A few weeks later, another protest struck.

Pimco employees walking back into the office with their coffees on October 30 confronted a small crowd outside the building, protesting the Richmond lawsuit. The group—wearing yellow T-shirts announcing their membership in Alliance of Californians for Community Empowerment—aimed to disrupt business until senior officials deigned to speak with them. Activist Peggy Mears, one of the two who had interrupted Gross's UCLA talk, read a letter addressed to Gross and El-Erian, asking that Pimco negotiate with Richmond. They chanted, handed out flyers, and held up yellow signs reading, PIMCO STOP BLOCKING THE HOUSING RECOVERY, and BLACKROCK & PIMCO INVEST IN COMMUNITIES NOT FORECLOSURE.

Finally, Pimco sent Dan Tarman, the head of communications, to listen. He stood, hands clasped behind his back, as activist representatives explained why Pimco should allow Richmond to buy the mortgages. A few feet away, closer to the manicured hedges, private security guards in suits and ties and matching rimless sunglasses looked on, unmoved.

The next day, Gross dedicated his November *Investment Outlook* to capital versus labor: "The era of taxing 'capital' at lower rates than 'labor' should now end," he wrote, and his fellow "privileged 1%" should support higher taxes.

"Having benefited enormously via the leveraging of capital since the beginning of my career and having shared a decreasing percentage of my income thanks to Presidents Reagan and Bush 43 via lower government taxes, I now find my intellectual leanings shifting to the plight of labor," he wrote.

Gross was acknowledging that his enterprise had been built on the backs of humble people saving for retirement, to buy a house, to make ends meet. In that way, Fink's self-serving speech had been right: they *were* working for widows and firefighters. And that justified Pimco's treatment of the Street, the intense focus and painful insistence on grinding out basis points.

But did that really hold up to scrutiny? If they were doing such a good job for their clients—those retirees whose pension manager had picked Pimco, Fink's widows and orphans—why were the managers getting so much richer so much faster? Was that right?

Gross was beginning to feel like he had to do something more. Whatever his personal conscience held, after the spat with Icahn, the scrutiny, and the protests, he had to think about his legacy. Being rich wasn't enough to be remembered well.

In his bigger moments, he also saw that the system he had helped to build was somehow broken. That this game he loved—the making money into more money, the orderly little numbers on his blinking screens, the bond market expanding and forming the more he explored—had ended up gaming the American public, the world.

That December, the *Chronicle of Philanthropy* published an interview on Bill and Sue Gross's "unorthodox" giving, their $15,000 checks. "We're very satisfied with what we've done so far," Gross told them. "The only question is, 'Have we done enough?'"

12

Secretariat

It was getting late. Mohamed El-Erian asked his ten-year-old daughter to brush her teeth. She ignored him. He said it again. Still she ignored him. He sighed.

It was not so long ago she would have immediately responded, he reminded her, and he wouldn't have had to ask multiple times; she would have known from his tone of voice that he was serious.

"Wait a minute," she said, and disappeared into her room. She emerged holding a piece of paper, a list she had compiled, of twenty-two important events and activities of hers that her father had missed because he'd been working: her first day of school, her first soccer match of the year, a parent-teacher meeting, a Halloween parade.

"Talk about a wake-up call," El-Erian said later.

His first reaction was to get defensive. He had a good excuse for each missed event: travel, important meetings, an urgent phone call, sudden to-dos. Then he stopped: this was not the way to respond. He could talk his trademark circles out of it, but maybe she was right: "My work-life balance had gotten way out of whack, and the imbalance was hurting my very special relationship with my daughter," he said. "I was not making nearly enough time for her."

He would say later that this realization landed extra hard for him. He'd lost his own father suddenly to a heart attack on December 12, 1981, when El-Erian was twenty-three. His father's death changed the course of Mohamed's life: El-Erian had been on his way to a doctorate at Oxford, following his merit scholarship and first-class honors degree at the University of Cambridge. He was on track for a comfortable, intellectually stimulating career in academia.

But when his father died one year into El-Erian's studies, his mother and seven-year-old sister needed support. So, El-Erian had to look for a more lucrative path than reading books and teaching. Money became a goal, a necessity, to fund his family's functioning.

"Before then, life had been predictable," he said. "I stopped planning after that."

How, then, had this caught him so off-guard? He'd devoted time and resources within Pimco to diversity, spearheading initiatives with a stated mission of helping the firm accommodate different life stages and experiences, to move it away from a homogeneous bunch of white men in blue suits. It was all a work in progress, of course: you could count the women partners on barely two hands. And somehow, over the course of 2013, the proportion of both women and people of color in the partner pool slipped, dipping below 11 percent and 20 percent, respectively. By the numbers, Pimco was *un*making progress. But at least he'd stated the diversity mission. Wasn't cosmetic improvement the first step? ("Dr. El-Erian's genuine efforts and hard work in this regard were well-known throughout the firm," his lawyer says.)

Anyway, he'd tried to set an example: despite his insistence on face time in the office and despite settling in behind his desk well before even the East Coast's sunrise (which did not align with Bill Gross's ten hours in the office, which also demanded mandatory attendance), and despite emails at all hours, he'd made a show of declining certain deadlines due to his daughter's events before. How was it possible he had still missed so much?

He had to make a change.

Meanwhile, another situation was growing untenable. Gross and El-Erian had long trumpeted their working relationship. They had their differences, structural ones in personality and management style, but in the summer of 2013, that relationship was deteriorating. Things were getting increasingly tense.

For El-Erian, there was the grind of constant messages and unreasonable demands. The ridiculous, unnecessary messes Gross created, constantly: saying things off-message on TV, torching employees for minor infractions. Gross would commit to a client event that involved travel and then back out at the last minute, leaving him to fill in, he says. El-Erian got up at 3:30 A.M. to get to the office before everyone, and he left after everyone. How was there always still more to do?

None of this registered with Gross. He saw only El-Erian's hollow insistence on face time in the office; his breezy economic doublespeak, words that slipped through your hands like rushing water; his push for "diversity," which Gross found vaguely offensive—Gross had prided himself on being equal-opportunity difficult, and he'd always felt he tried to seek out and promote women, as clients were always asking why there weren't more at Pimco. There just weren't as many women around to promote.

In El-Erian, Gross saw the equity push sagging, saw the poor performance in GMAF, and saw someone who enjoyed the yield of work more than doing the work—flying to see clients,* appearing on TV, being cited as an "expert" instead of performing and doing what was necessary to keep the firm going. El-Erian's absence while he flew around the world, his mushy words masking an inability to make a decisive call—to Gross, it was all increasingly intolerable. And then there was that spat over Parikh.

It felt now like Gross and El-Erian no longer saw eye to eye on the firm's direction, or over trades and strategy, or whom to hire, or what new products to push. And all that discord was arising against the backdrop of clients pulling their money, more and more each month. Gross and El-Erian had always kept up a pleasant public face, even

---

* Despite "access to private planes and expensive cars," El-Erian's lawyer says, "Dr. El-Erian did not use these modes of transportation. Indeed, while CEO and co-CIO at Pimco, he repeatedly refused to use the Netjets budget that was available to him and traveled via commercial airlines."

amid private disagreements, but now the discord was spilling out into the open, in front of employees.

Even with the increasing tension, the disappointments of GMAF, and the limping stock funds, El-Erian was nonetheless working on expanding Pimco's menu as intended beyond the classic old-school-Pimco bond products that Gross liked to call "bonds and burgers." There was now all the stuff with Ivascyn, the real estate and private fund–type stuff, which brought in fat fees. That was good for the company, but it looked increasingly distant from interest rates and bonds, the areas where Gross reigned, where he could parse information ratios or read economic tea leaves to forecast what rates will do. This stuff made Gross squirm.

"It just seemed like a lot of risk to me," he says. "Mohamed and I started to have disagreements in committee and outside committee—I kept saying this: 'We're drifting into risk space where I'm not comfortable. I don't know anything about these products that Ivascyn is selling. I'm glad they're making money, but I don't know what's in them! And he doesn't even come to committee.'

"Mohamed would go, 'Well, sure seems to be working, because we're growing and making more money,'" Gross recalls.

After a while, Gross figured maybe there should be two investment committees: one for the normal stuff and the other for the extra-maybe-too-risky stuff. That could be a solution. It was an idea, at least.

He suggested it to El-Erian: "You do one committee, because that's what you're comfortable with, and I do the conventional committee."

El-Erian rejected the idea. It made no sense, even on its face: Two committees running one firm? Bifurcating strategy and risk? How would you see when parts of the portfolio became accidentally overgrown, or when unrelated risks started overlapping? That sounded like the opposite of prudent risk management.

"Of course, he didn't think that was a good idea at all," Gross says. "It probably wasn't. But I was trying to control what I thought was a company moving into areas I didn't know anything about. Which is probably typical of a generational shift, in [some] ways. Not that they weren't risky, but it's probably something like me talking about the hits from the eighties and the nineties and not being into rap, you know. I can see it! That's the way things go. But I couldn't see it at the time."

Things came to a head one day in June 2013, soon after the memorably searing tantrum at Ivascyn. More than a dozen colleagues gathered for the regular Investment Committee meeting, but talk turned to Gross's conduct: he was acting erratically, and it was threatening to hurt the firm.

The charge was in some ways indisputable. Gross's behavior frequently required someone—usually El-Erian—to go around and smooth things over. Like Gross's tweeting: he loved to connect with his audience.

"I would tweet things, and he would come back and basically say, 'I'm always fixing things for you, for your fuck-ups,'" Gross remembers. Like his tweeting about specific companies.

El-Erian "was very concerned that [a tech company Gross tweeted about] was a potential client, I don't know," Gross remembers. "But I was doing my usual bit, about being too public." To Gross, communicating was part of his job. Oversharing had become a trademark, and look at what it had created.

El-Erian had to confront Gross about his tweeting, his lawyer says, because of "concerns expressed to Pimco's client-facing colleagues and passed on to Dr. El-Erian that clients were concerned about signs of Mr. Gross being distracted." For El-Erian, Gross's unending supply of unforced errors—not to mention explaining the performance of Total Return, his bad Treasury call—was ever more time-consuming. A neutral observer could imagine what he might be able to achieve, were he not constantly cleaning up after the aging founder. He might have time to brainstorm with the sales team about where to find new potential clients, or to push forward the "diversity and inclusion" efforts he was always talking about.

After the Investment Committee meeting in June 2013, fed up with pushback on his behavior, these supposed "messes" he made so constantly, Gross snapped. "I have a forty-one-year track record of investing excellence," he sniped at El-Erian. "What do you have?" This could only have been a reference to GMAF, the "global macro" fund, ranked last against its peers. And/or that he only managed 1 percent of the firm's total assets.

"I'm tired of cleaning up your shit," El-Erian shot back.

The room was stunned. It was clear El-Erian was losing his ability to calm Gross. Or he was losing the will to do it.

Gross could usually bounce back from bad interactions—traders cite as one of his best personality points that if a problem got resolved, Gross would walk in the next day with no apparent memory of the issue. El-Erian was different. The effect of Gross's barbs and the constant pressure had become cumulative; he could not reset. He was forgetting why he would want to.

The meeting ended. Later, now that their conflict was in the open, El-Erian told Gross that he, Gross, needed to change how he interacted with employees. He needed to tone down his aggression, to be less combative, to trust that employees could make investment decisions sometimes. These were grown people with trading talent, El-Erian said. We hired them for a reason.

Gross nodded. He'd always thought the brutal honesty, the combat, was the gig. But he knew, too, that he was difficult; he always had been. It had never really been a problem until now—in his mind, it had been an asset. But it was a point of pride at Pimco to be flexible, nimble, to react quickly. Gross could tweak something if it truly needed tweaking. He agreed to be less confrontational, or he'd try.

Gross seemed incapable of lessening his surliness. Maybe it was that he had declared the bull market in bonds over for real in April, again; or that he had to go on TV with a Band-Aid on his left cheek; or that June was his worst monthly performance since September 2008, prompting him to write in his July *Investment Outlook* that bond investors should not "jump overboard," but rather, should "have a cocktail, tell the band to stop playing dirges, because you're gonna be just fine with Pimco at the helm."

He couldn't keep his crabbiness contained. In Investment Committee meetings, El-Erian would try to describe stock strategies—

really, anything that wasn't about bonds—and Gross would stare off, looking bored. Sometimes he'd leave entirely, walking out of the room to check the markets on his phone, which had the effect of ending the meeting.

Frustrated, Pimco's Executive Committee created a task force in November to meet with the two and address their mounting difficulties. Even in that, Gross would not be corralled. In front of a handful of traders one day, he complained about all the scrutiny, the bureaucratic oversight. "I could run all the two trillion myself," he said. "I'm Secretariat. Why would you bet on anyone other than Secretariat?"

It wasn't the first time Gross had said something like this. But the attitude did not bode well for reconciliation with El-Erian.

Their divergence in style and skills kept bugging Gross: his IMF-style consensus seeking, how he managed to talk so much without saying anything, that he managed a rounding error of Pimco's assets and yet was co-CIO. It was annoying.

Which he continued to express. If their in-person communication was freezing over, their daily emails continued. Gross wrote to El-Erian on November 17: "Mediocrity awaits Mohamed—your model will gradually lead to that."

"Oh now you have really pushed me beyond any level of decency and acceptability," El-Erian replied. "You may well think that insults and intimidation is the way to deal with your colleagues. I do not. And I will not accept it."

El-Erian started voicing that he wanted out. Gross realized that losing a CEO, as client money fled their funds and as those funds underperformed, would be bad. He knew he needed to keep El-Erian, or the floodgates would open.

Gross offered him more power. Whatever he wanted. Gross could step back instead of him, somehow take a smaller role. (Of course he couldn't leave entirely while El-Erian was both CEO and CIO, and render the firm a dictatorship.) "You can't resign," one executive remembers Gross telling El-Erian. "We need you."

But none of these offers seemed totally genuine—in no small part because Gross kept undermining them, reversing course, denying he'd offered anything; suddenly saying instead that there would be no succession plan, that he, Gross, would walk down the stairs when he wanted to walk down the stairs. The muscle memory of leading, of overpowering, was too strong.

One crisp day in November 2013, as Gross remembers it, El-Erian helmed the day's Investment Committee meeting. He and Gross were spitting back and forth about risk in the firm. Gross saw an opening to make his point.

"Mohamed," Gross recalls saying, "we've got to get in front of the company, and at least I have got to alert them to the risk I'm seeing inside our committee." Gross saw that El-Erian didn't like this request, but they dutifully scheduled a meeting of the Executive Committee to talk through their differences in vision.

Gross prepared a one-pager to present his case. He knew El-Erian would perceive the suggestion as a slam on him, on El-Erian's mission at the company, on his work. He had to be meticulous, make his pitch airtight.

When the day arrived, El-Erian sat across from Gross and opened the meeting.

Gross commenced his presentation. For ten minutes he enumerated, in his whispery singsong, the ways he felt risk was building up in the company's disparate portfolios—in "private equity," in "real estate" holdings, real buildings that they now owned—and wrapped up his remarks by saying that things in the Investment Committee weren't copacetic. There was too much risk. The Investment Committee must be split in two.

The room was silent. El-Erian thanked him for his comments before beginning to present his own counterarguments: The private fund stuff was profit-generating; Ivascyn and the others were following the plan. It made no sense for the Investment Committee to be split in two. Doing so would create turmoil with clients; it was a bad idea.

"And so," El-Erian concluded, according to Gross's memory, "I am resigning as of tonight."

The group reared back in their chairs.

"From the Investment Committee?" someone asked.

"No, I'm resigning from the company."

The committee was shocked. For the next hour, the group went around and around, asking, "Mohamed, why?"

Gross remembers El-Erian responding, "Because Gross doesn't honor his priors." He seemed to be referring to some earlier agreement, some promise Gross broke.

"What does that mean, priors? What does it mean, what do you mean?" Gross recalls saying. "He would never say." El-Erian says, through his lawyer, that he "responded that Mr. Gross repeatedly changed his mind and broke his promises."

At the end of two hours, people calmed him down enough, [saying], 'Well, let's talk about it overnight, not do anything, don't resign now, because then we'll have to notify Allianz, and they'll have to notify the public; just don't do that.' So, he agreed not to."

They could figure this out. It was a matter of soothing El-Erian, of repositioning some things, of moving a few responsibilities to others, and of Gross's being less terrible. All doable.

If Gross was really trying to step back, to relinquish some responsibilities, reality was making it extra challenging for him. A stink bomb had gone off in the $28 billion Pimco Unconstrained Bond Fund, and obviously someone had to fix it. The default answer was Gross. This handoff of the fund was impossible to do nicely.

Unconstrained should have been the best mutual fund on offer, and it was then one of the company's most important mutual fund products. It was better equipped—equipped at all—to navigate sinking rates. Clients were pulling money from Total Return strategies, like the one Gross managed, and putting money into the Unconstrained funds, also known as "Go Anywhere" funds, because they were untethered from benchmarks, free from constraints such as how long-dated the bonds could be or what credit grade they carried or where the debt-issuing company was domiciled. Unconstrained funds could buy what would go up and avoid what would go down.

Gross would have loved that kind of freedom, to branch out from the Total Return framework that, with the bond downturn, was no longer the Old Faithful of returns. Plus, it was far more fun to manage a fund strategy that clients loved rather than one they hated. The Unconstrained fund attracted $10.2 billion in 2013 through October, the most money of any of its peers, according to Morningstar. Simultaneously, clients had yanked more than $30 billion from Total Return.

But even as the Unconstrained fund had drawn in client money, performance sucked. All year, it had been stinking up the place. Not that the years before had been covered in glory: Over the past five years, the fund had returned 5.2 percent, trailing 83 percent of similar funds. In 2013 through the start of December, it fell 2.1 percent, lagging 75 percent of peers. There were a couple of reasons this mediocre performance hadn't attracted attention: One, unconstrained funds had only recently become cool. Two, since 2008, the fund's manager was Chris Dialynas.

Dialynas, by then fifty-nine, was one of Gross's oldest friends. Gross and Dialynas and Howie Raykoff and their wives got dinner together pretty regularly, struggling between Raykoff's impulse to check out very nice restaurants and Gross's total ignorance on that front. They loved to talk about their house remodelings, their shared love of bond trading, the future direction of the market. They had fun.

They'd been through a lot professionally, too—decades of Pimco's growth, of growing rich together. Coming up with awesome trades together. Like the Ginnie Mae caper in 1983. Or less awesome ones, like the time Dialynas got in trouble with regulators for playing a prank on a bond saleswoman at Salomon before she left due to being pregnant, which got him entangled with the Treasury auction-rigging scandal in the early 1990s that helped lead to Salomon's collapse. Gross and Dialynas had to take a field trip to D.C. to explain the joke to regulators—that they were not involved in Salomon's bad behavior, only in an innocent joke on this lady Janice. Regulators found no transgression on their part, and Gross and Dialynas returned together to Newport Beach unscathed.

Gross valued Dialynas's trading and perspective as much as he treasured their friendship. But Unconstrained was the hot product across the fund industry, and Pimco's stank. So, at the start of December 2013, Gross took over the Unconstrained fund—partially out of necessity for the firm, but also probably out of envy, or greed, the need to manage the coolest product. No matter the motivation, it was seen as sad, humiliating for Dialynas, and more than a little mean of Gross.

Pimco announced that Dialynas would leave for a sabbatical—technically, his second, after he got burned out in the 1990s following that Treasury rigging thing and, instead of working, drove fast on the Pacific Coast Highway. Gross said in a Pimco publication, "Strategy Spotlight," that Unconstrained's "investment philosophy, process or approach" wouldn't change. But when he took over that December, he overhauled the entire fund.

Dialynas had built up a position in long-dated Treasuries and agency mortgage bonds, and Gross dumped those. Dialynas had accumulated bets on the U.S. dollar against the Chinese yuan, based on his long-held suspicion of China; Gross chucked those bets. Pimco Unconstrained ditched almost all the credit-default swaps it had bought, $3 billion on individual corporate issuers and another $4.4 billion in indexes, and sold CDS on corporate and sovereign bonds—a 180-degree strategy turn from betting against credit to betting on it.

Around the start of 2014, the Executive Committee convened for a meeting. Top of the agenda: the disintegrated relationship between Gross and El-Erian, now urgent. Pimco's management asked if the two would agree to a mediator, like a married couple. Gross said he would meet with whomever they picked.

A formal search began for someone to come in and reconcile the two chiefs; the process rolled through various bureaucracies until finally a session with the chosen mediator was on the calendar, and Gross and El-Erian were alerted to the meeting.

At which point Gross said, *No, I don't want a mediator; I never wanted a mediator.* But plenty of other people had been present and heard him agree to one. They had written it down, taken action. To

El-Erian, this was "indicative of [Gross's] resistance to change and not honoring prior commitments." (Gross maintains that he never agreed to a mediator, and says people hear what they want to hear.)

Many in upper management felt this was happening too often now: Gross would commit to something and then, later, reverse course, denying his pledge of support or at least acquiescence that everyone had witnessed.

This put El-Erian in an impossible situation. It was tiring, agreeing on a course of action—often just whatever Gross had said he wanted—only to discover that Gross didn't want to hear about it or was denying having asked for it.

Were they watching him lie? A liar knows what they're saying is false. What was accurate? With Gross, it wasn't clear.

Was it forgetfulness? Or his natural contrarian bent? Maybe he was too accustomed to following neural pathways that said the other party was always wrong. It was his nature that, whenever anyone asserted anything (on trading matters, on internal matters, whatever), his first inclination was to push back. Even if it was his idea in the first place. This trait made him a great investor, but it made him intolerable as a manager and coworker.

Or maybe he forgot strategically. Maybe he changed his mind and didn't want to say he had, so he denied the earlier condition, denied its reality to others and to himself. If he'd never changed his mind, he was never wrong.

His memory had seemed selective for decades—Pat Fisher recalls getting the silent treatment after hiring new employees and having to remind Gross that he himself had approved the hires, cajoling him into remembering. It never felt like lying then, to her, but that was a long time ago, and since then, Pimco had grown exponentially.

Whether he intended it or not, it was a manipulative power play: he was changing the rules so his colleagues and subordinates could never get their bearings. It helped keep him fully in control—for as long as his power was still effective.

Early into 2014, El-Erian decided he was done, for real this time.

He informed Pimco's Executive Committee that he would be departing, and that was that. He could not be cajoled further.

Pimco's fifty-six partners had a long-scheduled meeting on January 21, 2014. Many didn't know the reason, didn't know what they were walking into. They were surprised to learn they were there to elect El-Erian's successor.

El-Erian said he'd stay through mid-March. January to March is not a long runway to find an entire new CEO, not for an almost $2 trillion asset manager. But El-Erian was serious, and because Allianz was a public company, they had to announce whatever they were going to do quickly. Something that should have taken months would have to be resolved in days.

Pimco designated a committee to find a suitable replacement, which had approached a handful of internal candidates and considered a few external candidates, going as far as conducting informal conversations with Goldman Sachs's president and chief operating officer, Gary Cohn.

No one wanted to do it. No one was a Gross-whispering saint like Bill Thompson—maybe they could convince him to come back? As chairman, or something?—and no one was dumb enough to ignore the flashing warning signs of more trouble. That the hardest part—any actual transition of power and subsequent extraction of Gross from the company—was yet to come.

Only chief operating officer Doug Hodge was eager. As one former coworker put it, Hodge was metaphorically sitting at the front of the class, his rosy cheeks glowing, hand in the air, waving, waiting to be called on.

Hodge had helped grow Pimco's international offices, and since 2009, he had been chief operating officer. But he was a manager. He'd traded bonds at Salomon Brothers decades earlier, but at Pimco he had only ever been on the business side. His investing fluency extended about as far as that of a sophomore economics major; his public persona was polished, and he'd spent his life in or near the bond market, but he disintegrated into talking points if pressed too hard.

It was a moot point anyway, because the short list of CEO candidates was basically Doug Hodge. The partners voted. Hodge could tide the company over until they figured things out.

They decided, also, to split the role in two, half to Hodge and half to Jay Jacobs, the soft-spoken head of human resources, who'd worked at the firm since 1998, as "president." The way Gross saw it, Hodge was Mr. Outside—he could handle the image part, looking nice—and Jacobs Mr. Inside.

Gross considered Hodge and Jacobs "his" guys, people he had reared at the firm. That should help prevent the difficulties he'd had with El-Erian. Gross knew that they knew that he'd made them; they would be loyal.

Plus, at the moment, Hodge had time: he was in a lull between busy periods of coordinating family crimes. For over a decade starting in 2008, he had worked with college admissions coach Rick Singer to get four of his children into the University of Southern California and Georgetown as fake athletic recruits by falsifying athletic records and bribing coaches. He could have donated money the normal way, by buying a building, but that way was more expensive, north of $5 million (which wasn't out of bounds—he'd just gotten a bonus of $45 million in 2013). In 2018, Hodge tried for admission of a fifth child— "We don't have to talk in code," he said on the taped call; "we know how this works"—but the scheme was uncovered before he could secure his son's admission. (Later, Hodge would say he was an "easy mark," that he believed his money was going to "underfunded athletic programs," but that he did know Singer was faking the Hodge kids' athletic brand. "As a person who values honesty and integrity, I failed," he wrote.)

Meanwhile, publicly, Hodge had just been talking about restoring public trust in markets, saying that "as firms and individuals, we need to personify trustworthy values . . . Willful violations of the rules should not be tolerated by any of us." Elsewhere he'd lamented the "steady stream of news about mistakes in judgment (or worse) across the financial services sector," and he warned against "bad culture" that "can morph into a chimera that makes acceptable bad behavior that at best is unethical, or worse may be illegal." At the same time, he was wiring money to Rick Singer, which would eventually total $850,000, for what Singer called having "stretched the truth" on applications. "But," Singer told him, "this is what is done for all kids."

While Hodge settled into his leadership role alongside Jay Jacobs, Pimco addressed the other half of its top management. Given that El-Erian was supposed to be Gross's heir, the company now needed to create a viable "succession plan" for its founder. The result was a "deputy CIO" (DCIO) structure of the up-and-coming managers, to report up to Gross and succeed him one day: Andrew Balls, the head of European portfolio management and a former *Financial Times* journalist; Marc Seidner, an El-Erian protégé and fellow alumnus of Harvard Management Company; and Dan Ivascyn. The "DCIO" title irked some of its recipients, but okay.

Then, out of nowhere, Seidner quit, too.

He had also had enough. Instead of this new road to the top, he took a job overseeing fixed income at Grantham Mayo Van Otterloo, a competitor not known for managing bonds.

Okay, fine. Just Balls and Ivascyn would be promoted.

On January 21, the announcement went out. El-Erian was leaving the firm. "The decision to step down from Pimco has not been an easy one," he wrote in an internal note sent around the firm. He would retain a consulting role with Allianz,* but, otherwise, his future— "what happens longer-term"—was "an open question."

He wanted to spend more time with his family—namely, his daughter. He would later tell the press that story of her list of important life events, the twenty-two transgressions. That was why he was quitting, he said. Maybe he wanted to write another book, too. Certainly, he was not quitting because his job was miserable or untenable.

---

* "It was Allianz that asked Dr. El-Erian to stay on within the Group as chief economic advisor," El-Erian's lawyer says. "It was not Dr. El-Erian's idea. At no point did Dr. El-Erian suggest or request this, and it's a position that he still holds today, seven years after leaving Pimco."

He'd known since May 2013, since that list, he said, that he needed to get out. It had been a matter of doing it.

It was reminiscent of his departure from Harvard Management, in which he emailed the staff saying he was leaving for family considerations, among other things, to give his daughter a greater sense of family in her formative years. Now, years later, he was again emphatically pinning his departure on his family, his then-ten-year-old daughter.

A day later, the *Financial Times* published a very different story. The departure was due to "long hours and a frequently fractious relationship" with Gross, according to unnamed sources who also said the two had "often sparred" over strategy. El-Erian's "ubiquity" was another speculated source of tension, an unnamed industry consultant said. "A small group of senior executives" had known he was going to leave "for several months," the article said, before extolling the investing prowess of Dan Ivascyn and noting that Andrew Balls had really "established himself in a big way."

Pimco's account executives and client-facing teams went into overdrive to control the narrative. In the days following El-Erian's announcement, they called more than 3,500 clients—calling and calling and calling, until they got a living human on the other end of the line. Leaving a voice message was insufficient.

Gross and El-Erian made a point of flattering each other externally. El-Erian said of Gross, "His talents are truly exceptional, as is his dedication," and Gross said that El-Erian was "a great leader, business builder and thought leader."

In an interview with *The Wall Street Journal*, Gross affirmed that El-Erian's exit "had nothing to do with friction," but he did concede that he could be difficult. "Sometimes people will say, 'Gross is too challenging,' and maybe so. I would say if you think I'm challenging now, you should have seen me 20 years ago."

Gross told Bloomberg that they'd appoint more deputy CIOs in the coming weeks. "I intend there to be a number of heirs apparent," he said.

Clients seemed not too perturbed, whether because of all the PR or because, thankfully, returns were starting to look up. Total Return had tracked its benchmark in January, or close enough: it generated 1.35 percent while the Barclays Agg returned 1.48 percent. A fine start! The Unconstrained fund was also doing better, after Gross had turned the portfolio upside down. He'd boosted the portfolio's sensitivity to rates, more than doubling it by the standard measure. That set the fund up to benefit if rates declined in January. And indeed, the yield on ten-year Treasuries fell, from 3 percent at the end of 2013 to 2.64 percent by the end of January. This helped Pimco Unconstrained return 0.58 percent that month, which, annualized, would be 7.1 percent—pretty good. Gross hadn't lost his touch after all.

But the management transition was rumbling on uneven rails. The *FT* article hadn't ruffled many feathers externally, but that same reporter published another one five days later. Somehow he'd managed to get details on El-Erian's alarm-clock setting and sleep schedule—that his alarm went off at 2:45 a.m., that he usually got into the office by 4:15 a.m., and that he generally got home around 7 p.m. and went to bed before 9 p.m. These grueling hours showed El-Erian's dedication, the demands of the job, why he had felt he needed to tap the brakes. But it was so specific. Internally, the articles created an itch of paranoia. Who had leaked to the journalist? Gross read them again, getting pissed. The last line—that Balls had "established himself in a big way"—got lodged in his mind. A small suspicion was born.

Meanwhile, Neel Kashkari's replacement, Virginie Maisonneuve, who was in town, marched into Gross's office and made a demand. If he wanted anyone to think Pimco took equities seriously, then *she* needed to be a DCIO, too. She had a point.

A week after El-Erian's announcement, Pimco announced four more DCIOs: Maisonneuve; corporate bond guy Mark Kiesel; Mihir Worah, who had a Ph.D. in theoretical physics from Chicago and oversaw "real return" teams (aka inflation protection); and Scott Mather, an ex–Goldman Sachs guy who had started in 1998 with Ivascyn, who now ran "global portfolio management."

Amid the upheaval, Gross realized he needed to step up. Some of El-Erian's responsibilities had reverted to him—stuff he hated but could handle, if he rallied. The whole point of El-Erian's hiring had been to give Gross a path out, but now, as sole CIO and the public face again, Gross had to keep reassuring clients that their money was safe.

"Pimco's fully engaged," he'd tweeted from the Pimco account. "Batteries 110% charged. I'm ready to go for another 40 years!"

Pimco's public relations team had met and decided there was nothing to do but to take the high road. Gross and the new DCIOs would be deployed as the face of the firm, and they'd continue telling the world that Pimco was stable. So far, they were pulling it off.

Gross went on CNBC to drive the message home. The anchor opened by saying she'd been surprised by El-Erian's decision. "It was a surprise to us, too," Gross said. "What we know and all we know, is that he doesn't have a new job. And he said that, if one develops, that it won't be in the financial industry . . . so Wall Street and the City in London can breathe easier, I guess."

He added: "We're disappointed that he won't be with Pimco, that he didn't continue with the successor role, for *me*, as chief investment officer, but that is the way it is." Slightly off message, slightly petty, but fine.

On February 5, Gross published his monthly *Investment Outlook*, again reassuring the public. "Believe me when I say, we are a better team at this moment than we were before," he wrote. "I/we take the future challenge faced by all asset managers with close to a sacred trust." If a reader wasn't alert and looking for the petty undertones, the tiny cuts, they could miss them entirely.

Internally, no one felt reassured. There was a reason Gross had never been CEO, never wanted to be: he was no stolid bureaucrat. Everyone within the firm, from management to trade assistants, knew this, had always known it: Gross was a trader, a legendary one, not a manager. Many also knew or heard that Gross had hand-picked Hodge and Jacobs because they were pleasant little reeds in the wind, people he could bend to his will—which made the company feel functionally headless.

El-Erian's pledge to stay until March was sort of nominal; his 4 A.M. presence at the office became less reliable. The building's facilities team disassembled and moved El-Erian's desk before the actual end of his tenure. According to El-Erian's lawyer, this was done on Gross's orders, and was "sudden, overnight, and unanticipated," while he was still managing client accounts. Then, his lawyer says, El-Erian was "told to work from his office; and was then told that Mr. Gross wanted his office moved to another building," and finally was "asked to work from home."

"All of this played out in a public way, which was damaging to Dr. El-Erian's professional standing," his lawyer says.

Pimco had minimized the *FT* articles, but the placid image of El-Erian's departure could not hold. The fact that the changeover wasn't messaged for months, as is common practice, smelled kind of weird.

Veteran reporter Greg Zuckerman at *The Wall Street Journal* caught this strange whiff. He'd talked to Gross countless times over more than a decade, visited the Newport Beach office. He picked up the phone and started dialing.

13

Inside the Showdown

The story was brutal.

It was splashed across the front page of *The Wall Street Journal* on Tuesday, February 25: INSIDE THE SHOWDOWN ATOP PIMCO, THE WORLD'S BIGGEST BOND FUND. The news: El-Erian had left Pimco because, basically, Bill Gross was a terrible asshole. El-Erian had been pushed to quit by untenable friction with Gross, Gross's testiness, his unreasonable demands.

The reporters on the byline were, unfortunately, very credible veteran journalists. Kirsten Grind had worked her sources while on parental leave, and she and Greg Zuckerman had nailed the story.

The *Journal* reporters wrote about Gross's off-putting coldness; his awkwardness with employees; his violent moods; his insistence on avoiding eye contact, on silence on the trade floor. They wrote that he reprimanded those who broke that silence, even if they were talking about investments; that he scolded employees for failing to number the pages of their presentations properly, which would later show up in "communication demerits" on their year-end bonus.

The story detailed confrontations that seemed indisputably, unspinnably bad. Like the "Secretariat" outburst, and El-Erian's "tired of cleaning up your shit" comment. That Gross had ordered a strict trading freeze in 2013 that couldn't be worked around. That he didn't like dissent when he'd made up his mind about an investment—arguably a rigidity that could inhibit achieving the best performance.

As an example, the *Journal* cited a senior investment manager who thought a bond in Gross's fund was expensive.

"Okay, buy me more of it," Gross had reportedly replied, apparently just to be a dick.

Or another, weirder story, from the early 2000s: when John Brynjolfsson was sitting on the trade floor and failed to stand up to greet visiting clients. This didn't sit well with Gross; Brynjo would see "consequences," Gross told him. This was a test, Brynjo knew. He could have argued, but there was a right answer. Gross suggested that he write a ten-thousand-dollar check to Pimco's foundation, and Brynjo did. Less than a year later, he was made partner. "I knew he wouldn't have tested me if I couldn't handle it," Brynjo told the *Journal*. "He's a great motivator of top talent." (Following the incident, a colleague patted Brynjo on the back and, as comfort, told him they used to do the same thing on his old team at Goldman Sachs. If someone cursed, they had to put twenty dollars in a jar on the head trader's desk which, once full, became a lunch slush fund for the trade floor. "That makes me feel better," Brynjo says, because that figure—just twenty dollars—showed that Pimco was in a bigger league than Goldman.)

The Wall Street Journal quoted Bill Powers, the longtime partner who'd left Pimco four years earlier: Gross "routinely grew tired and wary of those closest to him who had assumed significant responsibility, power, and compensation," Powers said. "After a four- to five-year honeymoon period, the chosen one's halo would turn into a crown of thorns [to the point] where interactions with Bill would turn adversarial, short, and unpleasant."

Powers's quote conjured associations for any Pimco insider, memories of those who'd fallen through the trapdoor next to Gross's desk—Powers himself, El-Erian, plus many others who had basked in the favoritism and then had abruptly found themselves on the outs, often with new psychological scars.

The article shocked those outside the bond market. The infighting, Gross's stringent rules on the trade floor, the crown of thorns? It was a lot. The Wall Street banks who covered Pimco knew how tightly wound things were in Newport Beach, as did competitors who'd heard the horror stories or who had interviewed there and run away in terror. But outside of that, no one had had a clue, until now. Most people, even in finance, had seen only Gross's folksy TV persona, his often eccentric *Investment Outlooks*. They may have read in those about his preoccupation with his own stomach fat, his fear of "cameras" in automatic-flushing toilets, or a memory of brutally undertipping a waitress. But they were totally unfamiliar with his bullying, his brittle insecurity.

Some of Gross's comments—"I have a forty-one-year track record of investing excellence. What do you have?"—quickly circulated among the loose confederation of fund managers and writers on "finance Twitter"; the bloggers at the website *Dealbreaker*; the talking heads on CNBC, Bloomberg.

Reuters's Felix Salmon wrote that Gross had to retire. "There is no way for Gross to recover from this article," Salmon wrote. "He knows it, too." El-Erian's job had been "to manage Pimco's risks, and he felt simply incapable of managing the biggest risk of all." Salmon added: "It's time for Bill Gross to take his leave of the company he built and for him to watch it thrive under more professional, less idiosyncratic, management."

Of course, Gross wasn't considering that now—and if he had been, if he'd wanted out, now he for sure wouldn't. But the *Journal* article freaked him out. It was a "crusher," he said later, a takedown. He read it slowly, carefully. El-Erian's departure, betrayal, had wounded him, and this was salt. He was shocked and hurt.

Is this the person I am and have been? he wondered. He'd thought of himself as being part of a weird Pimco family, of sharing and leading his people, not as coercive or bullying. That was the most unsettling part. Were they right?

He could not for the life of him understand the huge reaction to his demands for silence, for avoiding eye contact. Why did everybody object to that? Did he have to apologize for being an introvert? Sorry for trying to work—he had to focus, to trade. Sorry if he wasn't also running around the office hugging everyone, saying, *Hi, Sally. Hi, Joe, how you doing?* That's not who he was, had ever been.

He had defenders in that ocean of snark. Venture capitalist Marc Andreessen, a total stranger but a fellow billionaire in the public eye, sent a series of tweets saying, "The behavior described is completely typical of any highly-successful, high-functioning organization in any field I've ever seen . . . High-functioning business organizations aren't Disneyland. There's always stress, conflict, argument, dissent. Emotion. Drama." That, to him, sounded like "Apple, Oracle, Intel, Cisco, Google, Amazon and Microsoft."

Gross wrote down a short defense on legal paper, counting out his 140 characters as always, and handing it over for tweeting: "Clients come first. Performance and service that's our mission. Always has been. Always will be."

But that afternoon, he seemed compelled to try for more damage control. Banking on the public charm that had served him well for forty years, Gross called into CNBC's *Street Signs*, while his favorite anchor, Brian Sullivan, was on.

"Bill, thank you very much for joining us," a cheery Sullivan said. "I'm assuming you're calling in to react to what you heard from Greg Zuckerman. Or maybe yell at us."

"All of this discourse about an autocratic style, from my standpoint, and conflict between Mohamed and myself, is overblown," Gross told him, seeming unnerved, ruffled.

Sullivan asked if the article had any errors.

"I don't want to quarrel with Greg Zuckerman and his article," Gross said, forgetting the other half of the byline.

Did he really demand no speaking, no eye contact, especially in the mornings?

Sure, Gross said. He is not a morning person. He needs five cups of coffee to wake up. But there was that 8 A.M. conga line, "to let employees know that it was okay to scream and shout and to let it all hang out," he said. Employees could even pick their own rock songs! Pimco was fun and a family. El-Erian left, Gross said, because he told us that he wasn't the man to carry out his own plan.

Sullivan asked Gross if he was friends with El-Erian.

"He's always been a good friend," Gross said. Their wives were involved in charity together, he said.

Gross's voice was sometimes difficult to understand on the line. Sullivan asked what was up.

"I'm on my wife's cell phone," Gross said. "We have a medical situation."

"Now I feel like a jerk," Sullivan said.

In truth, Sue was sick. Gross never spoke about it publicly, but his wife was recovering from surgery in the hospital. Gross was commuting to the hospital, keeping watch by her side. Separately, their son, Nick, was having business trouble, a music world partnership that Gross had funded in 2013 going south. Gross was unaccustomed to this level of stress.

He defended Pimco's culture directly to the *Journal* article's authors, Zuckerman and Grind, a few days later. The trade floor wasn't a gentle, beautiful place to be, he said. But "it's like dealing with family," he said. "You don't always produce a productive family by sweet talking and always being inclusive. There's a time for soft love and time for hard love. . . . I can admit to both."

Sometimes he made jokes, he said, and sometimes people didn't understand those jokes, and they were misinterpreted as insults. Or maybe it was sour grapes, because he was the ultimate decider, and that always sowed resentment. That was human nature.

"It's hard to see yourself through other people's eyes," he told them. With the recent changes, Gross said, he was sharing power, reducing his role in the Investment Committee, trying to pipe down. "It's a huge change," he said.

Gross hoped this would address the growing external perception that, without El-Erian, no one could stand up to him. People were welcome to challenge him—encouraged, even!

It was comforting that Allianz saw no problems. Michael Diek-mann, chief executive of Pimco's German parent, told the *Journal* that the insurer was "very happy" with the new management structure. Diekmann said it had finally answered "the long-term question whether Pimco is a Bill Gross one-man show or more than that." Allianz would continue its absent-parent oversight from Munich.

Doug Hodge told the *Journal* that few clients seemed to care about the damning article; only a handful had contacted Pimco in the aftermath. It was "remarkably quiet," he said. "They hire us not because it's happy talk around here, but because we deliver performance."

But the *Journal* article seemed to be all anyone in finance could talk about, for days; they were shocked by the distance between Gross's public persona and how he apparently acted on the trade floor. He'd seemed so down home, unpretentious, the bond market's Warren Buffett.

Contrary to Hodge's sunny account, rumors began to trickle through the media that clients were in fact beginning to worry, that pension consultants whose advice directed billions and billions of dollars had started putting Pimco on watch lists. If, previously, hiring Pimco could never get an allocator fired, now it was suddenly seen as high risk.

There was one other inflammatory nugget in the article: it reported that in recent years, Gross took home more than $200 million annually. This was actually way low—in 2013, it was more like $300 million, but publishing a lowball estimate is always safer than being too precise. Still, the reported figure made a splash.

Previously, information about Pimco's outsize salaries had been scant: *The New York Times* reported in 2012 that El-Erian received about $100 million in 2011, and Gross about $200 million. Those figures were immediately seized on by the media, especially given that 2011 had been the performance "stinker." Pimco's spokesman wouldn't confirm those figures at the time, but here it was again, the same figure for Gross, reported by other journalists. It now felt undeniable.

On a good day anywhere in finance, $200 million would be considered staggering—it was about ten times what the CEO of Goldman Sachs got in a year, about ten times what Gross's competitor at BlackRock, Larry Fink, got. But Gross defenders would point out that Gross took that home for 2012, the one year of decent performance sandwiched between two of the worst years of Total Return's history—the two years Gross misstepped, in his four-decade career, as he managed the most money any mutual fund had ever contained. Bad timing. It was his firm, and his firm did well.

Shortly after the story broke, a board member brought it up at a meeting. Bill Popejoy was one of five independent watchdogs for investors in Pimco's funds, and he led the board's committee on governance. Although two Pimco executives sat on the board (Hodge and Brent Harris), Popejoy said the board had learned about the Gross/El-Erian drama when they read about it in the newspaper, like everybody else. Popejoy, who at age seventy-five had been a trustee for twenty-three years, told the board that the $200 million figure "was so outrageous" that they "should get involved." He added: "If Pimco overpaid so outrageously, then we the trustees must be authorizing payments/fees to Pimco that were too high," he said.

In March, he went public with these thoughts. "I don't know if Secretariat made $200 million a year," he told the *Los Angeles Times*. "You could hire 2,000 schoolteachers for that money." Plus, Gross's performance had been "mediocre," and his management style sounded "bullying" and "worrisome," Popejoy said, "if what I read is true." He added: "You just can't treat people that way and expect things to be OK."

Allianz should look into Gross's conduct, Popejoy said, and try to rein him in—in salary and behavior. "I'm not suggesting he be replaced," he said, but Gross's salary "needs to be reviewed," and that perhaps $20 million would be more appropriate.

In May, Popejoy was off the board, after Pimco abruptly instituted age limits for Pimco Fund trustees, which affected Popejoy and one other person. Popejoy would later say this was revenge for his sharing his opinions on Gross and/or for butting heads with the board chairman, Pimco partner Brent Harris, over the lack of diversity on the entirely white and male board: Harris wanted to fill a free seat with a guy he knew who'd worked at Treasury, but Popejoy lobbied to appoint a woman or a person of color. In the end, he kind of helped achieve this: while Pimco filled the two vacant seats with two white men, including Harris's buddy, they also named a white woman to the board.

In mid-February, a group of El-Erian loyalists, including Josh Thimons, a volatility trader, organized going-away drinks for their departing leader. They sent out invitations, setting a date of March 10, and got to planning.

It quickly became apparent that this simple party was too politically charged. Paranoid RSVPs trickled back: people didn't want to come for fear of retribution. The internal opinion of the outgoing CEO had soured now that there was no longer any upside to supporting him; it was more politically expedient to shed any El-Erian allegiance. If they attended his farewell party, it would put a bull's-eye on their backs.

That Friday, a rattled Gross was again making the multi-hour highway trek between his home and the hospital in LA where Sue was recovering from surgery. As he drove, he got increasingly incensed. All these people reading these articles thought El-Erian was such a great guy, so nice, when really, he wasn't. They didn't know how manipulative he was—he'd manipulated *them!* They needed to know the truth, what had actually happened. Gross needed to clear things up. It was time to announce El-Erian's bad intentions.

Gross pulled the car over and took out his and Sue's phone. He couldn't think of whom to call, what reporters he knew; he could remember only Zuckerman and Grind, and he knew better than to call them. Schmoozing the press—that was El-Erian's thing! Gross's media relationships were more utilitarian, and transient—bond expert to bond reporter du jour. Oh, but what about Jennifer Ablan, at Reuters! She was always a friendly enough ear, though she also seemed to get on well with El-Erian. She might be able to shed some light on what the latter was doing.

This is the only thing I got, Gross thought, dialing.

She answered, and words started to tumble out. He explained: *Mohamed is trying to poison the press against me. I have evidence.* El-Erian "wrote" that damning *Journal* article himself, basically, he said. El-Erian was trying to detail their failing relationship, to get his side of the story out, obviously to hurt Gross. "I'm so sick of Mohamed trying to undermine me," he said.

Ablan interrupted, asking to see the evidence. After knowing him all these years, she wouldn't take him at his word that El-Erian had engineered the article.

"You're on his side!" Gross said. "Great, he's got you, too, wrapped around his charming right finger!"

This confirmed it: Ablan had been talking to El-Erian, too. El-Erian had probably been talking to all the outlets. No one would ever hear Gross out now; they all loved El-Erian. Gross couldn't compete with that; he was toast. His mind was skipping.

"I know El-Erian has been talking to you *and* the *Journal*," he said. He knew, he said, because he'd been monitoring whom El-Erian talked to on the phone.

Ablan dutifully took down what Gross said. And then she published it.

Her story was met with incredulity. Had Gross thought he was speaking "on background," not for attribution? No, he had clearly been on the record. Had he lost his mind?

The first reaction from Pimco was to deny: "Mr. Gross did not make the statements Reuters attributes to him," a spokesperson said. "He categorically denies saying this firm ever listened in on Mr. El-Erian's phone calls or that Mr. El-Erian 'wrote' any previous media article . . .

As a regulated company, PIMCO is required to retain records of its employees' communications to help ensure compliance with the firm's policies."

Gross had known immediately when he hung up that calling Reuters was a mistake. He explained to people at Pimco that he'd been under stress, because of his wife's surgery, the trips to the hospital; he wasn't himself. He was unhappy about the Reuters story, but what could you do?

According to Pimco's official account, Gross pledged to the Executive Committee not to comment further about El-Erian in the press. He also produced what he said were notes from the call, a transcript of sorts, red scratches of dialogue on a yellow legal pad. Pimco says Gross told them that he took the notes in his car, while pulled over on the shoulder of the 405, and later found them in the trunk of his car.

Hodge and Jacobs were livid. In the Reuters article, Gross sounded unhinged, fixated on El-Erian, bitter over the separation. He sounded like a man engulfed in the irrational rage of divorce, not a rational manager on an executive search.

In the wake of the article, El-Erian asked Thimons to postpone his going-away party. Things were tense, El-Erian explained. He didn't want to make it more awkward than it already was, especially for those who had to continue at Pimco.

Morningstar downgraded Pimco's firmwide "stewardship grade" from a "B" to a "C," mentioning the "fractious interactions" among management, uncertainty after El-Erian's and Seidner's departures, and Gross's "at-times tempestuous behavior." Morningstar analysts had visited Pimco on March 10 to ask if any of this drama would hurt performance, because if so, they needed to warn investors.

Gross was convinced that his now enemy was getting the better bullhorn and that the discord at Pimco was threatening to show up in real ways, where it mattered: with clients. He needed to tighten his grip on the narrative, on the firm. He needed to reassure the troops that he was their leader, now and for always; that they had no reason to fear. He needed to close ranks, make sure everyone was united behind him.

He called a companywide meeting, ahead of the quarterly Cyclical Forum that set Pimco's shorter outlook; he spent twenty minutes talking about El-Erian's departure. He wanted to give *his* version, share it with the entire firm, the traders and analysts who maybe had heard only snippets, left out as they were of Executive Committee and most Investment Committee meetings.

This stays in the room, he told the hushed assembled crowd. He didn't want it leaking.

He talked about how he didn't really understand El-Erian. That it turned out that El-Erian wasn't who we thought he was. El-Erian had said he wasn't the right guy to lead us forward, and he was de facto correct in this: He abandoned us, Gross said. He was a wolf in sheep's clothing.

To those in the room, it was clear from Gross's words that he was deeply wounded, as if he had lost a son or a wife. Angry, too. He seemed emotional, inappropriately so.

He went on that he, Bill Gross, would firmly take the helm, as he had in the past. We'll be stronger than ever. We're Pimco, after all!

His words hung in the air, tense and sour. They weren't landing: to many present, the speech sounded off-key, especially the "wolf in sheep's clothing" thing. That was a little much.

Nonetheless, when Gross finished, the room rose, a sea of suits at attention, giving a standing ovation for his speech. Hodge stood, Ivascyn stood, clapping, awkwardly, next to Gross at the front of the room. They knew what had actually happened, had been present during the fights, but they would put on a unified front for the troops.

Josh Thimons didn't stand. This, as everyone else in the room also knew, was bullshit.

Thimons hadn't been quiet about his misgivings over Gross's leadership. His coworkers recall his running commentary about how Gross was destroying the firm, his loud questioning of whether Gross was going senile. Thimons loved the place, and Gross's insanity or senility, or whatever, was destroying it. Thimons was already an enemy of the state, having planned El-Erian's aborted send-off. And this was bullshit. So, Thimons stayed seated, which, in a place that measures power in seating charts and standing ovations, was open insurrection.

The Forum revealed another split, in investing outlook: Gross faced off with his DCIOs over the U.S. economy's future. He thought everything was going to be kind of bad, forever. They didn't. Four of the DCIOs—Virginie Maisonneuve, Mark Kiesel, Dan Ivascyn, and Andrew Balls—tried to show Gross that he was being too pessimistic, that he was stuck in this murky old postcrisis "new normal" view of the world and missing the bright reality of what was actually happening in the country.

Mark Kiesel, czar of corporate credit, banged the table, vibrating his tuft of red-orange hair, to emphasize his point that the U.S. energy market was growing by leaps and bounds, and that it would propel employment and growth. The private sector was healing. Employment was picking up. Airlines, too! "You're paying more for middle seats!"

Maisonneuve said stocks would climb faster than the 5 percent Gross had forecast. Ivascyn said home prices were going to climb 3 to 5 percent for the next two years. In the end, they managed to nudge up Pimco's forecast for U.S. economic output. Ostensibly, a small victory, but internally, it felt pretty significant.

As usual, Gross processed it in the press. "The investment committee had been dominated by bond people," who tend to see the world as half-empty, he later told Bloomberg News. With the new structure, he said, "the committee is more evenly balanced in terms of optimism and pessimism."

Gross was on a hunt. He was watching, silently, as odd behaviors proliferated within the firm and as articles favorable to El-Erian surfaced in the media. Internal events kept showing up in the *Journal*, Bloomberg

News, everywhere, with conversations cited verbatim, sometimes right after they happened. How? Who?

Someone at Pimco was sabotaging him, them, from the inside. Someone Pimco had chosen, someone they were paying ungodly sums of money, was talking to the press, leaking damaging information, undermining the company in public and, slowly, destroying it. Pimco had a mole, maybe multiple moles. It was no longer safe within Pimco's walls. Someone was actively seeking to hurt the firm. Who would do that? The thought disgusted Gross, horrified him.

Suspicion grew in his head, began to take over. It could be anyone. His most trusted lieutenants, his oldest allies. He had no way of knowing who the traitor was. And all the while, they were clipping their fat coupons. It was eating away at him; he had to get to the bottom of it.

He wasn't wrong. There were people speaking to the press, dozens; he was one of them.

"There's a group of people that are hunting Bill," one person inside the firm said at the time. "Bill manages seven hundred billion dollars. A lot of people see that the day he retires, those assets are going to be released; they're going to be up for grabs."

And the stakes were particularly high: the SEC had been poking around Pimco for months, asking about how to value bonds, how to mark them, the firm's third-party pricing systems. Pimco was proud never to have gotten a Wells Notice, that dreaded warning of imminent enforcement action. Everyone was nervous that their luck might have run out.

To find the leaker(s), Pimco's general counsel David Flattum combed through emails and telephone logs. Gross printed some of the emails and put them in a three-ring binder, adding his own handwritten notes. He clipped in his observations, scrawled notes on legal paper or printouts about who the "moles" might be. He carried it around the office with him, everywhere he went, like a security blanket.

Gross and Flattum gathered a list of potential candidates, those most likely to be the spies, and brought them in for questioning. They enlisted DCIO Mihir Worah to aid them. People were abruptly pulled aside, seemingly at random. Gross was interrogating his employees, from members of the Investment Committee and managing directors down to lower-ranking money managers, analysts, and traders. Gross's binder sat open on the table during interrogations.

They found a Bloomberg chat room where a group of junior employees talked about everyone using code names, and they devoted an inordinate amount of energy to decoding these code names. The junior employees referred to Gross as "Papa." El-Erian was "Pharaoh." Josh Thimons was "JT" or "Justin Timberlake." Sudi Mariappa, "Suit & tie." And "MSFT" (the stock ticker for Microsoft, often fondly called "Mister Softee") was Marc Seidner. "Knives are out," they'd said.

In an interrogation, one of the chat room participants remembered Seidner saying something about how a mole would be someone who had the most to gain from a leak . . . maybe someone like Thimons? To Gross, this was circumstantial evidence, but evidence nonetheless.

Also: Gross was convinced that Hodge and Jacobs weren't protecting him. One day, he confronted them in a conference room just off the trade floor. As he whisper-shouted accusations, Hodge sat with his head in his hands, waiting for it to end. Gross thought for sure he'd gotten through to them.

Shortly afterward, a journalist called asking about that exact moment.

To Gross, this was proof: Weren't Hodge and Jacobs the leaks? Because if it wasn't them—no one else was in that meeting—then Pimco's email had been hacked. Someone had gotten into their system. Gross demanded a firmwide inspection of email. (Gross says he didn't do that.)

After a couple days of freaking out about their compromised system, Gross railed about the incident in an Executive Committee meeting. The rest of the committee gently reminded him that the meeting in question had taken place in a glass room near the trade floor, in plain view of more than sixty people.

Gross couldn't accept this. That wasn't right; they had met in *private*. It had been *private*.

After some coaxing—*no, we all saw you in that glass room, we assumed that you'd done that on purpose, made it into a show*—Gross paused. He closed his big binder. Oh yeah, he told the committee. Actually, that was by design; he'd meant to. He wanted to intimidate people, by yelling at Hodge and Jacobs for all to see. He wanted to make them examples, to send a message: *Don't leak.* (Gross disputes that this episode happened.)

Gross's suspicions didn't end there. He was looking at everyone sideways. But his attention began to focus on two men: Andrew Balls, the former journalist, and Josh Thimons.

For his part, Thimons already knew that Gross had an eye on him. He wasn't going to wait around, or go quietly. Thimons filed an internal complaint claiming that Gross had made sexist, ageist, and racist comments—he'd called a female managing director "Blondie" and had referred to another employee as "that old Egyptian guy." And he'd front-run his own portfolio manager team's good trades.

Pimco dutifully opened an internal investigation. Which eventually exonerated Gross. But Thimons's complaint had cast a protective bubble around himself: if Pimco took any action against Thimons now, he would have a very strong case that they were retaliating for whistleblowing. He was unfireable.

Gross's other target proved easier. There was robust logic behind it: El-Erian had helped to hire Balls in 2006. Bloomberg wrote a glowing profile of the Oxford graduate, as his two biggest funds were beating more than 90 percent of competitors, in which Balls praised El-Erian and bragged about his own (team's) investing prowess. At any other time, this would maybe not have caught Gross's attention, but now his senses were heightened.

And that *Financial Times* article, right after El-Erian left. So flattering—kind, even—to El-Erian. Balls used to work at the *FT*. It was a straight line: he still talked to his friends there.

David Flattum checked the phone logs and, indeed, Balls had talked to someone at the *FT*. In violation of firm policies. Got him.

Balls had to confess. Hodge and Jacobs forced him to make a written statement, signed and dated, saying he'd spoken to a reporter. Balls obediently wrote an account of first checking with El-Erian, still then the CEO, on January 22. Pimco's media policy was if the CEO says do it, it's okay. So this was within bounds. El-Erian had said he was concerned that the *FT* was working on a critical story, according to Balls's confession; the reporter was going to write that El-Erian left "because of Allianz or client dissatisfaction with Pimco investment performance."

"I said that I had received emails from several reporters that I had not responded to and would call a friend at the *FT* and speak to him on background to hear the narrative and point out inaccuracies," Balls wrote. "I spoke to the reporter who said that the story was close to publication and referred me to another reporter at the *FT* who I called. I then spoke to the reporter on background on the circumstances of Mr El-Erian's resignation. I spoke to Mr El-Erian afterwards to recount the details of the call. Mr El-Erian was the chief executive officer of Pimco."

He wrote that he'd also talked to a reporter at *The Wall Street Journal* in mid-February. But again, he did so at the request of El-Erian, who was still the CEO.

Balls apologized and offered to resign. Pimco's management felt the infraction was not ideal. But the firm was still reeling from El-Erian's departure. There'd been too much turmoil at the firm, too many damaging articles, and Balls was a newly appointed DCIO, whose funds were doing well. They had to hold steady. And . . . if they fired Balls now, under these circumstances, wouldn't he have grounds to sue? Or at the very least tell the press what things were really like inside the building? They couldn't do anything right now.

They agreed to push it off until the end of the year. At which time, yes, Balls would have to go.

They let Balls know. He got the picture. He agreed to keep up appearances, and looked forward to a fair compensation review.

But what about Gross's original mole, El-Erian? He was still collecting money from the company; he should not be allowed to profit from the firm he was actively working to destroy. El-Erian had also recently started tweeting, invading Gross's favorite social media platform, on which he had allegedly caused El-Erian such consternation. Gross could only imagine what kind of smear campaign El-Erian was preparing to mount.*

Gross asked the Executive Committee to fire El-Erian retroactively, or at least deny him part of his $50 million bonus for the first quarter of 2014. Some of his colleagues would recount that Gross wanted to smear El-Erian anonymously in the press, or to bait him into suing Pimco, believing it would hurt his chances at a new job. They remember him demanding that they present Gross in a better light to a newspaper reporter. He wasn't one to let things lie. He wanted to strike back.

The Executive Committee refused. They found his requests disturbing: it was so far beyond the bounds of anything resembling professional. What would clients say if they heard any of this? He was not handling this well. At this point, it became urgent to have a real succession plan in place. Maybe over a shorter time horizon, like a year. Or maybe less. Just in case things didn't settle down.

Hodge warned Gross that, at some point, he could be held accountable for his behavior.

Gross remembers that as Hodge pulling him aside and saying, "I could fire you, you know."

---

* "Not once did Dr. El-Erian use social media or any other media to say anything remotely critical of Mr. Gross," El-Erian's lawyer says.

14

Stealing the Firm

Bill Gross had a solution: a media tour.

If his image had been shattered, he didn't know it. Or he didn't let on. Or maybe he didn't think it was permanent: For forty years, keeping at it had kept him on top. Stay in the game, avoid "ruin," as card players said, and eventually you won. He would keep at it; he'd show them.

So, in late March 2014, Pimco allowed *Bloomberg Businessweek*'s Sheelah Kolhatkar to visit their Newport Beach offices. She was going to write a cover story about the firm's new structure, Gross without El-Erian. Pimco would show a new, positive face to the world.

Kolhatkar sat in the sunny office as Gross told her from his swivel chair about his morning routine, beginning with his 4:30 wake-up.

Step by step: He would make coffee, he told her, and feed treats to his cats; sneak a glance at the Bloomberg Terminal in his library, kiss Sue good-bye without disturbing her sleep. He generally ate two scrambled eggs every morning and would grab a box of Special K with blueberries to eat while driving his black Mercedes along the Pacific Coast Highway, his knees conducting the steering wheel as the highway went from hugging the cliffs of Laguna to passing the strip malls of Corona del Mar and Newport Beach. He would get his daily "black eye" at Starbucks—"two shots of whatever they shoot it with"—and then, around 5:30 A.M., he'd settle into his desk on Pimco's trade floor. An enormous red binder always sat on the windowsill behind his desk, full of printouts of the contents of all the portfolios Gross over-saw. Then, his 9 A.M. hour of stationary biking—formerly yoga—at the nearby Marriott.

Kolhatkar listened and took notes. She walked on the trade floor, past Gross's seven monitors at his U-shaped desk, past the big space next to it, where El-Erian's desk had been.

Gross talked about his relationship with El-Erian, and other executives past and present chimed in, too. Sure, he was intense, Bill Thompson said of Gross, but that's what made him such a great trader. El-Erian's task had been to push the firm beyond burgers and bonds, and yes, Gross conceded, there'd been some friction: "It wasn't all a smoothie, so to speak. There were some chunks of ice cream in the milkshake in terms of how to do it," Gross said. "Mohamed, coming from the IMF, was always a big meeting guy, the more at the table the better. I was always the-smaller-the-better because that prevents the consensual mush."

Kolhatkar sat in on an Investment Committee meeting that in-cluded a "spirited debate about whether it was possible to know how soon interest rates would go up"—a debate that Gross insisted couldn't have happened a few months prior. "The willingness of everyone to jump in—this to me is, like, man, this is really good," Gross told her afterward, while he ate a turkey sandwich. "The challenge of this new structure is making sure that the risk vs. return is being adequately adjusted for, without being 'the boss.' But I ultimately am responsible."

The big, looming question, he told her, was whether this "happy family of deputies" would translate into satisfied clients. "I'm sure they want us to be happy and joyful and have good lives, but their primary concern is that *they're* happy, which I think has always been our focus—you be happy first, and we'll worry about our happiness second. It's proved to be true with me: A happy wife is a happy life."

Of course, happiness within Pimco didn't naturally translate into good results, he said. Sort of the opposite, actually. "It's not always necessarily a productive process to have everyone leave the meeting with smiles on their faces. Maybe there should be a grain of sand in the oyster to produce the pearl, maybe there *should* be some conflict." He had to strike a balance between being too autocratic and too sweet, he said—whatever mix would produce the right results.

"Like a captain on a ship," he said. "We want to have a fighting team that sinks the other navy ships, as opposed to a fighting team that's happy and has to man the lifeboats. That's the danger in this—it's not all love and kisses and cheesecake dessert."

Kolhatkar went back to New York to write her article. She contacted Pimco to check facts. They waited. In the meantime, Gross's charm offensive continued: On April 10, he went on Bloomberg Television. Keeping at it. Despite (because of?) feeling totally unsupported. Anchor Trish Regan immediately asked him about the rumor mill following El-Erian's departure. Gross fidgeted and laughed awkwardly. She asked how he thought he'd been treated by the media?

"This whole past two months has been sorta silly," he said, his hair twitching with each jerk of his head. "*Breaking* news, Gross gets mad once in a while!

"Did Mohamed leave because Gross gets mad sometimes?" he asked, taking on the *Journal* story's perspective. "The answer's no. But it would have been helpful, from my standpoint and from the company's standpoint, for Mohamed to have spoken up and to have cleared the air and supported the company he so proudly helped build . . . and he hasn't. He hasn't spoken up, and that's a mystery to us and, quite frankly, an extreme disappointment."

Regan pinched her face in concern: "Any sense of why he didn't speak up? Does this get at some of the issues that you guys were dealing with internally?"

"No, I don't think so, and it's a mystery to us," Gross said, Regan nodding. "He simply said that he wasn't the man to take the company forward, and he constantly repeated that, without explaining it." Gross held up his hands, showing invisible boxes holding El-Erian's secret reasons. "He didn't really say that he had lost interest; obviously he's still interested in the markets." He had that gig as "chief economic advisor" at Allianz, and was already writing columns about finance for various outlets.

Gross collapsed the imaginary boxes with a shrug and started talking faster: "He simply said he wasn't 'the person,' and that's a mystery, and the additional mystery, as I've mentioned, is the fact that he hasn't spoken up." Gross bunched up his face in a childish approximation of confusion. "I would simply say, 'Come on, Mohamed, tell us why,' because the furor over the past two months in terms of the headlines really are quite exaggerated, and it's not indicative of what this company is, what this company was, and what this company will be in terms of our future structure."

"Bill, how has that made you feel?" Regan pressed. "Knowing that this was a guy you worked alongside and really was a trusted partner, your co-CIO, the idea that he leaves and—and doesn't say anything?"

Gross swallowed. "I thought I knew him better," he said. "We hired him, quite frankly, to be my successor, so does that make me mad? Yes, that makes me mad. Does that make me disillusioned? Not really, because, like I said, we have a future that's now probably better"—only one eye blinked—"than what we had in the past." Both eyes were now blinking rapidly, too rapidly, as he recited the firm's new structure. "This is a different type of company, that is inclusive, that yes, hopefully, Gross responds to in terms of allowing discussion, and allowing even potential disagreement."

Pimco employees watched this performance from the trade floor, jaws slack. Gross knew why El-Erian had left. What was he hoping to achieve with this? *Mohamed, tell us why?* Wasn't there a nondisclosure agreement? Was Gross intentionally baiting El-Erian, knowing he couldn't talk? This was a step beyond bickering parents. Now one was provoking the other and airing emotional problems on live television.

As the bright lights shut off, Gross unhooked his microphone. He was not supposed to say anything about El-Erian, and he had gone and done it. And this time there was tape, a transcript; he couldn't deny it had happened. But surely this was a minor boo-boo.

As Gross stepped off the set, Jay Jacobs was already calling an emergency meeting of the top executives. Gross was not invited; he was not even told about it. The group recapped Gross's Bloomberg appearance. They had to do something; this could not continue. They decided, without dispute: Gross would no longer be allowed to go on television. Or do any media. A temporary suspension.

Jacobs got to deliver the news. At the time Gross was busy trying to coax Paul McCulley back to Pimco, four years after his "retirement." Getting McCulley back would help Gross and the firm feel confident again, stable—like its old self. Everyone loved McCulley, "the [Dude from the] Big Lebowski" of financial markets. The rabbit sculptures McCulley had kept on his desk were still there, waiting for him; they'd even moved to the new building. McCulley could be a jolt of goodwill, if Gross could cajole him into rejoining the place he'd once called "Camelot."

Jacobs, a slow, quiet talker, took his time getting to the point, according to Gross, but finally told him: He was suspended from media appearances. The committee had decided.

Gross was furious. *I wasn't even allowed to participate in my own hanging.* "I'm part of the Executive Committee," he said, his thin voice vibrating with intensity. "I'm, if anything, a witness here. I don't care whether you have a tape of the discussion or not. . . . You wouldn't do that to anybody in this committee, let alone me. I at least deserve a hearing!"

Jacobs calmly reminded him that there was a transcript: *Mohamed, why are you leaving?* Even though he knew he was not supposed to talk about El-Erian.

"So, obviously," Jacobs said, as Gross remembers it, "Gross, you can't be controlled. So, obviously, we'll control you."

"You and I are *done!*" Gross shouted.

In the heat of the moment, he may also have said something about quitting. And why not? No matter how much Pimco management wanted to rein him in, they couldn't risk his quitting, not amid all the turmoil. It would destroy the firm. It was his trump card.

What they didn't understand was the firm *needed* him on TV.

Clients were still pulling their money, every month, from every offering in Pimco's mutual fund complex. Now it wasn't a macro, taper-related move away from bonds: It was just Pimco. Everyone else in bonds was seeing *inflows*.

The very next day, the *Journal* published an interview with El-Erian about his departure. "We always had different styles, which made us very good complements in serving our clients and leading the firm forward through both smooth and rough markets," El-Erian said. "That worked very well for a long time, until last year."

Every word seemed crafted to stoke Gross's rage, his feeling that El-Erian had fooled everyone into loving him. One day they would learn.

Even as their leader was acting increasingly desperate, even as they fretted about what horror would come next, Pimco's executives and analysts and traders were trying to carry on as if everything was fine. There was one redeeming factor amid the chaos: Gross *was* letting other people talk, even in Investment Committee—an improvement from having the twin pillars of Gross and El-Erian at the head of a rectangular table, taking turns leading the meetings. Now they were sitting at a round table, like the knights, as McCulley had always said—this place *was* Camelot!—and Gross was sitting back, somewhat uncomfortably, chairing only one of every seven Investment Committee meetings, letting his six DCIOs rotate chairmanship. Maybe he could actually loosen his grasp.

Four days after Gross's disastrous Bloomberg TV interview, Kolhatkar's big *Businessweek* cover story came out. The article was not ideal. It was fair. But the cover. There was Gross, his eyebrows raised, his gaze up and off into the distance, his palms raised, under a headline in huge letters arranged for Dr. Seussian effect: AM I REALLY SUCH A JERK?

Kolhatkar quoted Gross, speaking "in the singsong voice of a Dr. Seuss character," referring to himself extensively in the third person: "Our Gross has not been a happy camper for the last two months," he told her. "But an unhappy captain still has to steer the ship through the rocks."

It didn't improve from there. "It's been like a near-death experience, an emotional blow," Gross told her. "Whenever I read the newspaper, I say to myself, 'At least my wife loves me.'"

On El-Erian: "I begged, as much as a man in my position can beg. I didn't get on my knees, but—'Don't leave. What are you doing? Don't!' And at some point, it was, 'All right, already.'"

Of the empty space next to Gross's desk, Kolhatkar wrote: "One gets the sense that people go out of their way to walk around it, as if avoiding the chalk outline of a murder victim on the sidewalk."

The hoped-for positive angle had not panned out. But there was no one to be mad at.

So, slight damage control. Pimco needed to turn the focus back to its investing, which was doing better this year, finally, even as outflows continued.

New DCIO Scott Mather said in April on Bloomberg that Pimco was moving away from the "new normal" framework, that the economy was "going to head back to a new destination."

A week later, Gross called into the same show, saying that Mather had been "a little out over his skis, in terms of declaring the new normal dead." Actually, he said, Pimco was still pretty much on that same "normal" track!

Over the spring and summer, the chasm between the pessimists like Gross and the optimists inside the firm only grew. And the optimists, those who'd bet on the U.S. economy's growing, were outperforming Gross.

The deputies seemed emboldened by their new positions, maybe more so by beating Gross's performance. Kiesel and Balls were overweight longer-dated bonds, and that was the right spot to be. But they—and Ivascyn—were trouncing Total Return.

They could also be a little braver because the nuclear option suddenly felt available: they could leave. When long-haul Pimco people left, they often evaporated, blackballed by Wall Street like Jason Williams or burned out like so many others. But Seidner had shown them, reminded them it was possible: when he left, in January, he was the biggest name they'd seen walk out and get a new, real job.

A strange new power dynamic was forming. After years of expansion, with new products and new faces on TV, Gross was beginning to look like one fund manager among many. And kind of an average one—Total Return was becoming a drag, as money continued to pour out. Gross's power seemed now largely derived from the other fund managers, not the other way around. Ivascyn, not Total Return, was driving profitability. The next generation was rising.

In his own way, Gross seemed to be working on healing. In May, he sent an email to the Executive Committee asking each of them to reflect on all that had happened since Mohamed El-Erian's resignation: that they didn't fire El-Erian, that they *did* pay him, even as he was working against the firm; that El-Erian had been able to get a senior position at Allianz immediately, with ease. The not-firing of Andrew Balls, whom Gross had taken to calling "Mr. X." And, lastly, banning Gross from media. Were these the right choices? Did they think so then, and do they still think so now?

The recipients conferred and decided it seemed counterproductive to snipe individually. They should air it all out, talk through it together. A collective autopsy.

So they replied-all. In individual emails, they lamented the heartbreak of El-Erian's betrayal, how he was still wreaking havoc even in absentia, the hours of sickening decision-making. The general sense was that the choices were suboptimal but barely even choices: they'd had to pay El-Erian out, through gritted teeth, or risk an ugly, destructive lawsuit; keeping El-Erian at Allianz was a mistake but likely did help to control what he said in public, to some extent, and anyway it wasn't clear they could have stopped it. And they'd *had* to ban Gross from media, to give him a cooling-off period. They probably should have invited him to the meeting deciding that, yes. But the outcome was correct. The committee had to be able to enforce policy, or the firm's management would be a joke.

In Ivascyn's email, he tried to walk a careful line: Gross was the founder and deserved to control his own destiny. But they needed him to focus. Hodge and Jacobs were not the enemy; the enemies were external, at competitors like DoubleLine and BlackRock. Morale was suffering. People were starting to hear about Gross's behavior.

Gross had a fix for that. The same prescription as before. A PR campaign, more aggressive this time, to reverse the impression that he was an autocratic leader.

After that year's "Secular Forum" in May, Gross was reading the summary observations from one of the firm's prominent economic advisors, economist Rich Clarida. Gross was going to write up conclusions from the Forum that would set Pimco's framework for the next three to five years. There, in the text, he saw the perfect phrase: "the new neutral."

It was catchy, iterative, a riff on the success of "the new normal."

"Now we've got it," Gross said, circling it with a pen: the new *neutral*.

The communications team pushed the new phrase, and the financial press wrote it up. Pimco's united front, the thought leader in bonds (and beyond!), saw a new neutral, whatever that meant.

It was a bit more complicated to understand than the new normal, but basically it signified more of the same: it referred to the "neutral rate" that the central banks focused on, the magical level at which the Fed should do nothing.

Market estimates for that rate were too high, Pimco argued, and so were missing a quiet but steady rally. Nothing was going to return that much, but it was going to chug ahead peacefully. The new normal, but calmer.

Pimco focused on shorter-dated bonds, because the market was overestimating how fast the Fed would raise rates. The firm bought high-yield bonds, riskier stuff, expecting not a ton of profit but stability, low volatility.

"We've got a thesis here, we're sticking to our guns, our new guns, in terms of the new neutral," Gross said. "Believe me, by the end of 2014, Pimco's going to be at the top, not close to the middle."

That summer, the economy was doing well enough, but not gangbusters—the lukewarm middle that kept the Fed on hold, still supportive and with no movement toward raising rates. So, Gross doubled down on one of his favorite strategies, selling volatility, betting that market swings would be less wild than everyone else's anxiety told them.

Through that summer, as quietly as possible, Pimco conducted a volatility sale across asset classes: stocks, government bonds, corporate bonds, currencies. Anywhere the firm could structure it cleanly, Pimco was betting that price swings would be muted.

To express this view, strongly, Gross ordered a huge trade in the stock market, more than $10 billion notional. He sold sixty thousand contracts tied to the S&P Index, betting that stocks wouldn't move up or down more than 2 percent over a set period. The range: 1840 to 1920, on contracts expiring June 20, a strategy known in options land as a "strangle." Then he sold another ten thousand contracts, with a range of 1840 to 1940. He fashioned similar bets in interest rates and the main credit derivative index, betting they would bounce around in a narrow, prescribed range.

Markets were tranquil but tense. Prices were high, and the Fed was eager to change course. Buying and selling was thin, which can often mean gappy, volatile trading. Gross was betting huge, on the edge of a knife.

Rumors of Pimco's big trade rocketed across the market. It was a quiet, boring summer, so the Pimco bet became all anybody could talk about, across asset classes: Clients entertained themselves asking dealers about the "S&P Strangler," in utterly unrelated meetings. Banks chattered among themselves about it. Analysts cited it obliquely in notes.

Pimco had executed the bulk of the equity trade through one bank, aiming to keep things on the downlow, but that couldn't stop the gossip train. Not just because of the summer doldrums, not because it was Pimco, or Pimco in equities, but because it was so monstrously big, so heavily concentrated around a few "strike" prices.

Selling the contracts had netted more than $100 million, by some estimates, but if the S&P didn't cooperate, if it traded outside his range, that premium could get wiped out, fast, and then some.

The dealers who bought the contracts from Pimco had to hedge themselves, which meant functionally selling the same trade as Pimco's. Every day, dealers had to fiddle with their positions a little, to hedge themselves back to a neutral risk. Through this basic maintenance, the dealers themselves were acting as guardrails, pressure in the market, keeping things within the range Pimco had delineated. It became a self-fulfilling trade.

Unless there was some external disaster—and Pimco was betting there wouldn't be—the very structure of the trade helped make it work.

With this monster trade on, and working, and the press finally paying attention to Pimco's thought leadership instead of Gross's personality or the toxic culture, things were starting to look on track.

Reinforcing that feeling of momentum: in late May, Pimco moved into a brand-new building. When it was clear Pimco was outgrowing its squat old building, they'd considered actually moving. Some had floated Reno, for the tax break. They'd seriously considered an impressive, sprawling campus in nearby Irvine. But Gross couldn't imagine upsetting his routine, suddenly confronting new turns every morning. He liked driving in from the cliffs of Laguna to Fashion Island, stopping at Starbucks or Rose Bakery Café in Corona del Mar for a donut and coffee, and trundling in before the sun was up. His was the vote that mattered, so in 2011 it enlisted a developer, the Irvine Company, to build it a new twenty-story monument at 650 Newport Center Drive, not a mile down the block from its old offices.

The new building looked more polished, gleaming, with a smooth exterior of creamy Roman Classico Italian travertine, a departure from the bumpy white exoskeleton that crawled between the old building's windows. The glass of their new shiny windows optimized daylight for energy efficiency. Extra-tall columns guarded the set-back entrance. The building was assertive, domineering, despite the peacefully swaying palm trees lined up outside.

The new 380,000 square feet had a multifloor auditorium that could actually fit a respectable slice of the firm. It had a real broadcast studio. It was said to cost north of $60 million; Pimco was the sole tenant. *The Orange County Business Journal* said it was the most prominent new office building in Newport Beach in thirty years.

The new home permitted structural changes: trading was now spread out over three floors. Portfolio associates (who do the grunt work of babysitting a portfolio) were on the nineteenth floor, and portfolio managers (the higher rank) on the twentieth. This physical division put a fine point on what many felt was a growing chasm between the roles, a hierarchy with declining upward mobility. It hadn't been that way with Trosky and the ragtag group of the 1990s, but after the financial crisis and the influx of money and new hires, the strata got as formal as the dress code, an island of black shoe polish in flip-flopped Southern California.

In the new building, the elevator was more convenient than the stairs—which meant it was even harder for Gross to hide from others. "You see everybody," he says.

Despite the grandeur of what some had begun to call "the Fortress," the move was mocked in the press. There was chatter about the "curse" of a new building, that the minute a company decides to move to a bigger, fancier space, that's the top: the company's growth is done.

This wasn't the feeling inside the Fortress. The new office felt like a fresh season: sharpened pencils and brand-new notebooks. And there was another powerful factor contributing to the good feeling at the end of May: Paul McCulley came back.

Pimco made a huge deal about it. McCulley! Everyone loved McCulley! His return brought a glowing brand halo from years of his being right while also being lucid, accessible, engaging. He was also good with the media, which could only help. With his lolling Virginia accent and affinity for bunnies, McCulley had always been a welcome counterweight to Gross, a friendly presence, a cooling calm. His addition would demonstrate that Pimco was its old self and very much Leading in big economic Thoughts.

"Pimco will always be Camelot to me," McCulley told the press. He and Gross and Pimco were all perfectly aligned, he said: "There is zero, absolutely zero daylight between me and Pimco on the new neutral. In fact, there's the antithesis of daylight. Same church, same pew, same hymnal."

The Gross worship was intentional. Hodge drove the point home in a statement announcing the hire: "Bill Gross is one of the most talented and successful investors of our time," Hodge said, crediting "Bill's personal leadership in recruiting Paul to the firm."

In early June, Hodge hosted a firmwide meeting with hundreds of employees. In it, he took a moment to praise Gross's enduring skill and love for investing. Gross stood by his side as Hodge spoke, looking on approvingly.

"Forty-three years ago, he founded Pimco with a vision and a fire in his belly, and we are living that vision today," Hodge said. "We all owe so much. Thank you."

The room erupted in applause and another standing ovation. Hodge and Gross shook hands effusively, the audience of traders and research analysts looking on at what almost, terribly, became a hug.

If Hodge's fawning wasn't explicitly at Gross's behest this time, it was a wise political move: Gross was increasingly annoyed about the business side, Hodge's side of the company. They weren't pulling their weight; outflows were continuing. Performance was fine—Gross was doing *his* work. So, what was the business side doing?

In a private meeting with Pimco's partners in early June, Gross made these feelings known. Hodge had been presenting the business plan when Gross laid into him: How were they going to fix it? What was he doing, specifically, to limit Gross's outflows?

"Well, there's a committee," Hodge replied. They had a group explicitly looking at ways to turn sales around and hold on to jittery clients. They were working on it.

A committee: the absolute wrong answer for Gross, in any decade. Gross shot back: What was the point of having Hodge as CEO if there's a *committee*? *Hodge* should know the plan; *he* should know what they were doing.

If things seemed to be looking up to outsiders, and even as some of Pimco's rank and file allowed themselves to feel some hope, the tensions at its heart were worsening. They were struggling to keep a lid on it.

Gross's hunt for leakers had continued. The interrogations, the accusations, were escalating, and Gross wasn't showing any signs of stabilizing. He'd started saying that, in addition to "Mr. X," who was already clearly established as Andrew Balls, he was also hunting for a "Mr. Y." The leakers, the saboteurs. He clearly thought Mr. Y was Josh Thimons. While other names cropped up and receded, among them DCIO Scott Mather, Gross was sure about Balls and Thimons. But he was hamstrung in what he could do about it.

Sometimes the spell broke: in June, he replied to an email to Ivascyn saying something about how he, Gross, shouldn't be the decider on the Andrew Balls problem; he wouldn't be here long enough to experience the effects. The DCIOs needed to decide if *they* could forgive and forget.

Still, it should have been evident that sending Gross to deliver the keynote at the 2014 Morningstar Investment Conference that June was contraindicated. He had been banned from media appearances, after all. Maybe public speeches before a vast audience of wealth managers, journalists, and rolling cameras should have been scrutinized similarly. Somehow this had slipped through.

On June 19, the giant ballroom in Chicago was packed, teeming with clients and potential clients, the highest concentration of interested parties possible. Given Pimco's recent turmoil, everyone was paying full attention, if just to rubberneck.

The lights were blinding as Gross walked onstage, so he put on a pair of rimless sunglasses. The overhead speakers played a wordless cover of "Smooth," by Carlos Santana and Rob Thomas, as it had for every speaker and panel. Gross's was the only entrance anyone would remember.

As he took his spot onstage, he caught out of the corner of his shielded eye the giant picture of himself projected behind on a giant screen. "Actually," he said, "when you're seventy years old, you need things, you need props. Even guys need a little makeup and stuff. And so I put these on as I was getting dressed," he said, indicating the shades, "and I said, 'Man, that's a pretty cool-lookin' dude!'" He laughed, and the audience laughed, too.

He went on. His introduction about being a Bond King was kind, he said, though he'd been nervous about what would be said. Recent buzz indicated it could be anything from "General George Patton maybe berating a wounded soldier"—he lifted two limp fists, out to each side—"or a Wall Street version of Justin Bieber . . . or maybe just a Kim Kardashian impersonator. If you wanted to hear about my feminine side, which I'm sure you don't! Ummm. In any case.

"If you really wanted to know about me, just ask [Morningstar analyst] Eric Jacobson, here at the front table, 'cause I've told him a hundred times over the last few months exactly what a great guy I am, and he should be able to tell you as well; it should have sunk in by now."

This all reminded him of the movie *The Manchurian Candidate*, he said, in which soldiers were brainwashed during the Korean War to tell the American public that their autocratic captain was the "kindest, warmest, most wonderful human being they'd ever known in their life."

Encouraged by the audience's laughter, Gross continued the labored analogy, recalling how a Queen of Hearts playing card had been the trigger for the soldiers' brainwashed declarations. He said he wished he could hypnotize reporters to say such kind things about him—that he'd tried the reverse on himself, training so that when he saw the red queen, he would say, "Reporters are the kindest, bravest, warmest, most wonderful human beings I've ever met in my life.

"So, playing cards, it seems, can be great therapy," he said, before adding, "I've never been happier at work." He launched into an explanation of the new DCIO structure at the firm and said that Hodge and Jacobs were "exceeding expectations."

"If there's a happier kingdom on earth, it may be fifteen miles up the Santa Monica Freeway at Disneyland," he said. "But that's a fantasy, and I'm talking real time here. We're having a good time and we're a happy kingdom at Newport Beach," he said, and paused, looking down.

"For those of you that would like to have a memento of those red queens, I've got a surprise in my pocket; perhaps some of you after the speech can come up, and I'll give you one of them," he said.

He then went on to provide an elegant explanation of structural alpha—keys to the happy kingdom, he said, to the Mercedes that is Total Return, what they did better than anybody. He explained all their volatility selling, saying that Pimco was happy to sell insurance because it was so often mispriced.

No one was listening.

By then, Pimco had closed much of the huge position that had captivated traders that spring and early summer. That trade, so huge, so heavy it had forced the market into its own success, had succeeded by a hair: it had worked, but barely. Spikes of volatility that would come that autumn would have crushed the firm had they arrived any sooner.

But the ballroom in Chicago was fixated on the *Manchurian Candidate* thing, the Justin Bieber of bonds, the gratuitous Kardashian mention. The whole thing was a train wreck. Pimco's fleet of PR people had been watching, horrified.

The internet lit up with shock, alarm, amazement. The sunglasses! How did Bill Gross even know who Justin Bieber was? And why would anyone want to get in touch with Gross's feminine side?

After the speech, Gross handed out new business cards, as promised; on the back was the Queen of Hearts. This was a clear sign to others in Pimco management that he had planned this, and they had not known. He had printed business cards for the occasion. This wasn't a last-minute choice, an accident or an impulse. This was a premeditated deviation from what he had said he was going to do. Pimco's leadership could no longer even remotely anticipate his actions. Gross wasn't playing on their team; he'd gone completely rogue.

The next day, Gross visited Pimco's New York offices. He rarely went, due to his dislike of travel. This visit was supposed to be a big deal, but he felt the cloud of the day before hanging over him. He'd seen the coverage, the headlines and tweets; he knew the shtick hadn't landed as he'd hoped.

Hundreds of employees gathered at a town hall in their sleek Midtown office. Gross felt compelled to say something about the debacle. Hodge stood nearby, his cherry-cheeked face blank. The mood was uneasy, strained.

"I wish I could do it over again," Gross said, in comments that would quickly get to the *Journal*. "I wouldn't have worn the sunglasses," and "Hey, I'm not perfect."

He saw Hodge frown.

After his speech, Gross was supposed to be talking to clients. He remembers Hodge communicating: *Don't fucking do what you did yesterday!* Of course not. Hadn't he just said as much?

He was under a lot of stress, he would explain later. Not just within Pimco. He was having a tough time at home: Sue was healthy again, but his marriage wasn't going great. And their son Nick's business partnership was in an escalating war. It was looking increasingly like they were going to have to sue the other kid for mismanaging the finances.* There was a lot going on. Gross had excuses for his behavior.

His Morningstar speech had also cast a pall over Pimco's sunny headquarters. About half of the rank and file were openly wondering if Gross had lost it; if, in truth, he was going senile or something. This speculation was rampant among lower-ranking staff. Others, who'd been tossed out of Investment Committee meetings when their presentation documents weren't properly indented, felt this was

---

* They did sue, and the kid sued Gross and his son; the litigation would be amicably settled in December 2015.

consistent with the guy they knew: Gross had always been weird, unpredictable, abrasive.

The mood wasn't helped by Gross's recent *Investment Outlooks*. Certainly, the decades had seen some bizarre entries in his monthly missives. But in April 2014, he wrote about his dead cat Bob and how she would watch Gross on TV and also watch him get in and out of the shower. "I'm not a particularly shy guy, but then why was a female cat named Bob checking me out all the time?" he wrote. "Her obsession carried over to the TV, sensing when I was on CNBC and paying apt attention no less [*sic*]." Then, in May, he wrote about how a sneeze was "to be candid, sort of half erotic, a release of pressure that feels oh so good either before or just after the Achoo! The air, along with 100,000 germs, comes shooting out of your nose faster than a race car at the Indy 500." In June, he wrote about how he didn't have a cell phone: "I'm sticking with live chirping as opposed to Angry Birds for now. Virtual reality seems just a tad <u>UNreal</u> to me."

Those who worked most closely with Gross were most concerned. His decisions and actions were increasingly unpredictable. Pimco's management, trying to steer the thing with him, doubted they could trust him. If they could not trust him, they could not do their jobs.

His teams tried to keep doing their jobs. Investing continued; conversations with clients continued. Account managers struggled to explain away the sunglasses, the Queen of Hearts, Justin Bieber. He's always been nuts! Ha-ha. Just an eccentric guy.

Internally, for the past few months, Gross had kept asking for public support from his underlings. He was all alone out there; they weren't protecting him. Hodge and Jacobs and the others had to glue back together the fractured picture of him and Pimco, making sure they looked aligned. The communications team deployed employees to the media for "background" conversations with no attribution, about how they had joined Pimco to learn from the greatest, the legend that was Bill Gross.

Hodge wrote an obsequious and dripping "viewpoint," published that summer on Pimco's website, that praised Gross's investing performance over the decades. "We are unaware of any person who has created more wealth for more people in the history of fixed income investing than Bill Gross," he wrote. "In our opinion, no other manager has invested as much money, over as long a period, with the same track record."

A couple months after Gross's visit, the New York office was beset by new chaos: it was infested with bedbugs. Executives and employees were covered in bites. They worried that they'd taken them home and were now harboring bedbugs in their clothes, in their bags; that they'd now have to spend thousands to fumigate their apartments and houses, throw out their cloth furniture, cook their clothes and books in the oven, in the common tradition of unlucky New Yorkers.

Pimco evacuated hundreds of employees from the Midtown building, temporarily relocating them upstate. "This is an issue that is far from uncommon in New York City," a spokesperson told Fox Business's Charlie Gasparino, after he broke the humiliating story and it raced from him to *Forbes*, *New York* magazine, Gothamist.

Kevin Roose at *New York* magazine wondered "whether the infestation might be part of an elaborate revenge scheme concocted by a booted Pimco executive whose name may or may not rhyme with 'Bohamed Bel-Ferrian.'"

On August 19, Pimco's Executive Committee convened for a strategy meeting. As they took their seats around the table, they buckled up for a long one. There were real questions about generating returns and profit growth.

Early in the meeting, Wendy Cupps, the head of product management, started talking about some of the products she and her team had been working on for clients. Within minutes, Gross interrupted. Cupps was taking too much of a lead developing products without the consent of portfolio management, the people who actually invest the money, he said. Without sufficient quality assurance. "You're stealing the firm," he said. "Product is stealing the firm." He managed, somehow, to blame her for the operational problems in the stocks push.

Speaking of which, he didn't want to be in equities anyway. Why were they pushing into stocks? Stock markets were hitting record highs, they were way too expensive right now, it was a ridiculous time to be buying in. Pimco hadn't gathered enough assets to justify keeping that business line.

Cupps, one of the few women in or near any kind of leadership role, was doing everything her job mandated: helping the equities push, supporting portfolio managers, and developing new products. Her reports seemed to like her, hardly the Pimco norm. She had climbed her way up the ladder and earned an elected seat on the Executive Committee in addition to making partner in 2004 (then one of three female managing directors).

She was not "stealing the firm," as everyone present knew.

They all knew Pimco had a formal process for approving new products, which included getting past a committee almost entirely comprised of portfolio managers. And they all remembered that meeting in 2009, when Gross himself had demanded the push into equities so violently. *Do it faster, or I'll find someone else who will.* Even though that was now five years ago, it was Gross's risk; he should own it. Why was Cupps being subjected to this irrational and very public attack?

Cupps pushed back, saying Gross had no idea about her area. True enough, he said, but you don't need a weatherman to know which way the wind is blowing. She tried to remind him of that committee approval process, and of that 2009 meeting, his own insistence, the whole *everybody loves pepperoni pizza* thing. The others tried to object, too, with similar points. Eventually, they tried to resume the meeting, to move on to other topics. Someone mentioned real estate—

Gross started up again. Since when did we buy physical buildings anyway? Why are we doing that? They were overpriced and would be impossible to sell; we'll be stuck with them. And then what? Are we going to manage rentals now? Pimco needed to retrench, to go back to where it had been, doing what it was good at, he said. We don't need all these people.

Finally, he fixed his attention on Hodge, railing on about his incompetence in running the business side. His inability to stanch the bleeding of client money. Did he even know what Pimco's mission statement was?

Even as he raged, Gross could feel the meeting disintegrating under the heat. His attacks were so scathing, the group disbanded in shock. No work accomplished, nothing.

Gross watched as they left, quietly, in clumps. The air felt staticky, unsettled. He knew enough about social graces to understand that they were walking away from him, and not just literally. It was frustrating—the meeting was just a bureaucratic response to his real concerns about their strategy. It was becoming clear to Gross that Hodge was lazy and incompetent, and supporting him as CEO had been a mistake. But also. Maybe he'd misunderstood something, that power wasn't a muscle to be exercised—maybe it was more delicate, or finite and at some point, it could run out.

He had a vacation looming. He'd be out of the office for about two weeks, leaving those clumps unattended, free to foment a rebellion against him.

There was a palpable difference now. There was no give against his tirades now, none of the old deference, just bone crunching against bone.

He went home.

The next day, August 20, Wendy Cupps emailed the Executive Committee, reiterating just for clarity that, in Pimco's well-established system, "ALL PRODUCTS" were "APPROVED" by that portfolio manager–heavy committee, and each new product needed a portfolio manager "sponsor." Not only was her team *not* jamming bad new products through, she said, there was a long list of new products proposed by portfolio management that *her* team *rejected* for being below standards. She'd be happy to provide that list.

The group reconvened for a second day—without Cupps, who had a previously scheduled trip—and were shockingly productive. And, as his colleagues remember it, Gross came back with a new proposal for his own eventual exit. It had been almost a year of back-and-forth proposals and ideas, and he felt bad. He wanted to make clear that now, for the first time, he understood what had to happen. He'd been out of line, he said. He would step back as chief investment officer, he told them. Really, this time. He could see that it was clearly, evidently, the right moment. (Gross says he did not offer to step back at this time.) Also, he was sorry if he'd offended Cupps.

Some on the Executive Committee got the sense that he was trying to be helpful, even to extend an olive branch. At least to preempt their moving against him first.

But, Gross added, he had one condition. They had to fire Andrew Balls and Josh Thimons, his Mr. X and Mr. Y. He could go, but if he went, they had to go, too.

Gross followed his proposal with an email to management: He was about to leave for his cruise, with Sue. He would be off the grid. In his absence, could they work on a formal proposal for him? He'd come back well rested, less agitated, and he could look at what they cooked up.

Have a good time on your vacation, Hodge replied.

15

Minutes

With Gross away for almost two weeks, the office felt abruptly calmer. The DCIOs and others in management allowed themselves to feel a little hope, maybe. Like there was room for things to turn out okay. Maybe now, knowing he'd gone too far, he would actually work with them.

Hodge, Jacobs, and the rest of the Executive Committee made a PowerPoint, dating it September 5. Slide after slide detailed how they could structure the future. They clearly and deliberately enumerated Gross's demands, using his own words, in the hopes that he'd recognize them and maybe listen.

They titled it WHAT WHG ASKED FOR—William Hunt Gross. In case he forgot, or seemed to forget, or pretended to forget, that he'd asked for this.

Among the things he'd requested: Fewer client-facing responsibilities; fewer accounts to oversee; less of the managerial stuff he'd always hated; more of the pure investing he loved, playing with his toys of bonds and derivatives. An Unconstrained fund, the one he'd yanked away from Dialynas. Focus on bonds and burgers. Process to be completed by year end.

There was that one distressing point: Gross had clearly stated that his resignation as CIO was contingent on the dismissal of Andrew Balls and Josh Thimons, his two worst "moles." But to Hodge and the others, this was preposterous. With Balls, they had a plan, a legal agreement in place, and on top of that Gross had abdicated, had told Ivascyn it was up to the DCIOs. And Thimons was legally unfireable for whatever period might look retaliatory. All of which Gross had to know, was supposed to know.

Maybe if they quietly ignored that request, it would go away. Gross was so "forgetful," he might read the PowerPoint and be so pleased about the constructive path forward that he wouldn't notice the omission of his only demand.

They didn't even get that far.

When Gross got back from his time at sea and reentered his real life, his mind was clear. With a little perspective, it seemed, he saw what he had always seen: that Pimco was his, and Pimco was him. Suddenly, he could no longer remember why he had let them get to him. Was it just that one dumb meeting in which he'd raised, in his mind, crucial points about the firm's frightening direction?

Had all these new Pimco chieftains forgotten that he'd built this place *and* their fortunes? Did all these home-grown heroes think they were so smart because they were multimillionaires? Could they ever have gotten so wealthy elsewhere? Gross had made them rich, had made *them*.

So, why should he bow out?

Before he even got back to the office, before he even saw their carefully crafted presentation, he torched it and them. He fired off an email: he would never cut back; that wasn't at all what he wanted. He would never have asked for that.

As wary as Hodge and the others on the Executive Committee had been about Gross's response upon his return, this was beyond their expectations—a corporate leader flip-flopping on a real, previously agreed upon strategic corporate initiative. It seemed like either Gross was lying or he'd lost his mind. Had that even been a sincere request, or was it just to keep them busy and mollified while he was gone? Their inability to predict what he'd do was now normal.

Gross came into the office as usual on the morning of Monday, September 8, seemingly refreshed. He wasn't done.

That afternoon, he sent a new email to the Executive Committee, abruptly recapping his thoughts from that scorching August meeting.

Sent: Monday, September 08, 2014 2:36 PM
Subject: Summary and Minutes of August 19/20 meeting
After reviewing the summary minutes of our late August meeting, it strikes me that it evolved into more of a near term strategy meeting as opposed to a long term business planning session . . .

Totally cool, normal, professional tone. He wanted to raise just eight points, mostly refuting what the minutes showed. Among them: "While the minutes mention discussion of our mission statement, I recall no discussion whatsoever."

The minutes also said that portfolio management should focus on markets "(as opposed to growing assets under their supervision)," which Gross took as a "clear rebuke" to his contention that "Product"—he didn't name her, but Wendy Cupps—was charging ahead without the consent of portfolio management.

And Hodge had said that Pimco should "maximize wallet share" and "fend off fee pressures," which Gross thought was utterly wrongheaded. Trying to charge clients more money in this environment? They were letting profits drive the firm when they needed to be paying attention to fees, he said. Also, the minutes don't reflect Hodge's comment that Pimco is an active bond manager. It is! But by buying all the stuff like private equity and real estate, Gross said, Pimco was becoming *passive*—dependent on leverage for returns and along for whatever ride those markets took it on.

He was doubling down.

His language was mystifying, disorienting. "Passive" has a clear meaning in investing, which is close to the opposite of how he used it. Passive is an index fund that buys every stock to get the average performance of the market. Ivascyn's private investing business was at what's understood to be the opposite, "very active" end of the spectrum, making large concentrated bets on a few carefully chosen private companies or buying those distressed mall loans. Things that were not being achieved by any automatically updating spreadsheet. Was he saying the strategy was just borrow money, buy a building . . . and wait?

Ivascyn replied privately, only to Gross. "Nothing is passive," he wrote. They were not just along for the ride. And the private structures ran very light leverage—actually lower than what Gross used in his funds. And, also, the private funds were doing well, boosting the company's brand.

In Gross's reply to Ivascyn, he cc'd the rest of the Executive Committee. He reiterated that Ivascyn's strategies were not truly active, saying that if Pimco could sell passive products like private equity, then they should consider doing more.

Ivascyn replied yet again, keeping the committee on the thread: okay, again, private investing is super active. More active than buying a bond and holding it and just hoping the issuing company did well! Also, he wrote, the private funds only got material fees if it made money for clients—unlike some traditional funds "where we have taken out plenty of fees in recent years while generating no alpha or negative alpha for our clients."

"You have always told us as PMs that our primary focus is investor returns," he wrote. "I thought this is a key to PIMCO long term success."

"Best of luck," Gross wrote back. "No one was willing to confront the critical long term decisions that my e-mail spoke to." And, he added, "these back and forth emails, by the way, are constructive, not destructive. Other exec co members should take note. You should have a REAL discussion, not an agenda-determined outline that invariably runs out of time."

Some of his subordinates suspected, were starting to feel sure, that Gross's rage was less about business strategy and more a manifestation of deep fears, of pain, the emotional residue of El-Erian's departure, the betrayal and violence of that rupture, the humiliation; Gross's own fund's outflows, the fading bond era where he'd mastered the market; the firm that had grown so far beyond his scope, in complexity and size and strategy and head count; that he might have to give up his seat one day; that for all his billions, he might be mortal.

Even as they could see all this, those on the Executive Committee struggled to remain empathetic.

In any breakup, there is a moment when a switch is flipped and the investment in the relationship drops to zero. Gross didn't realize it, but sometime in the days after his return, the lights had gone out.

They tried to find a resolution. On September 10, Mihir Worah met with Jacobs, Hodge, and Flattum. He was increasingly acting as the intermediary and healer, trying to bridge the chasm between Gross and everyone else. He told them he'd spoken with Gross—"Good Bill" this time, he said—and thought Gross would settle down soon and agree to reduce his duties.

That same day, top executives assembled again at Worah's request, this time with Gross. Gross laid out his newest proposal for how he could step back. Although he had just said a few days before that he would never withdraw, he now, again, seemed to have realized there was no more backtracking.

In the meeting, he enumerated how they could transition his funds, how they'd find his replacement. With Hodge, Jacobs, Cupps, Worah, and Flattum listening, Gross proposed sharing his role with a co–chief investment officer and said they could start a search for that person immediately. Or he could oversee only the fixed-income part of the business, and everything else could be the purview of Worah.

In the co-CIO scenario, he proposed continuing to oversee Total Return with said co-CIO for another year, until December 31, 2015, at which time he would step down quietly. It would be orderly. Then, he said, he would just run the Unconstrained fund and a few other select portfolios.

Pimco's top brass sat listening, silent. To most of them, under other circumstances, all this would have sounded almost reasonable. A month before, it would have been close to what they had wanted to hear. But now it was too late, far too late. He'd torched them so many times that the meeting almost seemed like a farce, a scene in a play they were all performing.

They didn't bring up his earlier emails; it wouldn't do any good. They asked a few logistical questions, but this counterplan sounded like another fakeout. December 31, 2015, felt hundreds of years away. It left too much room for him to trick them again. If he'd behaved in a normal way, maybe they could have created a long-term glidepath, made him a chairman emeritus or something. But he'd demonstrated that he couldn't stay within the lines, even if he painted them himself.

There was one more thing, Gross said. Balls should resign. "Now's the time," he said.

Ah, but you don't have the votes, Hodge and Jacobs said, according to one attendee's recollection. They'd held a vote, and he had been outvoted.

Gross was surprised—they'd held a vote without him? It was that same feeling he'd had in July, some thread slipping through his fingers.

Okay, he said to himself, feeling desperate. *I'm CIO. If I can't fire him that way, I'll ask him.*

Hodge asked Gross if he could leave the room.

Gross gathered his papers and stepped out. Despite the Balls setback, he felt optimistic. His proposal was good. He'd found a way forward.

As soon as he'd gone, the Executive Committee minus one articulated the obvious.

First off, the timeline Gross had suggested was far too long. Then: He had no clear succession plan for the remaining funds he managed. What would happen to Unconstrained? Would he just die managing it? How would they explain this to clients? How was this even really a plan? The discussion felt empty. Even considering his suggestions seemed futile at this point. No one believed they could trust him anymore.

Finally, the conversation wound around to what was beginning to seem inevitable, an idea that had been taking shape in their minds: if he wouldn't leave peacefully, they might have to fire him.

Truthfully, the Executive Committee had already started planning for this, out of necessity. Following his Bloomberg TV debacle in April and his threat in the aftermath to resign, they'd discreetly begun "contingency planning." Hodge and other top executives had built a "Transition Committee," and over the last few months, they had made a list of Gross's biggest accounts, still hundreds of billions in assets, and carved them up, in the hypothetical, deciding who might handle what.

Fortunately, the next step was already obvious. Ivascyn was a clear favorite for the next CIO. Everyone loved him. The power and money wouldn't totally go to his head, they knew, because he already had some power and because he was not volatile or abusive: He'd chaired a committee overseeing Pimco's trade floors and money management teams around the world. His fellow money managers had elected him to represent them on the Executive Committee, for several years. Most important, he was credible. His Pimco Income Fund had beat 97 percent of peers in 2013 (and 99 percent over three and five years), and his private funds were raking in hundreds of millions in profit.

The jockeying would be one level below—who would get the Total Return fund, for example, and in what order? As always in finance, it was crucially important whose name was flush left. Gross's appointed successors were indeed first in line, but some had proven too loyal to Gross—like Mihir Worah, who'd stood alongside Gross in the employee interrogations. That wouldn't look good once the war was over.

Pimco's quarterly Cyclical Forum was at noon that Monday. Top-level investment professionals flew in from around the world to gather in Newport Beach to debate short-term economic conditions and decide trading strategies. Just like normal.

Which meant Andrew Balls was in town from London.

Gross had his assistant buzz Balls on the trade floor and ask him to come meet Gross. The two stepped into Gross's office. *It's down to you or me*, Gross told Balls, according to one person's recollection of the meeting. At the end of an upcoming Executive Committee, one of the two would no longer be working at Pimco.

"Guess who?"

"Me?" Balls said.

"No, me," Gross said, "because they're going to vote for you, not me. You're going to win. But I want you to resign anyway." Balls needed to step down, Gross said, for the good of Pimco.

Not now, Gross said. Talk to Jacobs, Hodge. Talk to your family. Talk to Flattum. Take a few days, consider it. Do what you need to do. Come to the Executive Committee meeting tomorrow.

Balls made some noises about thinking about it. The meeting went on for an hour. Balls left very confused.

Gross felt it went well.

The next day, Gross again collected all his papers, this time to testify before the Executive Committee. He kept his notes with him now, because he was seventy, he forgot things, so sometimes he wrote things down—but, also, this was crucially important.

Balls didn't show for the meeting. No matter; Gross would convince them of his view that Andrew Balls, admitted mole, leaker to the press, Pimco saboteur, should be fired. When he was done, Hodge and the rest of the firm's top deciders would understand, and agree.

He made his case confidently, laying it all out, splaying his hands before him as if to underscore: Here are the facts. I didn't make them; I just have them. And now you have them.

When he finished, there was hardly a beat before Hodge said that Gross didn't have the authority; he was not authorized to ask for the resignation of a managing director.

Gross tried to push back, to tell them that he'd just spoken to the firm's lawyer who'd said that nothing in Pimco's bylaws prevented him from—

Hodge interrupted: have you tried to force Balls to quit?

No, Gross said. He hadn't. Asking isn't forcing. Asking to *consider* isn't even asking.

His denial hung in the air.

Ivascyn, Hodge, and the rest were stunned. They'd all watched his earlier overt attempts to have Balls fired, and they knew about his most recent demand; *asking* versus *forcing* was a distinction without a difference. There was no way around it. He didn't forget, and he wasn't confused; he had to be lying.

Dan Ivascyn was fed up. This was ridiculous, and dangerous. For months Ivascyn had been grousing to his colleagues, voicing his displeasure. Gross's behavior had gotten so unpredictable, and more so since El-Erian left.

Ivascyn had watched the drama unfolding with El-Erian and Seidner; had watched Gross throw Dialynas under the bus and take over Unconstrained; had watched Gross's binder of snitches grow fat and had said then that he'd like very much to steer clear of all that, to keep his head down and do his work, if that was possible. Which it wasn't. As it became apparent that things would not improve, Ivascyn had made moves.

That Thursday, September 11, he'd talked to a lawyer. And on the weekend, Ivascyn visited some of his peers to talk through the future of the firm. They needed to figure out how to get out of this flaming pit of chaos, and what things could look like in the future.

Ivascyn told others in Pimco management that he was near the end of his rope. He was used to Gross's being nasty—they all were—but lately, the functioning of the firm was imperiled. It was irresponsible. If it continued, Ivascyn would have to leave.

It wasn't just Ivascyn. One by one, a handful of critical partners had told Pimco management the same thing: They were ready to leave. Jay Jacobs was done. Wendy Cupps had said that she, too, was done. They could not work with Gross any longer.

Stories about Ivascyn's insurrection spread among employees like a fever. After Seidner left in January, they'd all heard his analysis: that no normal person could work for Gross. He was articulating an abstract concept that many were feeling more every day. With these new, serious, high-level threats, lower-ranking employees were grappling with the idea of a Pimco without Bill Gross.

On some level, Gross knew not to antagonize them. But things were moving fast, and sometimes his impulses proved dead-on, so he let himself: For the already-scheduled portfolio manager meeting, he devised a plan, a seating chart. He spent a lot of time constructing it. He'd used seating, in Investment Committee and other gatherings, to reflect who was in his favor before. But for this meeting, it seemed unnecessary: the room wasn't even full. At the large, long table with him: Mihir Worah and Virginie Maisonneuve. Ivascyn, Balls, and Mather weren't at the table. Ivascyn was in the first ring of chairs, and Balls and Mather in the fourth row. Far from the rest of the grown-ups.

The arrangement was an obvious snub, petty and childish. It seemed built to humiliate them. Which was lost on no one.

On Thursday, September 11, Gross heard that three managing directors had threatened to resign: Ivascyn, Cupps, and Jacobs. Then, a few hours later, he heard about two more. Never heard which ones. It didn't matter: he could feel the growing consensus.

It was them or him.

He'd been pulling people aside to tell them that they wouldn't have the votes to fire him, that if they tried to stage a coup by themselves, he would know it was they who'd done it. But with each day, he was less and less sure that this was true. And they probably knew that.

For all his "power," the dynamic felt strangely familiar, tailor-made to agitate him. It was a lifelong discomfort: knowing he was about to face some situation everybody else could read but that, for Gross, was beyond comprehension. It was like he was back sitting in his car, not that long ago, outside his high school reunion, too anxious to go in alone, waiting until he saw his childhood best friend, Jerry, who was already inside. Finally, Gross slunk into a corner of the party. Jerry spotted him and went over immediately. He knew this was a difficult situation for Gross.

"He can go into the bond market and lay down a half-a-billion-dollar bet, and I'd have a heart attack doing that," Jerry says. "But walking into a reunion, no problem, even though I don't know all the people or don't know what's gonna happen; that's not totally comfortable for Bill."

A roomful of social cues he wasn't going to catch; full of people of whom he was supposed to have some partial understanding; filled with memories of shared experiences, some degree of warmth. Everybody knew him now, even if they didn't know him then. They'd come up, beer in hand, and say the weirdest, most inappropriate things. Invariably, they asked him for "bond market" advice. Gross would squirm, unsure how to respond, unable to tell how serious his answer should be, what they actually wanted from him. It seemed like they just wanted to say things *at* him. Usually, he would try to shield himself, to prevent these conversations in the first place; he'd sit next to Jerry and ask *Do you know who that is?* and Jerry would say no, and they'd ask somebody else. Gross needed that buffer, someone to sit with.

Right now, to Gross, that didn't apply. In this situation at Pimco, the question was one of legality. The lines were clear; he wasn't looking for clues.

That Saturday morning, September 13, Bill Gross went over to Mihir Worah's home to talk. Worah was his last real ally; he was still loyal. Gross explained the back-and-forth, all the proposals, and asked why people felt hell-bent against him; he didn't understand.

Worah gently explained. The whole Balls thing: the business side really wouldn't let it go.

Gross asked Worah what he would do, as a voting member of the Executive Committee, with power over Gross's fate, should it come to that.

Worah said he could never vote against him.

With Worah's and his own votes on his side, the committee didn't have the majority to oust him. So, Gross thought, he had time.

But by Monday, he'd had another change of heart. He knew what this was asking of Worah: Stopping a coup that was already unfolding would make him a dead man. "Matter of fact, you may already be a dead man," Gross mused. But there are some things you can't go alone—family, cancer, opposing open corporate insurrection, things like that. Worah had to vote against Gross.

So Worah cried, and Gross cried, and they hugged and knew what had to happen: the knives were coming, and Worah wouldn't stop them.

By then, Hodge and the others were convening daily, figuring out how to do what had to be done.

The Executive Committee scheduled a special meeting on Saturday, September 27. These things took planning and preparation, and even this long lead felt too short. But the air was so toxic, and the risk in those resignation threats so pressing, that some started asking to move the meeting up.

This wasn't ideal: it would be difficult from a disclosure standpoint for a partially public company to conduct an emergency management transition while the market was open. And generally the big decision-makers were supposed to be in those markets whenever they were open. But urgency prevailed, and the committee moved the meeting from Saturday to Friday.

On Tuesday, September 16, Gross was notified: an Executive Committee meeting, on Friday, the twenty-sixth, at two o'clock.

So, that was his deadline, then. His mind raced. He had to find a way to get the upper hand again, to get out on his own terms.

Gross called the main telephone line of DoubleLine Capital, a rival bond shop north of Newport Beach—a straight shot up the 405 Highway, then along the 10 East, in Downtown LA. The receptionist answered, and Gross asked to speak with Jeffrey Gundlach, please.

Gundlach was not an obvious choice for a phone-a-friend, mainly because he and Gross had been positioned as enemies for their entire careers. They were both big fans of the mortgage market, and Gross had felt Gundlach's performance numbers creeping up on him for the past few years.

Even closer parallels motivated Gross now: Gundlach had founded

DoubleLine almost five years earlier, after an ugly departure from Trust Company of the West. Gundlach had spent his then-twenty-four-year investing career at TCW, running its Total Return Bond Fund, and had generated outsize profits for himself, the firm, and clients. Like Gross, Gundlach had seen the mortgage crash coming and had invested accordingly. But toward the end, he felt that TCW management wasn't compensating him for all the money he was bringing in, and was overlooking him as a leader. Tensions escalated into corporate warfare until, one day, Gundlach left in a huff, with lawyers literally pursuing him down the stairwell and out the building, dress shoes clacking on the concrete steps.

Gundlach ended up taking forty-five of his sixty TCW employees with him, to start his own thing. In the nasty litigation that followed, wild anecdotes spilled out, built for maximal damage and of varying degrees of relevance to the actual case: One employee had smuggled out a thumb drive of proprietary information by stuffing it in her bra. TCW had raided Gundlach's second office and discovered his stash of weed and paraphernalia ("bearing evidence of recent use"); twelve sexual "devices," including two glass dildos; thirty-four "hardcore pornographic magazines"; and thirty-six "hardcore sexually explicit DVDs and video-cassettes." Gundlach responded by telling investors, "I had every expectation of privacy in these spaces, which stored vestiges of closed chapters of my life." Later he would add that not all of the findings were his.

But nothing stuck to the man who'd often called himself a genius and also "the Pope" and also "the Godfather." Eventually a jury found him liable for breaching fiduciary duty to TCW, but the jury made him pay $0 to TCW for that breach, and made TCW pay him and his three codefendants $66.7 million in back pay. Asked how he felt about the verdict, he smiled and said, "It's sixty-seven to zero."

Investors loved him, his employees loved him, and DoubleLine flourished. It became one of the fastest-growing mutual fund managers of all time.

The details hardly mattered to Gross. Gundlach's history indicated that they were one and the same, both so undeniably talented in investing and business-building that they offended, threatened the useless bureaucrats who wanted to leech off their profits.

When Gross called, DoubleLine's receptionist, Melissa, said Gundlach couldn't be reached. Gross left a message. Melissa relayed the information that a "Bill Gross" had called.

This sounded very obviously like a prank call. This happened to Gundlach a lot. His growing notoriety attracted intense fans and also, of course, trolls. Gundlach told her to check the number.

It was a 949 area code, she said.

Gundlach went into the office of Ignacio Sosa, a former Pimco product manager who'd sought refuge from the insanity by joining DoubleLine a few months prior, opting for a two-hour daily commute to Los Angeles over clocking into Newport Center Drive. Did he have Gross's phone number? Of course not, he replied. So they crouched around a computer screen and searched online: "949 area code."

Orange County. Oh.

Gundlach told Melissa to call the guy back, find out if it was really Bill Gross. She returned saying it was definitely him; she could tell from his voice.

Gundlach called him back a couple of hours after that.

A still-distraught Gross picked up. "Oh, hi, Jeffrey," Gross said. "Is it Jeff or Jeffrey?"

It was "Jeffrey," as Gundlach felt Gross already knew. They moved past it.

"Pimco doesn't want me anymore," Gross told Gundlach. "They are going to push the button and fire me."

Gundlach was surprised by the news, but it resonated. "I can't believe they'd actually want to get rid of you—that seems like a monumentally stupid thing to do," Gundlach said. "But I've seen that kind of thing done before, I've seen monumental stupidity before."

Gross said he didn't want to retire yet. Or get fired! He wanted to keep managing money. Less money would be okay. He just wasn't ready to tap out.

"Sounds like you're in a big hurry," Gundlach said. "You want to get together?" Why didn't Gross come over to Gundlach's house? They could talk through it all in private. At the very least, Gundlach could share his experiences. He smelled an opportunity, too, some kind of "dream team" scenario to be cooked up here.

The next day, at around 4 P.M., a driver delivered Gross to Gundlach's home. For the next three hours, sitting in the covered outdoors of Gundlach's Tuscan villa–style home, the Pacific Ocean in the hazy distance, Gross unloaded everything that had happened, talking quickly, detailing the past twelve months: the falling-out with El-Erian, the ridiculous muzzling, his TV ban, his mole hunt, his Mr. X, the mismanagement of the company he had built. He vacillated, veering wildly from a firm resolve to preempt "them" to an equally strong resolve to force them to fire him. He kept referring to the "PE guy," which seemed to mean Ivascyn.

He was speaking so forcefully, seemed so pissed. It all felt familiar.

Gross seemed mournful, too, depressed and despondent. He described to Gundlach photographs he'd seen of Nazi soldiers aiming guns at civilians lined up with their hands raised. Gross said he'd always wondered why the civilians didn't run. "Now I understand," he said. He saw himself in the victims. He wouldn't run, either; he wouldn't give them the satisfaction. If they were going to do it, they had to do it. "They're going to have to shoot me in the head."

Gundlach tried to reassure him, in his way. He told Gross that all those decades of outperformance in Total Return were, ironically, what was undermining him now: the fund had gotten too big to manage. Too much success creates failure, every successful person knew that.

"You are running too much money," Gundlach remembers telling him.

"Absolutely," Gross said. Smaller is easier to run. In fact, that's what he had proposed to Pimco! He had asked for that, for maybe $40 billion, $50 billion—nothing outlandish, just a respectable pile of money for him to invest. He didn't want to run the flagship fund.

But no, Gross told him, mournful again, they'd said, "We want you to leave soon."

The meeting was not without its tensions. The two had been rivals over the years, on occasion insulting each other obliquely in the financial press. Gundlach had even taken over the mantle of "Bond King" in the press in recent years, sporadically, though he told Gross he'd never encouraged the media in this. As Gundlach remembers it, they talked about their legacies, who they would become when they died. Gross said he was like Kobe Bryant, and Gundlach was LeBron James—the young upstart, not yet the legend. "I have five rings, you have two rings—probably going to five," Gross said. (Gross denies saying this.)

With their egos butting, they inched toward a mutually beneficial idea: was there a future for Gross at DoubleLine? The words hardly fit together, but they tried to envision it. Gross said he'd be willing to work for one dollar. Gundlach understood this to mean they could work out the details later.

Gross did have to disclose one thing. Bit awkward, but if he was going to join DoubleLine, he had to say it. Gundlach assured him that nothing would leave the house, so Gross shared: The SEC had been poking around Pimco for many months by now, "learning" how Pimco marked bond prices, peeking into its third-party pricing systems and its compliance department, specifically related to its Total Return ETF. Gross himself had been interviewed, at length.

This was also big news, but manageable. The SEC was playing catchup in the bond market, so it had been sniffing everywhere.

For his part, there was one thing Gundlach needed to make very clear if they were to proceed: He was not going to share leadership. He'd built DoubleLine from nothing, and it would remain his. Gross could come aboard as a money manager, doing his own thing, but he would not ever be co-anything with Jeffrey Gundlach. And, it would follow, there'd be no equity.

They agreed to keep in touch. Nothing firm, no decision.

On his way home, Gross called Sue. He told her he just wasn't sure. Something felt off.

Gundlach wasn't sold, either. A "dream team" may not have been a good or even possible idea. They were so similar. Nonetheless, DoubleLine people drafted a press release about Bill Gross joining the firm. They readied to push the button, just in case.

By now, Allianz had realized the gravity of the situation.

Since buying the majority stake in 2000, Allianz had always maintained an arm's-length, absent-parent relationship with Pimco, and this was by design. Some at Pimco had sustained an air of superiority, like it had done Allianz a favor by selling it any ownership. Pimco demanded this distance, and usually it worked out fine.

Allianz was kept apprised of the deteriorating situation from its perch in Munich, but now that the wheels were fully coming off, CEO Michael Diekmann had to intervene. He booked a flight.

Before Diekmann's arrival in California, Gross sat down with the former head of Allianz Global Investors, Joachim Faber, who'd overseen the 2000 Allianz deal and whom Gross liked, and retired CEO Bill Thompson, whom he still trusted and whose gentle manner could still soothe him. (Pimco executives had been asking Thompson for help; Thompson kept an office down the way, and they'd trek over to consult the Gross whisperer, hoping to gain some insight.)

By phone and email, they worked out a plan. As Gross remembers it, they worked on Gross's sketch for how to transition himself out of the firm that for decades had defined him, that he had defined. He would resign now, as CIO, as chairman of the Investment Committee, and as a member of the Executive Committee and the Partner Compensation Committee—surrendering all the real sources of his power. His bonus would be cut by half or more; that was fine. He would take a reduced role, relinquishing Total Return entirely and accepting a small portfolio, maybe a couple of tens of billions. And he wouldn't set foot in the Pimco offices again. He would manage his little portfolio elsewhere, where his presence, and personality, wouldn't upset anyone.

The plan was a whittled-down version of his proposal of just the week before, his punishment far more draconian. But at this point, it was the best he could hope for, and he knew it.

Diekmann arrived on the seventeenth. Gross's leaving was an expensive disaster but, now, probably, an unavoidable one. Diekmann's objective had to be only mitigating the damage; he would do what he could.

On the morning of September 18, Diekmann sat down for breakfast with Gross. They knew each other of course, but hadn't interacted too much over the years, so a stiff formality ran through their conversation.

In Gross's recounting, Diekmann proposed the plan Faber had worked out with Gross and Thompson, which would give Gross a "sidecar"—he remembers Diekmann using that word, *sidecar*—of twenty or thirty billion dollars to manage, off on his own. They both hoped this would resolve what was threatening to become intractable. Pimco, and Allianz, would benefit from the continuity of the aging founder still at the firm, but off to the side, happily working for the most loyal clients. They could avoid a public blowup. This could be done smoothly, without rupture. They could all be "headed in the same direction," Gross remembers Diekmann saying.

Diekmann said he would take the plan to Pimco's management, Gross recalls. They would meet again in a few hours.

Diekmann went to meet with Hodge and Jacobs. A few hours later, Gross made his way to his own appointed meeting with them. Gross distinctly remembers Diekmann pointing to him, saying he thought Gross was going to like what he was about to hear. A smile.

This put a little spring in Gross's step: The sidecar was a go maybe! This war would end. He walked inside.

And was immediately blindsided. Hodge presented Gross with an entirely different transition plan. Pimco would announce his retirement at year end, praising his accomplishments over his long career—a "champagne and balloons" press release, to Gross's mind.

Which was not at all what he was expecting. He asked about the "sidecar" structure: what had happened to that? He could just manage a small pile of money, remember? He'd even agreed to work across the street, in an entirely different building, if having him around was just so difficult. Even that wasn't enough?

Jacobs demurred. The idea was unconventional at best. Logistically, it made no sense; optically, it made no sense. How would they explain it to clients? He didn't get into all that with Gross right then—it wasn't clear anymore that Gross could see reason, in that moment or in general. They told him they could consider it, at least, but not for tens of billions—maybe one or two.

To Gross, the offer they were presenting was termination, but termination dressed up and drawn out a few months so Pimco could hide it from the public, pretend it was nicer than it was. With a humiliating press release, like he was some fossil, a pile of dentures that needed praise—not the Bond King, godfather of the industry, pioneer, legend, billionaire, celebrity. He'd endured enough humiliation already, and indeed was prepared to suffer more, but this wasn't what he'd agreed to.

They said it would help ease the transition of his duties and responsibilities if Gross stayed on through December. But Gross heard only that he would be "allowed" to remain and that if he didn't accept this new proposal, he would be fired immediately.

They explained that Gross couldn't be an employee of Pimco. They needed to part ways. But they could figure something out, some structure that could work. Jacobs offered to have Pimco help Gross start a new company or fund, Gross recalls.

"That's a bone even a dog wouldn't pick," he said in reply. He left the meeting without an agreement.

Outside, the internet was abruptly cresting with a newly viral story about Mohamed El-Erian, a powerful and noble CEO who stepped back from influence and riches to spend more time with his daughter, thanks to a list of twenty-two reasons. El-Erian had written an essay for *Worth* in June, and interest in it had suddenly and inexplicably been renewed, so he was everywhere: in the *Telegraph*, the *Daily Mail*, the *Independent*, the *Huffington Post*; on *E! Online*. Pimco employees of all loyalties chattered, with no apparent substantiation, that El-Erian had engineered a media blitz to push Gross over the edge.* Rumors swirled about El-Erian talking with Allianz about a potential return.

Around the same time, something slipped: on September 23, *The Wall Street Journal* broke the news about the SEC probe. Kirsten Grind, Gregory Zuckerman, and Jean Eaglesham published a story saying the regulatory body was looking into whether Pimco had artificially boosted returns of its Bond ETF; that the ETF's "huge early gains" had probably helped attract investors; that the SEC's probe had intensified in recent weeks; that Gross himself had met with the investigators.

The article wasn't heavy on details, but the SEC had caught on to the odd-lot pricing mechanism Pimco had exploited that gave the Total Return ETF a killer head start, trouncing its own mutual fund counterpart—just as alleged in Jason Williams's lawsuit.

Pimco had kept the investigation under wraps for so long, only for it to break now, at the worst possible moment, as everything was coming to a head. Pimco's management had known that this could eventually get out. Under normal circumstances, such news leaking would have felt like a disaster, but at this moment, it was not their biggest problem.

"Friday at two" still loomed. Gross had some dignity left; he wouldn't show up for it. He wouldn't be fired in front of all those people. He would find a solution before then and preempt their little plan.

He called Dick Weil.

Gross had reached out to Weil in the summer, amid the chaos with El-Erian and the wounding press coverage. Gross had heard a garbled

---

* Through his lawyer, El-Erian denies participating in developments within Pimco leading up to Gross's exit. The "catalyst" for this crest of news, his lawyer says, was "an editorial meeting for Dr. El-Erian at Reuters arranged by Allianz and in which reporters asked about a conversation with his [sic] in May 2013. The Reuters write-up was picked up by other media outlets, which was encouraged by the general focus on work-life issues."

rumor that he was at risk of getting fired, and he was nothing if not a risk manager, so he called Weil. Weil had said something about how Gross would always be welcome to join him at Janus. But at that time Gross still thought he could persevere, and said he intended to stay at Pimco. Conversations had petered out.

Now things had changed.

Weil was not dumb. He saw the opportunity; he'd been trying to get the spotlight on Janus for years, to only middling success. He told Gross the firm would have an office ready.

Gross called Gundlach and left a voice mail: he was leaving Pimco but wouldn't be joining DoubleLine. Thanks, though.

Well after the sun went down that Thursday night, a half day before the Executive Committee would meet, Gross slipped into Pimco's offices and walked around the empty trade floor. He wrote out little love notes on trade tickets and printer paper for the dwindling number of people he still considered allies, the few he still respected.

"Keep doing a great job," he wrote to Ben Emons. Another, to Qi Wang. "Look after her."

He tucked the notes into envelopes, sealed them, addressed them, and placed them on the desks of fifteen or sixteen soon-to-be-former colleagues.

He scrawled one more note, adding a predictive time stamp:

TO: CEO, PIMCO
This letter will confirm my resignation from Pimco as of Sept 26, 2014
at 6:29 AM PST
William H Gross

16

Bye-Bye to Those Days

Even that note was late.

On September 26, at 5:28 A.M. Pacific Standard Time, Janus Capital announced: the legendary bond investor William H. Gross was joining its ranks.

Pimco, and Allianz, were shocked. In Munich, Allianz's shares immediately slumped; its executives frantically called Pimco in Newport Beach to confirm, ridiculously, that Gross had quit. Reporters who covered Pimco full time were shocked. Traders up and down Wall Street, at hedge funds, at bond shops across the country, were shocked. Financial celebrities, accustomed to early information, stared at their blinking screens, wondering if there was another William H. Gross.

By the time they and the rest of the world found out, his Falcon jet was parked in Denver, Colorado, and Gross was inside Janus's offices in Cherry Creek. He'd already managed to assemble almost everything he wanted: his own fund, no management responsibilities, and at least some of his pride. He had no severance package, no golden parachute.

Gross would manage the Janus Global Unconstrained Bond Fund, which had a grand total of $13 million under management—*million* with an *m*. He would open the Janus Newport Beach office, a couple thousand feet from Pimco's headquarters. The building was a carbon copy of Pimco's building, but with one extra floor. A rumor floated around that the developer had added it just to one-up Pimco. (They had not.)

On the morning the news broke, the market seized. Things had felt jittery for weeks, for a handful of unrelated reasons. But Gross's departure jolted traders, and a tremor of terror pulsed through the bond market, rippling out across the different asset classes: Gross *was* Pimco. The implications of this could be huge. Given the extent to which he had called all the investing shots there, did this mean that his favorite trades would fall out of favor? How violently? Would this spark a huge sell-off in bonds, or in the emerging market economies he seemed to support single-handedly?

The calculus was quick: Pimco was about to get hit with a huge wave of client redemptions. It was unavoidable.

Redemptions meant Pimco would have to dump securities onto the market, wholesale. Whatever Pimco liked—get out, *fast*.

The market for Pimco's, Gross's, favorite things plummeted. Government debt of Brazil and Mexico dropped. The corporate issuers Pimco favored fell off a cliff. Gross's most treasured derivatives and swaps, TIPS, all of it. Traders pulled up Total Return's list of holdings on Pimco's website, updated every sixty days, and scoured it for securities to lean on, strategizing where to apply pressure, where to break them.

Traders weren't alone in their speculation. Regulators, too, were nervous that Gross's fall might be the dreaded "systemic" event they'd feared since the financial crisis, the earthquake they were always trying to predict and prevent. From the minute the news broke, regulators hit the phones. The SEC; FINRA, the Financial Industry Regulatory Authority; and other oversight bodies phoned Pimco, trying to assess the potential impact of Gross's departure; they called top executives at its rivals, at hedge funds, brokerages, exchanges that hosted trading. *How bad could it get?* they wanted to know. Would it cause instability across financial markets? Was this the thing? They would keep calling the biggest fund companies, quizzing them about any client demands to pull money, any disruptions in the bond market.

Everyone watched the market, monitoring for signs that the system was buckling under the trading volume.

One security reacted positively: Janus stock shot up 43 percent, for its best day ever.

The financial press struggled to digest the news. Print reporters furiously tapped out updates off scraps of information; TV producers scrambled to book guests who could explain what the hell had happened at Pimco and who were willing to go on record and put their face to it.

Pimco hurriedly crafted a statement, which crossed the wires at 6:37 A.M. Pacific time: Gross had resigned and, though he had already left, "will leave the firm, effective immediately."

"Over the course of this year it became increasingly clear that the firm's leadership and Bill have fundamental differences about how to take Pimco forward," Hodge said in the statement. "As part of our responsibilities to our clients, employees and parent [Allianz], Pimco has been developing a succession plan for some time to ensure that the firm is well prepared to manage a seamless leadership transition."

The firm, Hodge seemed to say, had *not* been caught out; while perhaps Gross had gotten the last laugh on the exact timing, Pimco had been perfectly prepared.

Pimco management whipped together a series of meetings to vote on the next CIO, though there was little doubt. It would be Ivascyn, but the managing directors had to vote.

Pimco announced that Scott Mather, Mark Kiesel, and Mihir Worah—Worah conspicuously got last billing, a perceived slight for his allegiance to Gross—would take over management of Total Return. They were already on it, batting away vulturous hedge fund traders as they tried to front-run a fire sale.

Which was almost unavoidable. After Bill Gross left, from October to March, clients pulled more than $100 billion from Total Return. Pimco somehow had to meet those redemptions.

It was busily holding part of that fire sale in-house. Using that old favorite 17a-7 provision, it sold about $18 billion in securities to other Pimco portfolios. This didn't offset the pulled $100 billion, but it helped.

It 17a-7-ed a ton of Gross's beloved Treasury inflation-protected securities from Total Return into Ivascyn's Income Fund. By the end of March, TIPS would be the biggest position in Pimco Income Fund, which had held little to none for years—a fund its clients had purposely selected for its focus on generating income, extra cash flow, which is arguably the exact opposite of what TIPS do.

Externally, Pimco's traders nimbly sold bond indexes and the most heavily traded stuff they had, raising cash. They held tight to the securities the market was battering. They wouldn't allow the circling hedge fund fighter fish to destroy them.

"Pimco is at battle station alert," Bill Powers said. "Everyone has to pick up the pieces of Bill's departure. And they're doing their second reorg in a year, with Mohamed having left earlier . . . It's hard to imagine people working harder and with more focus than arriving at four thirty in the morning and leaving often at six at night, and working weekends." But, Powers said, "this is their time to convince them that the process, the structure, is in place, that it works, and that it will outlive Bill Gross."

Pimco was well aware that it had a small window in which to win over the consultants and clients whose knee-jerk reaction was to run. Starting that Friday morning, the client services people worked the phones, calling everyone they could get ahold of, from the huge pension funds to the individual investors. Come visit us, they said. You'll love our new structure. In some ways this *removes* an overhang, you know? Because Gross was going to have to go eventually, and it just wasn't clear what we were going to do then. Now it's clear! We are strong and ready to go!

It was an uphill battle. Almost immediately, reports of Gross's unpredictable behavior popped up. Traders and journalists rehashed details of the *Journal*'s February story, and new tidbits made their way out: Gross had phoned Gundlach, of all people, and had met with him. The day the news broke, Gundlach gamely recounted the story of their meeting to Jennifer Ablan. Gross had been about to get fired, sources told a CNBC reporter, for his "increasingly erratic behavior."

That word, *erratic*, kept showing up. There it was again on NPR, and again in *The New York Times*. It was a loaded term, implying that Gross wasn't just mean and nasty. It wasn't just how he treated people. *Erratic* suggested that he had been downright unstable, which at some point could raise a corporate-level problem. Fund managers, and a fund's board of directors, must uphold their fiduciary duty, and part of that is the "duty of prudence," or, basically, acting right, with "care, skill, and caution."

It presented a bit of a conundrum, too: Pimco's management knew that if it got out just how erratically Gross had acted, they would look justified in firing him. Except that even in their own narrative, they hadn't actually fired him; he'd quit. If the public learned all that they'd been struggling to keep a lid on, Pimco might win the battle against Gross but lose the war. Clients might demand to know why management hadn't taken action sooner. Many were already appalled: In a business about trust, the "key man" had been unstable for a full eighteen months? Had there been no adults in the room? Had they no control over their "erratic" founder, no committees or rules or bylaws? Wasn't this supposed to be a real company?

From Pimco's standpoint, they could argue he only really became unfit at the very end, and, in that way, the problem resolved itself right as it became a problem.

Hodge gave his first post-Gross interview to Kirsten Grind at the *Journal* on Saturday, saying there was an "overwhelming" sense of relief at Pimco; that following Ivascyn's appointment on Friday afternoon, the gathered Pimco employees had celebrated the only way they knew how: by rising in an impromptu standing ovation. "There's a sense of optimism and enthusiasm," Hodge said.

On Tuesday, September 30, Ivascyn and Hodge went on CNBC. They were ready to set the new tone and direction, to assuage client concerns, to quell the storm. It was a disaster. The two men sat at aggressive angles, leaning as far away from each other as humanly possible while still staying in the frame—a perfect visual of their oil-and-water pairing. They stumbled through the questions, sounding rehearsed, looking pained. Hodge looked shiny and squirmed as he answered questions by reading or reciting too-practiced answers that didn't correspond to the questions asked. As Hodge spoke, Ivascyn fidgeted, refolding his hands, scratching his face, his sunken eyes darting. He shifted around like he was guilty of something or had somewhere better to be. When it was his turn to speak, he also appeared to be reading carefully.

Hodge dodged anchor Brian Sullivan's questions with bromides about how energized and optimistic and "ready to go" Pimco was. "Bill was going to leave eventually," he said. "We all knew that, whether it was on Friday, next year, or the year after."

It went on forever. They said "moving forward" or "going forward" almost a dozen times.

People at Pimco watched from the trade floor, mouths agape, in horror. How was this supposed to help? This was not better.

The PR department pushed fluffy profiles of Dan Ivascyn to the financial media. He loved NASCAR and country singer George Strait. For runs on the beach, he liked to listen to reggae. He was almost normal, which at Pimco passed for cool. "If you saw him on a Saturday, you'd never guess this guy was the CIO of Pimco," said his former boss, Scott Simon. "He looks like a dude walking around the beach in Newport. You'd never guess this guy was that guy—he's just too normal. He's just a guy. But I'll tell you something, he's a great investor. Just flat out. He has an incredibly good innate sense for risk-reward."

Ivascyn lived near the office, the *Financial Times* wrote, on a "pretty peninsula near the ocean, where he can take advantage of the beach to go running or play volleyball." Most critically, he was a dog person, unlike the leader who'd written a paean *Investment Outlook* to his dead cat, Bob. This was important: they were opposites.

This manifested on the trade floor, they said: happy huddles of

brainstorming analysts and traders were already springing up, naturally, crowding around desks as a new spirit of collaboration dominated. Maybe on a relative basis, but of course they were still Pimco.
Maybe anything was an improvement.

In the meantime, some employees who'd fled Pimco earlier that
year, fed up with Gross, began to trickle back. It was safe again. Within
weeks, Pimco announced the hires of prodigal money manager Marc
Seidner and a rates trader who'd left with a splash in the summer.
They rehired respected economist and Nobel laureate Michael Spence,
who'd been a consultant until that February. They bulked up the
equities and alternatives teams—precisely the ones Gross had wanted
to jettison.

Pimco was resolute that no one would leave, not now. This resolve
made it easy: they would simply throw money at any potential problem.

Conveniently, a giant portion of the profit pool had just been released to the partners: Pimco retained 30 percent of annual profits from
Allianz, and every year, Pimco's partners sliced up that pie among
themselves, with Gross receiving his fixed 20 percent. El-Erian's and
Gross's combined $520 million, give or take, was now up for grabs,
released back to the partners to do with what they wanted.

Which was lucky, because otherwise, the comp situation looked
dire: The tools built to incentivize growth were poised to backfire. M
units were plummeting in value.

Even before Gross quit, it had been a long shot for Pimco to boost
profitability enough to make M units valuable. But now Pimco was
looking at years of unavoidable, unstoppable outflows. The M units
would be functionally worthless. The newly freed-up $520 million
could fill in the M unit–shaped hole.

This addressed the partners, but not the peons. Top brass went to
Allianz, asking for a special award program to help retain talent. Allianz conceded and gave Pimco $279 million for the lower tiers—"all
employees that are not participating in the Pimco profit pool." Double bonuses through the next year.

Allianz was in no position to bargain; it had to keep this new leadership as happy as possible. So, the partners kept their fattened profit pool *and* got more money for the rank and file.

On October 2, Michael Diekmann announced that, after eleven years, he would end his tenure leading Allianz the next year, after he turned sixty, the normal age limit for Allianz board members.

As Pimco's managers frantically worked to restore calm, they poured resources into fixing the Total Return Fund. And it worked: performance bounced back. The managers undid Gross's bet on medium-term government bonds and bet on short-dated corporate bonds. The fund was still hemorrhaging client money—$48 billion in October alone—but, somehow, over the months, Total Return began to beat its peers, and within twelve months, it was back on top, beating almost all.

Black eye, two shots. Bill Gross picked up his regular order at the Starbucks in Fashion Island mall. It was 5:30 A.M., his regular time. Still dark out. The near-final step of his morning commute, roughly the same path for almost fifty years. As Pimco reinvented itself that fall, Gross had resumed most of this daily routine. His drive in every morning, from his cliffside mansion, his coffee order, his Bloomberg Terminal. He'd worked so hard to preserve it, but for the second time this year the man pathologically bound to his routine was forced to relocate. Now he took a right out of the Starbucks, instead of a left, to his new office on Newport Center Drive, in a not-yet-finished building constructed to be almost identical to Pimco's.

A few months after his move, the Starbucks moved locations, which he couldn't control.

Gross walked into the building this cool morning, and nodded silently in greeting to the security guard. He stepped into the elevator and rode up to the eighth floor. The Janus Newport Beach outpost consisted of just him and his new assistant, at first. Gross was the first tenant in the brand-new structure; it was still being built out. It was a tomb, dead silent.

Gross and his assistant set up in a corner in their sunny portion of the eighth floor. Gross had the corner office, of course, and eventually there would be a conference room and a few other nooks and cubbies for traders and assistants. They had plenty of room to expand.

His desk faced Pimco, so that, as he sat at his terminal, their building loomed in the middle of his huge window's frame, behind his screens, all day, every day. It would be a great motivator. Palm trees swayed below, top-heavy. Light reflected off their tall black windows, sometimes so much it created an annoying glare.

The same technician would beat him into the office every morning to turn on his terminal and log him in. Otherwise, at seventy, he was freshly on his own. He had to use terminal functions that he hadn't needed for decades. Had to trade securities that had always been someone else's purview. It was all down to him.

The quiet of the office was welcome. Pimco had always seemed so loud, even with his insistence on silence on the trade floor—the irrepressible sticky drum of keyboards, the coughing, the chatter he somehow couldn't squelch. He hoped this office would provide a haven, so he could get his mind back to trading. He would pick up where he left off, before his performance lost its shine. To pull the thread taut over a few bad years, restoring the long line of his track record.

At this new Potemkin office, he could finally put behind him all the problems that had accumulated at Pimco over the decades: the politics and posturing, the backstabbing, the flagrant undermining of the firm, employees leaking secrets to the press, flouting policies right in his face with no repercussions. He was still reeling from the shock—that, somehow, he had no ability anymore to punish anyone, in his own company. That the years of reducing his own cut of the profit-sharing pool and of being an at-will employee like the rest of them, of graciously parceling out ownership and control, had served to unbind him from his power. Until finally he was betrayed by the very people he'd hired and trained and built, people who were still in diapers when he was carving out the market they now took for granted, the one that had made them all so rich.

Now he was left looking from the outside at his own firm. He thought of his question "money, power, fame"; the five conspirators did it for money and power.

But of course he wasn't done. He would prove that he was still the Bond King to them, to everyone. Money would hemorrhage out of his former firm, the clients he'd served so well these many decades abandoning Pimco and following him to Janus. He would get up every morning before the sun with that singular focus: *showing* them. Proving that Pimco was missing out on a great deal. That's what he always said—about his first wife, about every client who fired Pimco, about anyone who couldn't recognize what he was.

On October 9, he sent out his first *Investment Outlook* as an employee of Janus, accompanied by a letter explaining his move. In keeping with tradition, it was bizarre. "Being asked to dance seems to have become an important part of my life over the past month or so," he wrote. "Had there been a reasonable way to continue there, I would have stayed to my last breath," he wrote of Pimco. "But slowly and with great hesitation, I came to understand that it was time for me to leave. It happens sometimes to founders! But that is water under the bridge, as they say. I don't plan to address it further. Now let's talk about the future."

He knew onlookers were wondering: Why Janus?

"I want to return to a simpler role, completely focused on markets, investment performance and serving my clients. . . . When I asked [Weil] whether Janus might provide me with that simple opportunity, he responded with a very enthusiastic 'yes,' let's dance together. I am excited to work in a true partnership environment with people I trust."

He titled this *Investment Outlook* YOU ONLY DANCE TWICE, saying that almost all marriages had some "missing link," and in his, it was . . . having never danced together. "My 30-year marriage with Sue has been one of those—me the frog and she the princess—but never one of ultimate completion or fulfillment—until now," he wrote. "Happy as we were for all those years, there was always something missing, a trivial last puzzle piece to be sure, but a noticeable one nonetheless, at least to me: *We had never danced!*"

Sue had finally asked him to dance, on September 2, he said. On the cruise ship, just before his fiery return to work. "Maybe it was that extra vodka martini on her side of the table, maybe, as she said later that night, it was my 'fluffy hair,' or maybe it was just the fated last piece of a puzzle coming together on the perimeter of what to me has been a uniquely wonderful marriage. Whatever. We danced!" Indeed, now that they had danced, his marriage was "just like a fairy tale," he wrote. "Picture perfect."

In a way this was a gesture, a bouquet for Sue. Over the years, he'd gifted her sweet *Investment Outlook* intros periodically, in tribute to her wry rejoinders, her enviable speed at picking up pennies from the ground, her skill at replicating a Picasso. He'd freaked her out a little in the aftermath of his departure from Pimco, his agita over the lies being spread about him. But he could express his gratitude during what he knew was a tough period, and this *IO* bouquet was something he knew how to do, something he could present to her, publicly.

The *Investment Outlook* was accompanied by a webcast, Dick Weil in a tan suit interviewing Gross, both in leather chairs, discussing financial markets and what investors could expect. Gross was embarrassed by a Band-Aid just under his right eye, from a minor procedure. It did not help his overall look.

He was still down on markets: The eternal bull market in bonds was over, he said, as he often had in recent years. The era of historically low and falling interest rates was coming to a close, and with it, the days of double-digit returns. "Times have changed," he said. "It's too bad for Bill Gross, too bad for Janus, and too bad for investors. . . . Bye-bye to those days." Maybe not great salesmanship, but everyone had always valued his candor.

Gross kept up his TV appearances. Everyone did still care what he thought, at least in bond markets. He just had to keep at it, he knew. That charm would work again.

But that was all just confection, stuff he did for attention. What truly mattered was performance. If anyone understood the benefit of a strong start, it was Gross: If the numbers weren't spectacular in the first weeks and months, his track record would become nearly impossible to drag higher. Start with killer numbers, and the average is hard to hurt.

Gross figured a huge wave of clients would follow him, terrified by the obvious mess that was Pimco. Analysts estimated $25 billion, minimum, would flow to him. Morningstar forecast that "tens of billions, if not hundreds of billions" would leave Pimco, and much of that would likely follow Gross. It could be a flood. He couldn't know how big; he had to be ready.

At the outset, to ensure his own success, Gross pumped over $700 million of his own money into his new fund. This helped get it going, gave him enough to play with. It also got it past $1 billion, a key threshold for many institutional investors. He was paving the way.

Putting in his own money meant he had to pay fees on it to Janus. In his haste to get hired, he hadn't really bothered negotiating a salary. It just wasn't top of mind. Former Pimco board member Myron Scholes, a Nobel Prize–winning economist, had joined Janus in July as chief investment strategist, so Gross told Weil just to give him whatever Scholes got, which turned out to be not that much. There were about two hundred Janus employees who made more. Taking into account the fees he paid on his $700-plus million, Gross was effectively *paying* Janus for the privilege of working there.

This didn't bother him too much; it would be worth it.

In November, Janus announced that George Soros's family investment fund was investing $500 million with Gross. Sometimes clients needed a first mover, someone to follow. Big pension funds were not known for staking new ground, bravely going it alone.

"An honor to be chosen & an honor to be earned as well," Gross tweeted from Janus's account. He had to make good, to Soros and the other handful of clients who had bravely followed him. And to prove to Pimco, once and for all, who the loser was.

The only way to do that was in the market.

He could still use his "structural alpha" trades and ideas, if they still worked, which he thought they would, or should. Selling volatility, investing in short-dated corporates instead of cash—that stuff was perfectly transferrable. But much of its success relied on time, the "true odds" gamblers talk about—a long enough time span, a big enough data set, to reveal his 51 percent advantage. In the short term, he risked getting a random sample where the market vomited for no reason, or surged for no reason, where relationships between investments went sideways. In the true odds, he wins; without them, he could lose. If his strategies still worked, the only way to get the advantage was time.

But he didn't have time; he knew that. He would have to press harder. He'd long been more of a hedge fund manager in a mutual fund wrapper, taking more risk and making more concentrated bets than a boring fund for retirees maybe should. Now that was even more pronounced and on display, for those who took the time to look. He tethered himself to the market's roller coaster, taking on massive amounts of risk to try to carve out his old caliber of performance. If he worked hard enough, pressed hard enough, squeezed reluctant basis points out of the market, he could do it.

Over the months, money flowed out of Total Return at Pimco, but it didn't flow to Gross. That first year, the total in his Janus Unconstrained fund reached only some $1.4 billion. He made noises about how that was great, he'd *wanted* agility, to be nimble in markets—that was the fun of it. But, of course, it was a disappointment. He'd worked so hard for his clients, putting them first, the whole time, literally for decades; where was their loyalty?

At least Dick Weil was being rewarded for his: Janus's profits surged 18 percent in the last quarter of 2014, as it saw net new client money—$2 billion worth—for the first time in over five years. "Bill Gross is our Peyton Manning, that game-changing level of talent for us," Weil told Bloomberg News in Denver. "People are looking at us."

In January, those dogged *Journal* reporters Kirsten Grind and Greg

Zuckerman reported that half of the assets in Gross's new fund represented his own money.

Gross was so tired of those two. In advance of publication, he tweeted, "Thanks @KirstenGrind @WSJ for upcoming article—yes I do believe in and invest in Janus Global Unconstrained Bond Fund!"

The fund had already lost 1.1 percent since he'd taken over. In February, investors pulled $18.5 million from his fund; it was going the wrong way. And 2015 was already not stacking up right: he was down 0.8 percent, trailing 96 percent of similar funds, according to Morningstar data. Neither his "since inception" or "this year" numbers looked how he needed them to look.

Across the way, in the marginally smaller building, Pimco wasn't faring much better with its proud equity push. In May 2015, just months after Gross's outspoken rejection of its equities business, Pimco finally killed it. It closed three active stock mutual funds. Virginie Maisonneuve left in June, and they didn't replace her.

Gross's point about equities, buried in his rage, had ended up being correct: it didn't make sense for Pimco to pursue the business. They had never managed to attract much money: When Pimco gave up, the funds to be closed were still counting client assets by the millions. Piddling. No one internally would ever say Gross was right, because the strong feeling was that he hadn't been: equities had been his idea all along, no matter what history he tried to write later.

And it was unfortunate for Pimco that Maisonneuve's departure further depressed the firm's already precarious diversity numbers: she'd been one of eight female managing directors, out of sixty-three.

Then, in August 2015, Pimco experienced another first: after years of investigating Pimco's practices, the SEC had issued it a Wells Notice, a formal warning indicating that some regulatory action was coming.

It wasn't very damaging in itself. Wells Notices are like the HPV of asset management; a lot of firms get them. But those within Pimco remembered Jason Williams, now in Montana. Was this his doing? The SEC was claiming similar things to what he'd claimed: that Pimco had gamed the pricing system.

Other "whistleblowers," former Pimco employees, had filed complaints with the SEC, too. They offered to talk to regulators. There was plenty to find, if they looked hard enough, according to these ex-employees. Gross had extended words and rules and pricing systems beyond their intent, yes, they said, but it was also the whole place. The portfolio managers railing at compliance, pushing for looser oversight, stretching terminology to their advantage as far as possible, in order to clear a path for their alleged misdeeds. These ranged from manipulative allocation practices; liberal abuse of the 17a-7 exemption; conflicts of interest; and overt trading on material nonpublic information with a "'wink and nod' approach." (The SEC has not taken action related to these allegations.)

From Pimco's standpoint, there might be a way that this Wells Notice could be good: it was an opportunity to tie up the loose ends Gross might have left behind. They could give themselves a clean slate; any wrongdoing had been on Gross's watch. The worst actor was gone.

In that way, Pimco got away with it, whitewashed decades of firm-wide envelope-pushing and loophole-exploiting, pinning it all on their bad old founder on his way out the door—the bad old founder who helped create the market where they would continue to play. Gross had helped to swell the finance industry, and it was now disproportionately massive relative to the economy to which it was attached, with correspondingly disproportionate salaries and bonuses, protected by defensive layers of jargon and derivative complexity so no one would try to get wise.

Without him, Pimco could finally graduate from being founder-run into the ranks of the Established Firms. It could cleanly be a place for thought leaders; a nice, staid firm different only in its insistence on excellence and its great, very long-term track record. All the downside of Bill Gross—the embarrassing emotional show-and-tell every month, the wrangling with the ethics of being capital and feeling bad for labor, the rawness—had gone with him. But all his inventions and decades of achievement, the loophole exploiting that helped make the game wilder (until the game became a crisis and the government had to intervene), his inspiration to send Dan Ivascyn to Boston to fake-buy a house, laying the foundation for Pimco's insight and global authority and influence and coziness with power—the entire upside of Bill Gross's legacy, theirs to keep.

To settle the odd-lot charges, Pimco ended up paying nearly $20 million—something it could easily absorb—without admitting or denying that it had violated anything.

After about a year at Janus, Gross could see his new track record forming. By October 2015, he'd lost more than 1 percent and was trailing over 70 percent of comparable funds.

Then, in November, news broke that George Soros had pulled his now-$490 million. Soros had been the only big-name investor to follow Gross, and now he was gone.

As Gross flailed, failing to best Pimco in the markets, he took a different tack. People were getting the wrong impression about who the loser was. He didn't care for the aspersions he was hearing, that he might have *lost his touch*. He began to say more loudly that he'd been pushed out. That he'd been fighting for the little guy, arguing for lower fees—which he had, for years! In the 1990s, in his book. Even in *Investment Outlooks*. And in 2014, he'd argued to the Executive Committee that, given the lower projected returns, client fees should come down, too.

As he thought about it, it seemed that this was what had done him in. The pushback to that populist ideal. He had threatened their own fat wallets, their cavernous houses and collections of fast cars, with all his crusading on behalf of clients. That, and that they'd wanted his share of the profits.

He felt compelled to set the record straight. In the weeks that followed his ouster, he'd written a thirty-one-page mini-memoir, a pamphlet, of what had Really Happened. People had always told him he was a good writer, so he put those skills to use, recording everything while it was still fresh in his mind: El-Erian's eleventh-hour request to be co-CEO. Balls's betrayal, selling Gross out to the press. How Gross had only ever sought to help the little guy—to his own detriment. His own fury.

He called this IO MURDER ON THE PIMCO EXPRESS. That text would help him now. He hired LA lawyer Patricia Glaser, and, that October, sued Pimco.

Actually, Gross alleged, he had been *fired* from Pimco, forced out by a greedy "cabal" that was "driven by a lust for power, greed, and a desire to improve their own financial position and reputation at the expense of investors and decency." They wanted his slice of the profit-sharing pool, and feared his push for lower fees, the lawsuit said, artfully accusing Pimco both of not letting him hoard the wealth and of not helping him share it. The complaint was informed by MURDER ON THE PIMCO EXPRESS in tone and character and phrasing and festering.

Gross asserted constructive termination and breach of contract. He'd left four days shy of the end of the third quarter, and so, was owed his third-quarter bonus. But this wasn't about the money, he wanted to make clear. Any proceeds from this lawsuit he would donate to worthy causes, through his foundation.

The reaction was surprisingly elegiac. Like something had ended when he wasn't looking.

"It's a very sad day for the money management industry," John Brynjolfsson said on Bloomberg TV. "It's a sad day for Pimco, and it's a sad day for Bill." Brynjo's almost Seussian characterization echoed Gross's own assessment: it was too bad for everybody.

Gross, Brynjo said, had "been able to channel some of that ego, some of that narcissism, into positive directions," for the past sixty or so years. "I'd have to say the past three or four years have been a sad chapter and, unfortunately, not the way that Bill should have moved forward toward the twilight of his career."

For Pimco, that he wouldn't let his vendetta die was inconvenient at best; clients only wanted things to quiet down. They wanted to be able to stop thinking about Pimco all the time.

Pimco had to keep it together. So, it presented a blasé face. The suit was "a legally groundless and sad postscript to what had been a storied career," the firm said. "Pimco has moved forward since Mr. Gross's resignation. It is time for him to do the same."

The expensive battle would rage for more than a year.

Gross's determination to beat Pimco, in the market and in court, consumed him. For all his riches and for his old age, he commuted and clocked into work every day, trapped by his own inability to let go. Even if a better self wanted to be golfing in Indian Wells all the time, he could not indulge. Now the thing that got him out of bed was to triumph over those who had overthrown him and his undying desire to "prove" it, to *show* them.

Every day at 3 P.M. California time, he checked his fund's performance against Pimco Total Return and Unconstrained, to see who was winning. "I have a happy night if I'm doing better, and a not-so-happy night if I'm not doing better," he said.

He knew he was short on time.

"If you can be actually honest with yourself, which I don't think anybody can ever be, there comes a point where you would know, hopefully—to be crass about it—that you're losing it, that you're making mistakes, you're not as focused as you used to be," he said. "That hasn't come yet, but I know that happens to people in their seventies and eighties. That's how the cookie crumbles. So far, I think I'm okay."

In November 2016, Sue Gross filed for divorce. She hired Laura Wasser, the attorney who'd shepherded splits for Angelina Jolie and Britney Spears.

Gross felt totally blindsided. He knew things hadn't been good. He'd been making excuses for her absence to friends and neighbors for years, saying she was shopping with her sister, out on a hike, out of town. He had noticed that things were worsening in recent months, sure. She had moved out that summer, for space, to their spare homes up the road in Corona del Mar and in Los Angeles. When they met for dinner at Bandera, a nearby restaurant, in October, he demanded to know if she was coming back. He'd gotten angry, and, embarrassed, she'd walked out of the restaurant; he chased her to her car and screamed as she hurried to shut the door: "That's what you always do—you run!" She peeled out of the parking lot.

That was the last time he saw her before she filed.

Even so, divorce had been unthinkable to him. But as he adjusted to the pain, it became clear: She wanted war. Well, that he could deliver. "Feel peaceful while you can," he texted her in December. "War of the roses ahead and I can predict the winner!!! 😈"

On another day that month: "YOu are a piece of work and surely not a friend—for a long time—a coward too to not say why you really wanted a divorce. I feel utterly betrayed and will not shy from letting people know," he emailed her from his Janus account. "You are disgusting---all will know---and I do mean all."

She was out for his money, he knew; the Wasser hire said as much. Wasser had explicitly told Bloomberg News just that year: in California "you can sit on the couch and eat bonbons while your husband's at work, and you'll still get half of everything." Well, not this time.

In the weeks after she filed, he emailed Sue over and over, accusing her of having an affair, and extinguishing any hope she might have for "an amicable high road divorce." (A representative for Sue Gross said that Sue never had an affair.) As his emails to her escalated, he wrote to her sister and brother-in-law, too.

He drew the painfully obvious parallel himself: he was experiencing his second "divorce" in as many years.

"You should have known with the PIMCO lawsuit [then ongoing]," he wrote in one flame-mail. "I was passive---even after being fired[,] until they attacked me unfairly in the press---it was only then that I went into attack mode myself. Same thing here---I would have taken the high road---

"I trust no one now - especially you."

Sue proved a formidable opponent. Bill alleged in a court declaration that she had cut off the utilities at their Indian Wells house, the home of her hole-in-one trophy that had given him so much consternation; the lack of filtration turned their pool green. He claimed she would pop by their compound in Irvine Cove unannounced and leave with valuable possessions. She told him she was "going to do whatever she [had] to do to get [him] out of the house," he recalled. (A representative for Sue Gross says the property was maintained by the same property manager for twenty-five years; that Sue did not cut off the utilities; that the pool was never green; that she never went back to the home without approval from the lawyers; and that she never said that.)

She persevered, and won the compound. It was one of the three houses she kept in the even split.

But Bill Gross could not exit gracefully. Before surrendering the house, he went to a drugstore and bought spray bottles that promised to smell like farts and vomit, and went around the 13,819 square feet of the main residence, spritzing liberally. Sue discovered the empty bottles in her trash cans.

Other parting gifts Sue said she found: dead fish and dirt in the air vents; the cord to the treadmill severed; flowers decapitated in their pots; the remote controls for TVs, drapes, and other technology all missing; balls of human hair in the drawers; and the eyes and mouths scratched out of the portraits of their three cats that Sue had painted on pieces of furniture.

Gross said he saw Sue at their son Nick's concert and he feared she had a knife. He says he was concerned about theft, so he hired Empire Intelligence to keep him updated on Sue's and her relatives' whereabouts. Which led her to file for a restraining order, matching the one Bill took out against her after the concert incident. (A representative for Sue Gross says Sue has never carried a knife outside of her kitchen, and did not have one at her son's concert.)

Having been dislocated from his home of thirty years, Bill Gross was looking to snap up property in Irvine Cove, to reestablish himself in his same neighborhood. Irvine Cove is a gated community, so at least to some extent he also needed a home base if Empire Intelligence was going to get any relevant intelligence.

So, in the summer of 2018, when a few houses came up for sale there, Sue spent $37.8 million to make sure Bill couldn't get them.

A few weeks later, a home across the street from that of Sue's sister and brother-in-law came on the market, and both Sue and Bill bid on it. Her bid was higher, but he offered cash, and won, spending $36 million.

There were other costs, ones that Bill Gross didn't predict and couldn't price accurately. When his son got married, in Italy, Bill found out from his dental hygienist.

His lawsuit against Pimco at least found a satisfying-enough resolution: After a protracted, discovery-rich battle, Gross and Pimco settled in March 2017. Pimco sent $81 million to the "William and Sue Gross Family Foundation," though soon the "Sue"-involving foundation would be replaced by "the William, Jeff and Jennifer Gross Family Foundation," his remaining family, his non-Sue children. Gross topped the gift off with his own money, to tip it over the $100 million mark. By some philanthropy world definitions, that's the threshold for a "megagift," which gave it a chance at roundups from the year's biggest donations. Maximum yield.

As part of the settlement, Pimco agreed to dedicate a room in its headquarters to the cofounders. It did not specify which room, and some in the building joked that it would be the bathroom in the basement.

"Pimco has always been family to me, and like any family, sometimes there are disagreements," Gross said in a joint statement with Pimco. "I'm glad that we have had the opportunity to work through those."

"Bill Gross has always been larger than life," added Ivascyn, whose Income Fund had just surpassed Total Return as Pimco's biggest. "Bill has had an enormous influence on Pimco and the careers of many who have passed through its halls."

An influence on many—an understatement if Gross had ever read one. But it would have to do; this would have to count as his hole in one. Of the life and empire he had built over forty-five years, only his commute and half his money remained.

The world he'd built was cruel, petty, filled with boys pulling wings off flies—but it had been his. At the end, it had turned its brutality on him. His power had evaporated and, with it, any hope for justice; he could not exact revenge on the people he'd built, on the company he'd built, on the markets he'd built.

By almost any of his metrics, he had *won*. He had gamed every ranking he met. That question he used to ask in hiring—power, money, or fame? He'd gotten all three. Money, of course—that had come first. Fame, his own favorite answer—he'd had all the headlines and TV interviews he could ever have dreamed of. And power—the present moment notwithstanding, hadn't he been influential? He had been king, had had a kingdom. He'd joined the stable world of bond investing, paper resting in a vault, and had helped transform it into a casino. He'd taught disciples to play like he did; his enthusiastic embrace of mortgages, derivatives, and complicated structures had charged their growth, and when they destabilized the entire U.S. economy, he had helped write the government's guarantee, which has now expanded to, arguably, everything. Gross was always one of the few willing to say out loud that investing was just gambling, but in the end, he made it more and less of a gamble.

Whatever the cost, he'd had an effect.

He knew better than to be unhappy, or at least to admit it. He was alive and a billionaire, and those things had to count. But as his laurels receded in his mind, as it seemed more and more as though he were ending the game with the same-colored chips as everyone else, his worse instincts fought through his more sober reflections.

In September 2020, he issued an *Investment Outlook* by press release, titled TATTOOED, in which he called his youngest son, his only child with Sue, a disappointment. "Guess there is always one tattooed (black) sheep in every family," he wrote. "Nick is mine." Then he pivoted to how the global economy had been "tattooed" by coronavirus.

He was also in a fight closer to his literal home—or, rather, the beautiful home he'd bought for his then–"life partner," Amy Schwartz. He'd met her through Bill Powers, of all people, in 2017; she was a former tennis pro in her late forties then. They loved to golf together.

He'd gifted her a $1 million Dale Chihuly sculpture, which they'd installed in the yard of the beachfront mansion. When the statue— twenty-two feet of cobalt-blue glass, stabby tubes, and some fat globes sitting on the ground—was damaged by the elements (perhaps falling palm fronds), they added what looked like a soccer net above it for protection.

Except that the net obstructed the view of their next-door neighbor, who attempted to get them to remove it. They would not. Eventually, the neighbor complained to the city of Laguna Beach, which sent Bill and Amy a letter saying the sculpture and netting needed permits.

And then Bill and Amy started playing loud music, with speakers right near the property line, at all hours. From July into October. Including Led Zeppelin and 50 Cent and the theme songs from the TV shows *Green Acres* and, most frequently, *Gilligan's Island*.

When the neighbor texted Amy at almost midnight on July 31, asking for them to turn it down, Gross wrote back: "Peace on all fronts or we'll just have nightly concerts Big Boy."

In October, Bill and Amy sued the neighbor for invasion of privacy, among other things, saying he'd been watching, photographing, and filming them, including in various stages of undress while they swam in the pool. The next day, the neighbor sued for harassment.

So, that winter, as most people sheltered from the pandemic, Bill and Amy attended court in Santa Ana. They testified that they just enjoy music, in particular the theme from *Gilligan's Island*. "We've learned lyrics and we act together with hands and pointing. It's like a little play," Gross testified. "We play it because it makes us real happy. Half the time we start dancing, and when we finish, we're looking at each other like it's a good time."

One critical exhibit: A video of Gross crouching in his boxers behind the wall abutting the two properties; 50 Cent's "In Da Club" is audible. Gross is dancing, pointing his fingers, swaying, as his neighbor films him. After a while, Gross crouches, apparently hiding. The 50 Cent song peters out. The music changes to the *Gilligan's Island* theme. Gross looks up, beyond the wall, to his neighbor's camera.

"We're gonna subpoena that, boy, so you'd better erase it," he says, peeking through palm trees. "That's harassment. *Harrrrrrrrassment!*" he says, lunging forward as he growls the last word, before he creeps back to his own house.

In December, Gross tried a new tack: In an open letter to his neighbor, he said the situation had gotten out of hand. They'd lost sight of things at a particularly tacky time. "Those who know me and my history also know I do not willingly back down from a fight," he wrote. "But this situation has escalated far out of proportion to the actual issues at stake, which are petty in comparison to a world in which thousands are dying and suffering every day, while many more are out of work and desperate to pay the rent and feed their families."

They should end their fight, Gross said, tally what they'd already spent and would spend in legal fees and court expenses, and donate that total to Orange County food banks and other charities.

The neighbor declined, his attorney saying, "This is just billionaire Bill Gross trying to buy his way out of accountability for his horrible behavior."

Gross went ahead and donated half a million anyway, renewing his offer, in another self-published press release, for his neighbor to join him.

In December 2020, the judge sided with the neighbor, ruling that Bill and Amy had indeed been harassing their neighbors. She barred Bill and Amy from coming within five yards of the neighbors (except when they were on their own property) and banned them from playing music (above sixty decibels) outside their home when no one was in the backyard pool area. She tossed Gross's claim of harassment.

Gross said in a statement that though he was "disappointed in the outcome," he would abide by the terms of the decision. That month, a press release went out announcing that Bill Gross had signed the Giving Pledge.

He's had time for one more reinvention. After four years of dating, he and Amy got married, in April 2021, in a small ceremony in Indian Wells, overlooking the Vintage Club golf course awash in bright desert sunlight. They were surrounded by a small group of family and friends and giant vases bursting with white roses. Afterward they climbed in a golf cart with a JUST MARRIED sign and tooled around the enclosed community. A local write-up said the couple will "split their time between homes in Laguna Beach, the China Cove Beach section of Newport Beach, and their Indian Wells house," a radius of about 100 miles.

At the commission of an editor at the *Orange County Business Journal*, Gross wrote about his philanthropy, saying that giving makes for a happy life. He explicated lyrics from an old 1960s song, "Happiness Runs," seeing a "self-contained, inward-looking, self-satisfaction that equates happiness to being content with yourself as a person" and also something about "the Buddhist philosophy of impermanence and the priority of the moment."

"Have I achieved that level of folkie (or fogey) happiness? Well, I just married the love of my life Amy Schwartz, so I'm a little closer. But I also know that a lifetime of giving provides happiness that can be measured as much by self-satisfaction as by quantity."

Before, success was asset growth, trading profits, an S&P strangle with the right range. Now he has again changed the benchmark: success is seeing what he's done, and being satisfied.

He seems to have recovered his structural ability to forget, to start again, fresh. It has allowed him to approach the table unclouded by unhelpful emotion like regret. It's the posture a gambler must take: the system works, it just didn't work that time. If he keeps playing, he'll get the true odds.

Epilogue

Gross eased into a chair at the bar at R+D Kitchen at Fashion Island, in the shadow of the Pimco building across Newport Center Drive. The restaurant was a favorite of many Real Housewives of Orange County. You could spot them a mile away, their glistening, artificially smoothed faces remarkable even in Newport Beach.

Gross had been gratified to see many things lately: Pimco portfolio managers were appearing as experts on panels at prestigious but pay-to-play conferences, which Gross had boycotted as fluff for self-important bureaucrats.

Best of all was Doug Hodge getting swept up in the massive college bribery scandal, charged with wire fraud. He would plead guilty and serve nine months in prison. Gross couldn't have orchestrated anything better.

But now that Gross was retired—from the bond market, from the stamps market, from the war of his broken marriage—he was trying to practice serenity. He hadn't broadcast the news beforehand, not even to Dick Weil until the night before. It was his news. When he announced in February that he was retiring, he was at first gratified to see Pimco take out a big advertisement, on page B5 of *The Wall Street Journal*, congratulating him:

48 years. 2500+ Employees. Millions of Clients Served. One Investing Legend. PIMCO congratulates Bill Gross on his legendary career, and the enduring success of the firm he helped found nearly 50 years ago. He hired and mentored many of us and inspired many more. The principles and processes established during his four decades of leadership still help us pursue excellence for our clients every day.

Once the initial warmth wore off, the message came into focus: it was an ad for Pimco, for themselves. Small and petty as ever. "Still" pursuing "excellence." Don't worry, he got it. They invited him to the annual reunion; he declined.

He wondered if things could have been different. Asked himself honestly what might have happened. *Would you still be over there as the Bond King, at your desk at seventy-three? Would you go 'til eighty?*

But he knew. "I would still be encased in my little cocoon." Maybe the showdown was unavoidable, maybe this sorry outcome was the only one possible.

"There was a definite need for winding down and phasing out, for sure," he said. "Not in a way that I would choose, and I don't think even Pimco would choose, in retrospect. But that's the natural evolution, not just of life, but of business life. You rise to the top, and then you gradually erode, and out. But it's hard to see that when you're the Bond King and you're doing well, and [when] assets, in part because of me, are at two trillion . . . who could possibly object to that? Because it was a success story not just for me but for the company that I helped to build, beyond imagination. It's a fairy tale. So, why strike the clock at midnight? It's like there's not even the possibility of a pumpkin. Just put on that slipper and stay married.

"You can have a bad performance, but the prestige that it builds, that takes a long time to erode," he added. "It wasn't unrealistic to imagine that this was something that could keep going on and on."

There's no good way to do it.

All the hedge funds were trying to do it now, too, setting up weak successors behind aging founders. Even the control-freakiest among them. Private equity, too. All trying to preserve and perpetuate the machine they'd built, turn it into some kind of legacy, as if it were more than a better hand crank to squeeze money out of companies; out of building materials and hospitals and sludge dredged from the ground; and out of workers. The junior guys at these firms, they wanted the machine to keep working, too, but for themselves. They didn't care about legacy, only that the crank kept squeezing. The thing wasn't sacred to them like it was to the founders, like it was to Gross. The young ones couldn't see that Gross and his peers had created these beautiful machines out of nothing, out of their ability to wring out better numbers, and from there, they had learned to shift things to their will, to pick which companies would get money and which wouldn't. It was so much more than a game. Now, in the hands of those who had inherited it, it looked cheaper.

And maybe it really had been a partnership dedicated to enriching clients. Maybe people there still did believe that, even today. Bond traders used to speak credulously about how they were lowering the cost of capital by being bond traders. Now, as the Federal Reserve has been outright buying corporate bonds in the market, plucking them up alongside Pimco and BlackRock, surely the system's fundamental absurdity has become obvious. Gross and Pimco figured out that the government needs the markets to function, wants the stock market to go up, wants companies not to go bankrupt. So, people can battle over basis points in the full security that things will never be allowed to go too far down. And even if they do go down, for a professional money manager, it's almost never their problem.

There are many people to thank for this, but Gross is chief among them.

As Gross looked at the whole, watching as his peers across the industry shuffled their own organizations, putting younger men in orderly lines to manage their firms after their departure one way or another, to ensure their own legacy and some degree of immortality, he saw the primary difference: the other aging founders retained power at the executive level, allies.

"That was my failing," Gross said. "I should have made sure that the Executive Committee wasn't stacked, that I had a friend on the Executive Committee."

Of all the betrayals, he said, the one that wounded him most was by Dialynas, his friend of almost forty years, his trade floor protégé, his frequent dinner buddy.

In Gross's last week at Pimco, when they were preparing to fire him and appoint a new CIO, they needed to gather a selection committee—two portfolio managers and two account managers and whomever else. Somehow one of the portfolio manager spots on the committee came down to Chris Dialynas.

He was on vacation, up at Lake Arrowhead, when they called. "You've got to get back here, for a special meeting," they told him. Dialynas said no, but they browbeat him until he agreed—or, at least that's what he told Gross.

So, he came back on that Saturday and voted. He wasn't on the Executive Committee, so he wouldn't have voted to fire Gross, but he voted for Gross's replacement, which to Gross was tantamount to firing him. Dialynas didn't have the guts to turn them down and stay on vacation.

The message to Gross was clear: "Friendship only goes so far," he said.

He was in the process of transitioning to his new life of golfing full time, but that didn't mean he'd retire from being famous. He went on Bloomberg TV and mentioned his Asperger's diagnosis, and people responded with sympathy. Sue had told him, before anyone—he'd been reading that Michael Lewis book *The Big Short*: in it, a character ticks through a checklist of the symptoms:

"A lack of spontaneous seeking to share enjoyment, interests, or achievements with other people . . ." Check.

"Difficulty reading the social/emotional messages in someone's eyes . . ." Check.

"A faulty emotion regulation or control mechanism for expressing anger . . ." Check.

Gross went down through the list with the character, checking each off. (Except the one about not being coordinated. Not true here. Pretty athletic.) He took the book to Sue, who scanned the pages and basically said, yeah, I know. So, in 2016, Bill Gross saw a psychiatrist, who agreed. "I think it's at the margin, which is perfect," he says, of his case. "The positive qualities and some of the negatives. Yeah, I wish I didn't have some of the negatives, but it allows you the possibility of using this successfully."

He'd discussed the diagnosis obliquely in an *Investment Outlook*. But no one had seized on it, realized that perhaps that was why he'd misread things so badly, why he couldn't understand today's unending demand for openness and gentle words and feelings. People should understand that. He wasn't *just* an asshole.

Now, his empire lost to him, he saw that much of his drive was that thirst for affirmation. For external validation. He wondered now if it tied back to his cold Canadian parents, his father who never played baseball with him, the Dr. Spock parenting generation. Children seen and not heard. He could remember reading the funny papers with his father on a Sunday morning—that was his only memory of being close to him.

"How can you possibly think you shouldn't hug your child?" Gross lamented. "But back then that's what [you were] supposed to do. It doesn't make sense, does it? Because human nature wants to touch, wants to hug. That's what I tried to get through being famous—not being touched, but being connected. I assumed—emotionally, not intellectually, I always knew intellectually it was bullshit—but I assumed emotionally that the attention and the fame, that people would love me. Intellectually, I'd say, *Oh, I know that's bullshit*. But then I'd forget about it."

So, he'd used whatever playground worked to do it, which, for him, was financial markets. Decades of pushing the bounds, inventing and innovating and pushing relentlessly onward, leaving his competitors constantly in his dust, rushing to copy him, to follow him, to capture some of his magic; leaving the raggedy handful of regulators who chased them all around exhausted and ineffective.

In some ways, he can see what that wrought, that in his constant forward tilt he neglected everything else, to his own detriment. And that it was gone now.

He was trying to change, he said. He had to. He could do it. Just the other day he was dancing to a Justin Timberlake song. He'd been going on helicopter rides and zip-lining in Kauai. Everyone else zip-lining there had been in their thirties, forties, and fifties. *What am I doing here?* he'd thought to himself, laughing.

He was hanging out with his golf buddies. He was even making new friends, initiating conversations in the clubhouse between rounds, with total strangers. Women, even. Him! Giving out compliments. He wasn't flirting; he was experimenting with opening up to the world. When he tried dating in the months after Sue left, one date pointed out that maybe it wasn't great that he'd been taking Ambien for almost a decade, so he stopped for a while. He could not change who he had been and what he'd done, and maybe he wouldn't have even if he could. But he could try now to remake himself with what he had left. Which was some hair, a lot of money, and a little fame.

"My new life is different from my old life," he said. "In part it's because I know I have to make a new life.

"I can improve on what I was. I can do it."

Things with Amy were great, but even that took a while, Gross said, and real effort. Sometimes at the beginning he would catch himself in the mirror and think, *What the fuck is she interested in me for?* "It could be brushing your teeth or it could be when you get a sign—when, potentially, the cover or the mask comes off, and you become human and you reveal your real self," he said. He knew from how he was treated at Pimco that his mask must be gruesome. But Amy was sticking around, for whatever reason.

Gross ordered a water, no food. A short man about Gross's age, in a straw hat and a casual button-down shirt, walked up and stuck out his hand. "I don't care what they all say," he said. "You did right by me." Gross had made him money for years, and he appreciated that. He thanked him.

Gross smiled and shook the man's hand and thanked him for his kind words.

"That happens all the time," Gross said. Though, he added, it was unlikely anyone would come tell him that he sucked.

Author's Note

In the years I spent writing this book, I heard a lot of rumors about myself. I heard that I paid for stories. (No one in journalism does that; tabloids do.) I heard that I was conspiring with either Bill Gross or, alternately, with Pimco to make the other party look bad.

Of all the rumors I heard, two stand out.

My second-favorite rumor started because it was taking me so long to write and revise this book. No one could believe I was still working on it. Many within Pimco assumed that I'd been bought out, paid to not write this book. One figure I heard was $10 million. This made me laugh because, in a compensation structure only a public radio journalist could love, I had been *not* publishing this book on my own for free.

My very favorite rumor is this one.

When I landed in Los Angeles in September 2014, I was a beat reporter at Bloomberg News with the biggest story in my world breaking right now, and I had zero meetings lined up. Bloomberg sent me to go "get the real story" of why Gross had been quit-fired. It sounded daring and exhilarating, until I found myself sitting in my hotel room in Santa Monica with nothing to do because not a single person would speak to me.

That was bad enough, but there was one reliable thing I did have to do, an age-old part of being a beat reporter: doorstepping. Showing up at the home of whoever had just lost their famous spouse or had been accused of a crime, outside the office of a freshly disgraced politician or bank CEO. Sometimes this practice does yield good interviews, which is why people do it. But more often, you get only a horrified look as the person peering out a cracked-open door takes the measure of your morality, your absolute lack of shame.

As a low-level beat reporter, I had no real choice. I had to doorstep Bill Gross. Unlike the best reporters, I can feel shame, so I was horrified. But my options were doorstep or risk my paycheck.

As I thought about my unhappy fate, I discovered that what I had decided was a loophole. I'm from Virginia, where you could plausibly show up on the doorstep of a person recently hurt or wronged with a casserole. And, as luck would have it, I had just visited a contact who'd given me a Tupperware container full of homemade seven-layer brownies—her grandmother's recipe, even, written out on an index card in a pinched cursive just like my grandma's.

I decided that doorstepping with baked goods in hand felt adjacent to acceptable. People do that!

So, disgusted and ashamed but armed with the cousin of an excuse, I drove up the steep incline of the Pacific Coast Highway, past a beach with the ocean's crashing waves, toward the staggering cliffs onto which Bill Gross's house was said to cling.

I pulled up to the gate of Irvine Cove, where a lady in a uniform sat in a box. She turned to me.

"Hi," I said, smiling. "I'm here to see Bill Gross? Is he here?"

". . . yes. Is he expecting you?"

"Well, no. But I have these . . . brownies? To give him?"

She stared at me.

I suddenly grasped that no security guard would accept gifts from a stranger for a billionaire with enemies. "You can't take the brownies, can you?" I said.

"No."

"Right, of course, anthrax. I totally get that. That's fine, that's what I thought! Thank you! Sorry!" And I sped off, hooking a left back out

Pacific Highway 1, toward Los Angeles, skin crawling at my own capacity to harass another person.

I reported to my boss that I had tried, and then I buried the memory of the incident as deep inside as I could. I didn't think about it again until years later, when a source told me he'd heard a funny story about me: that I'd knocked on Bill Gross's front door dressed as a Girl Scout.

When I heard this, my stomach dropped, as if I had been caught doing something bad, as if I had *actually* done this. But, wait—dressed as a Girl Scout? It didn't even make sense. What utility would the costume have had? Was I conducting some kind of sexist sting operation? Hoping to trick Bill Gross into talking to me by . . . being a Girl Scout? For a journalist, it feels weird to be seen as a character in the story; you're supposed to be a lens. But it's even weirder to see yourself in creepy, infantilizing cosplay.

What I had just experienced was Pimco's special game of telephone, the circuitous route of information traveling from person to person, getting increasingly mangled, with new and often gross twists. I wondered how far the brownie story had traveled. Who had given me the costume, Bill Gross himself or someone down the chain?

This game is how I heard unsavory rumors, things I cannot and will not print. Some stories were arguably relevant, like the prevalence of in-office "romances," often between bosses and their reports. Others were less edifying.

These stories have come to me from even the most lovable of my sources. And they tell me the things in good faith, with the intention of revealing someone's bad character or moral wrongdoing. To illustrate a climate that's otherwise hard to describe, an office where the people with power are (with about four exceptions) white men. How do you prove the air is polluted if not by measuring the pollution?

I had a similar challenge: at a firm where workplace relationships are common, boundaries consistently muddy. Maybe that's part of the problem. Very often these stories crossed into areas that were not at all my business: it's not in my interest to report the personal lives of people working at Pimco; it's not my job, and I am literally uninterested. But that's not what Pimco thinks: for years, its leaders expressed anxiety that I was digging into people's personal lives to write a salacious book, despite my assurances otherwise. Of course, there has never been a need to dig, given that it has all been presented to me on a silver platter, whether I wanted it or not.

All this should paint a picture of an environment that is self-obsessed, irrationally anxious, and insular; that cannot see the world it built; that assumes that everyone lives in that world, too—that everyone responds to the same incentives that world does (money) and respects the same priorities (owning planes and special cars that can be driven quickly)—that their jokes about women are universally funny; that thinks it's reasonable to assume that "cougars" want to "hunt" for "fresh meat" (i.e., men who work at Pimco and are, therefore, rich and, it follows, desirable partners) at the bar in town, The Quiet Woman, whose logo is the body of a decapitated woman (get it? she finally stopped talking); that everyone wants to play poker, go golfing together, fraternize at strip clubs.

And all this informs this book's focus on why one white man was mad at another, or at the rare not-white man, with so little room for the anger or experience of any women or people of color. There is precious little of that in general, as evidenced by the demographic breakdown of who has worked and still works at Pimco. Those women and people of color who do make it in the door are, for the most part, kept on the fringes, far from the power center. It's worth noting that one of the main players often cast to me as the villain is one of the few people of color who did make it to that power center, and achieved the corresponding riches.

. In the past few years, three women have filed high-profile discrimination lawsuits against Pimco (one suit is ongoing, with three more women having signed on); one partner resigned after being investigated for "inappropriately touching" a lower-ranking employee; twenty-one current and former female employees have written a letter to management alleging abuse and discrimination; and one employee left following his wife's allegations of abuse. *The Wall Street Journal* tallied that, at the start of 2021, the company had never had a Black partner in its fifty years. And this is only what's reached the public eye or made it to court; many more cases and complaints never get there. Pimco is willing to file motion after motion, dragging out the process and whittling down a plaintiff's bank account. There is always a high cost to speaking out, but as with everything it does, Pimco puts in the extra work to ensure that theirs is a premium product.

Over the many years of study and robust sample of sources, from years of being practically immersed in this place and its culture, I have drawn a few conclusions. I've learned that staying too long in a crucible of toxicity and insecurity has long-lasting, corrosive effects on the mind. I have not yet figured out if becoming unfathomably wealthy makes a person maximally petty, or if that extreme pettiness is a pre-existing condition that helps effectuate the wealth accumulation; or if most of us harbor the capacity but our vindictiveness only becomes visible when enough money reveals it. I have gathered that any hypothetical $10 million would not make me any happier. And, depending on the situation and structure, keeping going is often the best cost- and risk-adjusted option.

Acknowledgments

This book had a long and arduous journey. It only exists thanks to the immense support of my team and the endless kindness of friends and family who, for years and years, cheered me on and listened to my woes and told me I could do it. It is impossible to express my profound gratitude, but I'm gonna give it a go.

I am incredibly grateful to Flatiron Books and Bob Miller, who guided it on that difficult path. I must thank my spectacularly talented, incisive, and funny editor, Meghan Houser. And to Zack Wagman, for valiantly getting us across the finish line.

I am eternally indebted to Christy Fletcher and Sarah Fuentes of Fletcher & Co., who saw the book in the pile of words I proposed and fought for it (and me) in demoralizing circumstances.

I am so grateful for all the people who shared their stories with me over the years, for this book and otherwise. For trusting me to listen and to recount your experience. I don't take that lightly. And to all the many reporters and editors who published good and hard-won stories that informed and filled this book.

Thank you to Quinn Heraty for protecting and encouraging me. To Peter Griffin, for shepherding me forward, for gently showing me that rabbit holes are best avoided. To Rima Parikh and Emily Berch, who contributed their precision and helped keep this thing between the lines.

I am so grateful for all of you who tended to me through this long process. I am indebted, to a staggering extent, to my book's informal board of advisors. Matt Levine and Jessie Gaynor, who believed in this project before it deserved it: you amaze me with your generosity, and I benefit from your genius every day. To Kirker Butler, Karen Harryman, Scott Cameron, and Bill Gerber: your hand-holding and humor are a beacon. To Clare Lambert, Kelsey Miller, Laura Stampler, and Gary Shteyngart, for helping me understand what book writing is, and for soothing me when I wanted to escape it. To Silvia Gonzalez Killingsworth, for sharing your abundant gifts of editing and thinking. To Wagatwe Wanjuki, for your kindness and clarity. To Jeff Cane, for your vast expertise and encouragement. To Carly Romeo, for babysitting me. To my therapist, Michelle.

I have so many to thank for material support: Martha and Clive Gurwitz, Andrew and Simone Ziv, Andrea Korb and Greg Hardes, Lauren Cook Hummel and Charles Hummel, Megan Hannum, Billie Whitehouse, Rosy Macedo, Amanda Askew, Lindsay Fortado, Chloe Waddington Maloney, and Justin Leong.

To friends, coworkers, colleagues, and bosses, for kindness, support, and inspiration. A not-inclusive list: Cardiff Garcia, Katherine Bell, Geoff Rogow, Leslie Picker, Tae Kim, Felix Salmon, Emily Flitter, Amanda Aronczyk, Alex Goldmark, MOMCHAT, Siena de Lisser, Lauren Wagner, Huaising Cindy Ko, Amy Berg, Hilary Fischer-Groban, Jessica Pressler, Neil Chriss, Alexa Meade, Jody Shenn, Isa Berner and Manu Boursin, Lindsey Rosin, Kat Greene, Alexandra Scaggs, Sujeet Indap, Jacob Goldstein, Sarah Gonzalez. I treasure you; thank you. I can hang out now!

To Bloomberg News for the most rigorous training an aspiring journalist could dream of, and to NPR for the honor of my job.

I am so grateful to my parents, who dutifully printed and read atrocious drafts. You taught me how to think critically and act charitably. To my sister and her family, my grandma and Sasa—I feel lucky to know you, let alone be related to you. To Ann Lane: your help made this possible.

To Demi and Sam, the best dogs. Thank you for letting me stuff my face in your fur when the going got tough. To my baby—thank you for your patience, and for being amazing.

This project has been oddly intertwined with my relationship with my spouse; we started dating in September 2014, and more than anyone Scott endured all the derivative effects of this project's process. Scott, you have been unfailingly supportive, and so, so generous. Thank you. All the extremely late nights and weekends this thing absorbed, all the vacations we never took. All the times you peeled me off the floor. I am so grateful you're my partner. We can go on our honeymoon now.

Notes

This book is a work of nonfiction. Everything recounted here happened to real people; everything in this book has been meticulously accounted for. While researching and writing, I interviewed hundreds of sources over thousands of hours. I attempted to speak with as many people who had passed through Pimco's halls, or interacted with it in the market, or recommended that clients invest their money with it, or tried to regulate it, as I could. I reviewed thousands of pages of documents, investment notes, legal filings, court transcripts, news stories, and Pimco's own self-published coffee table book of its history, titled *The Beach*. The narrative presented here is my careful synthesis of all that information, all those conversations and recollections. I wrote it in good faith, and I believe it is accurate and fair.

I was not present for many of the conversations reproduced in this book. I worked to reconstruct scenes using the recollections of participants, wherever possible conducting multiple interviews for more precision. But, of course, memories decay and even contemporaneous impressions differ; no two people experience the same moment the same way. Where memories were irreconcilable, I noted the differences in the text.

Despite my repeated efforts to engage, a few parties either offered extremely limited participation or declined to participate at all, instead sending me letters from their lawyers and demanding to review the manuscript, a practice that is unacceptable in journalism. Without their participation, I did everything I could—talking to their friends or allies, studying old quotes or testimony, even reviewing old interview notes from fellow journalists—to understand and represent their views.

I often thought of the process as looking through a time-traveling microscope, seeing multiple blurry outlines of events and carefully homing in on the overlap to bring the image into focus—or as akin to the story of the blind men and the elephant, a parable I learned from a thoughtful source in 2012: I only know what I know, the source said. I'm feeling one part of the elephant, and I can't see the rest. Another guy touches the tail and says, "Hmm, it's ropelike." One touches a tusk and says, "Ah, smooth and impenetrable, sharp." Another touches its ear: "leathery and floppy." Another, the body: "vast, sturdy." Individually, they are a little right but mostly wrong. Together, they describe the truth.

This was my process in collecting these memories: I found as many blind men as I could and wrote down what they remembered. When I began, I never knew what part they had felt. I listened and wrote down what they said, and then I asked another, and another, and another. I reached out to as many people as possible, occasionally enduring their abuse, thanking those who declined politely and interviewing the ones who agreed.

There are three settings: "on the record," which means every word can be attributed using the source's name; "on background," which means the information must be attributed to "a person familiar with the matter" or similar; and "off the record," which means nothing can be used, only known and used invisibly to help guide away from mistakes and closer to the truth.

These settings carry different weights. "On the record" is the most powerful: the speaker is attaching their personal accountability to their comments. "On background" depends on the source, their history of honesty, and the extent to which their account jibes or conflicts with those of others.

Quotes that are not cited in the following notes are from personal interviews or messages or sourced documents. Those cited here are from the publicly available sources I used in writing this book. Speech that is only paraphrased based on an interview subject's recollections of a conversation is included in the text but is not enclosed in quotation marks.

Introduction

1 **"I will take Mary to task"**: Bill Gross, "PIMCO Co-CIO William Gross Intvd on Bloomberg Radio," Bloomberg News, November 9, 2013.

1. The Housing Project

10 **"We needed to get a feel for the rest of the country"**: Bill Gross, "Pimco's Bill Gross on Scoping Out Subprime," *Bloomberg Businessweek*, June 9, 2011.

10 **"a little froth"**: David Leonhardt, "2005: In a Word; Frothy," *The New York Times*, December 25, 2005.

10 **"the Bond King"**: David Rynecki, "The Bond King," *Fortune*, March 4, 2002.

10 **"Instead of sending them to Armonk"**: Gross, "Pimco's Bill Gross on Scoping Out Subprime."

11 **"to get the real information"**: Devin Leonard, "Treasury's Got Bill Gross on Speed Dial," *The New York Times*, June 20, 2009.

12 **"The extent of the lending malpractice"**: Gross, "Pimco's Bill Gross on Scoping Out Subprime."

13 **"slowing under its own weight"**: Jeff Collins, "Pimco Predicts Soft Landing for Housing," *The Orange County Register*, May 10, 2006.

13 **"At that point, 'For Sale'"**: "Pimco Exec Cites Fallout from Housing," *The Orange County Register*, June 5, 2006.

13 **"stable disequilibrium"**: Bill Gross, "Mission Impossible?" *Investment Outlook*, Pimco.com, May 16, 2006.

15 **"the shadow banking system"**: Paul McCulley, "Teton Reflections," *Investment Outlook*, Pimco.com, September 7, 2007.

15 **"Minsky moment"**: Paul McCulley, "The Shadow Banking System and Hyman Minsky's Economic Journey," Pimco.com, May 26, 2007.

19 **"same old discussions"**: Allianz, Letter to the Shareholders, Fiscal Year 2000.

21 **"Anonymity, not notoriety"**: Bill Gross, "Miracu(less)," *Investment Outlook*, Pimco.com, August 1, 2001.

22 **"unresponsive mule"**: Paul McCulley, "Time: Varying Variables Vary," *Investment Outlook*, Pimco.com, October 19, 2006.

23 **"Reality is a delicate fabric"**: Bill Gross, "Reality Check," *Investment Outlook*, Pimco.com, November 30, 2006.

23 **"Timing is everything"**: Gross, "Pimco's Bill Gross on Scoping Out Subprime."

2. In the Beginning

24 **"There's an ill wind blowin'"**: Bill Gross, "100 Bottles of Beer on the Wall," *Investment Outlook*, Pimco.com, January 29, 2007.

28 **"very avant-garde"**: Steven L. Mintz, Dana Dakin, and Thomas Willison, *Beyond Wall Street: The Art of Investing* (Hoboken, N.J.: Wiley, 1998).

43 **"Would you consider"**: Craig Karmin and Ian McDonald, "Harvard's Loss: El-Erian," *The Wall Street Journal*, September 12, 2007.

3. The Turn

46 **"It was a great shot"**: Bill Gross, "On the Course to a New Normal," *Investment Outlook*, Pimco.com, September 1, 2009.

48 **"AAA? You were wooed"**: Bill Gross, "Looking for Contagion in All the Wrong Places," *Investment Outlook*, Pimco.com, July 2007.

48 **"worse before they get better"**: Kai Ryssdal, "Bernanke Cites Concerns with Economy," Marketplace.org, July 18, 2007.

49 **"effectively no value"**: "2 Bear Stearns Funds Are Almost Worthless," Reuters, July 17, 2007.

49 **"know-nothing" Fed**: Jim Cramer, "Watch the Full Rant: Cramer's 'They Know Nothing!'" CNBC, August 2007.

49 **"It was a time not to lose"**: Seth Lubove and Elizabeth Stanton, "Pimco Power in Treasuries Prompts Suit Gross Says Is Nonsense," Bloomberg News, February 20, 2007.

50 **"The complete evaporation of liquidity"**: Sudip Kar-Gupta and Yann Le Guernigou, "BNP Freezes $2.2 Bln of Funds over Subprime," Reuters, August 9, 2007.

50 **"I remember the day"**: Paul McCulley, "After the Crisis: Planning a New Financial Structure Learning from the Bank of Dad," Pimco.com, May 10, 2010.

50 **"the effect of U.S. subprime loans"**: John Ward Anderson, "E.U. Central Bank Injects More Cash as Markets Tumble," *The Washington Post* Foreign Service, August 11, 2007.

51 **"howls of coyotes"**: Robert Shiller, "Bubble Trouble," Project Syndicate, September 17, 2007.

51 **"the whole alphabet soup"**: Brooke Masters and Jeremy Grant, "Finance: Shadow Boxes," *Financial Times*, February 2, 2011.

52 **"smoked"**: Christine Benz, "Our 2007 Fund Managers of the Year," Morningstar, January 3, 2008.

53 **"When Humpty Dumpty cracked"**: Julie Segal, "War Stories over Board Games: How Bill Gross and Warren Buffett (Almost) Saved America," *Institutional Investor*, April 2017.

53 **"unlikely master"**: Deborah Brewster, "Man in the News: Bill Gross," *Financial Times*, September 12, 2008.

53 **"BOND KING" CAN REALLY THINK ON HIS HEAD**: Michael S. Rosenwald, "'Bond King' Can Really Think on His Head," *The Washington Post*, October 11, 2008.

53 **"the guy you want to hear from"**: Barbara Kiviat, "Even Bond Guru Bill Gross Can't Escape," *Time*, September 18, 2008.

53 **"one trillion went to two"**: Segal, "War Stories over Board Games: How Bill Gross and Warren Buffett (Almost) Saved America."

4. The Crisis

58 **"It gave me a sense of risk"**: Bob Campion, "Bill Gross Reveals Lessons from Blackjack," *Financial Times*, October 17, 2010.

59 **"that gambling instinct"**: David Lynch, "OC trader makes bonds a profitable game," *The Orange County Register*, August 10, 1992.

59 **"Vegas taught me"**: David Rynecki, "The Bond King," *Fortune*, March 4, 2002.

60 **"We welcome him home"**: "PIMCO Announces Mohamed El-Erian to Rejoin Firm as Co-CEO, Co-CIO," Marketwired, September 11, 2007.

62 **"Nice hat"**: Erin Burnett, CNBC, January 3, 2008.

62 **"We decided that things were critical"**: Mohamed El-Erian, "When Wall Street Nearly Collapsed," *Fortune*, September 14, 2009.

62 **"I'm not used to setting my alarm"**: Nelson D. Schwartz and Julie Creswell, "Pimco's Boss, Armed with Billions in Cash, Tackles a Monster," *The New York Times*, March 23, 2008.

63 **"the ark doesn't have any leaks"**: Ibid.

63 **"What Happens During Delevering"**: Bill Gross, "There's a Bull Market Somewhere?" *Investment Outlook*, Pimco.com, September 3, 2008.

63 **"Bear Stearns has made it obvious"**: Schwartz and Creswell, "Pimco's Boss, Armed with Billions in Cash, Tackles a Monster."

66 **"2005, 2006, into 2007"**: Mohamed El-Erian on *Charlie Rose*, PBS, July 24, 2008.

67 **"Unchecked"**: Bill Gross, "There's a Bull Market Somewhere?"

68 **"sitting on their hands"**: "Gross: Big Investors Avoiding Bank Debt for Now," CNBC, September 4, 2008.

68 **"You can say that I'm talking my book"**: Katie Benner, "Pimco's Power Play," *Fortune*, February 20, 2009.

68 **"Gross is begging the Treasury"**: Michael Steinberg, "Bill Gross Politicking for His Own Bailout," Seeking Alpha, September 5, 2008.

68 **"This is a bilateral monopoly"**: Benner, "Pimco's Power Play."

68 **"Journalists should flood the zone"**: Steven Pearlstein, "Pearlstein: Government Takes Control of Fannie Mae and Freddie Mac," *The Washington Post*, September 8, 2008.

69 **"had been preparing for catastrophe"**: El-Erian, "When Wall Street Nearly Collapsed."

70 **"banks might not open"**: Ibid.

72 **"Seven hundred billion was"**: Laura Blumenfeld, "The $700 Billion Man," *The Washington Post*, December 6, 2009.

72 **"Critics described Paulson as a 'Dr. Evil'"**: Ibid.

72 **"Our Favorite Asshole Banker"**: Hamilton Nolan, "Financial Crisis Taking a Toll on Our Favorite Asshole Banker," *Gawker*, November 14, 2008.

73 **"healing process"**: Mohamed El-Erian, "'Messy Healing' Process for U.S. Economy: El-Erian," CNBC, January 15, 2009.

73 **"When you lose half your 401(k)"**: "What Bill Gross Is Buying," *Forbes*, January 6, 2009.

74 **"In a way, we've partnered"**: Benner, "Pimco's Power Play."

75 **"When Mohamed and I wanted to wish"**: Jennifer Ablan and Matthew Goldstein, "Special Report: Twilight of the Bond King," Reuters, February 9, 2012.

75 **"We tried to move ahead"**: Benner, "Pimco's Power Play."

76 **"In for a nickel"**: "What Bill Gross Is Buying."

76 **"most incredible value"**: "Big Brother Investing," *Forbes*, December 25, 2008.

76 **"Pimco's view is simple"**: Bill Gross, "Andrew Mellon vs. Bailout Nation," *Investment Outlook*, Pimco.com, January 8, 2009.

77 **"if we're lucky"**: "What Bill Gross Is Buying."

77 **"The opportunities are just enormous"**: "Big Brother Investing."

5. Constructive Paranoia

78 **"Over the next several decades"**: Bill Gross, keynote address, Morningstar 2009 Investment Conference, Chicago, Ill., May 28, 2009.

80 **"Corporate bonds have the stock guys salivating"**: Russel Kinnel, "Stock Managers Go Bonkers over Bonds," Morningstar, June 1, 2009.

80 **"I can remember enduring her criticism"**: Bill Gross, "I've Got to Admit It's Getting Better Getting Better All the Time," *Investment Outlook*, Pimco.com, March 1, 2005.

82 **"Stocks will be more of a subordinated income vehicle"**: Peter Cohan, "Bill Gross, the $747 Billion Man, Declares the Death of Equities," AOL, February 26, 2009.

83 **"run out of gas"**: Jonathan Lansner, "Bill Thompson: Ex-Pimco CEO an Engine for Charity," *The Orange County Register*, January 4, 2013.

83 **"constructive paranoia"**: Sam Ro, "EL-ERIAN: These Are The Institutions And People Who Shaped The Way I Think," *Business Insider*, September 25, 2012.

86 **"road map"**: Seth Lubove and Sree Vidya Bhaktavatsalam, "Gross Vows This Time Different as El-Erian Leads Equities Push," *Bloomberg Markets*, June 24, 2010.

91 **"The revolving door between Treasury"**: Neil Barofsky, *Bailout: How Washington Abandoned Main Street While Rescuing Wall Street* (New York: Simon and Schuster, 2013).

91 **"to value precisely"**: Felix Salmon, "Where Else Could Kashkari Have Gone?" Reuters, December 8, 2009.

91 **TREASURY'S GOT BILL GROSS ON SPEED DIAL:** Devin Leonard, "Treasury's Got Bill Gross on Speed Dial," *The New York Times*, June 20, 2009.

91 **"Gross was one of those guys":** Devin Leonard, "Neel Kashkari's Quiet Path to Pimco," *The New York Times*, December 31, 2009.

93 **"If you're in a marriage":** Katie Benner, "Pimco's Power Play," *Fortune*, February 20, 2009.

6. New Normal

95 **"It's been significant":** Eric Jacobson, "Gross: It's Been a Fixed-Income Decade," Morningstar, December 28, 2009.

97 **"genetic makeup":** Bill Gross, "Consistent Alpha Generation Through Structure," Reflections, *Financial Analysts Journal* (September/October 2005).

98 **"penalty box":** Deepak Gopinath, "Pimco's El-Erian Shuns Banks That Break His Rules," Bloomberg News, September 23, 2005.

101 **"Short Skirt/Long Jacket":** Joanna Slater, "The Obsessive Life of Bond Guru Bill Gross," *Globe and Mail*, October 22, 2010.

101 **"the last thing [Gross] wanted":** Seth Lubove and Sree Bhaktavatsalam, "Gross Vows This Time Different."

103 **"the most fervent supporters":** Devin Leonard, "Treasury's Got Bill Gross on Speed Dial," *The New York Times*, June 20, 2009."

104 **"uncertainties regarding the design":** Deborah Solomon and Damian Paletta, "Treasury Names Nine Firms for Toxic-Asset Program," *The Wall Street Journal*, July 10, 2009.

104 **"The program has been dramatically scaled back":** Katie Rushkewicz Reichart, "Fund Times: PIMCO Passes on PPIP," Morningstar, July 9, 2009.

107 **"on a bed of nitroglycerine":** Bill Gross, "The Ring of Fire," *Investment Outlook*, Pimco .com, January 26, 2010.

7. Stinker

110 **MEXICO EASES CRISIS:** Anthony DePalma, "Mexico Eases Crisis, Selling All Bonds Offered," *The New York Times*, January 18, 1995.

111 **"The right hand is buying from the left":** Jennifer Rubin, "Exclusive Interview: Bill Gross of Pimco," *The Washington Post*, April 7, 2011.

111 **"We've been supporting Treasuries":** Megan McArdle, "The Vigilante," *The Atlantic*, June 2011.

113 **"preserve capital, preserve capital":** Ibid.

113 **"Everything you buy and hold":** Catherine Tymkiw, "Why Pimco Cut Its Bond Holdings," CNNMoney, March 31, 2011.

113 **"Gross got out of Treasurys":** Rubin, "Exclusive Interview: Bill Gross of Pimco."

114 **"showed that he's more than capable"**: Felix Salmon, "Pimco Datapoints of the Day," Reuters, February 14, 2011.

114 **"He has been talking about"**: Cullen Roche, "Bill Gross Sells Government Bonds. Does It Matter?" Pragmatic Capitalism, March 11, 2011.

114 **"If there were really a problem"**: Paul Krugman, "Stocks, Flows, and Pimco (Wonkish)," *The New York Times*, April 19, 2011.

116 **"Political brinkmanship"**: Nikola G. Swann, John Chambers, and David T. Beer, "United States of America Long-Term Rating Lowered to 'AA+' on Political Risks and Rising Debt Burden; Outlook Negative," RatingsDirect, Standard & Poor's Global Credit Portal, August 5, 2011.

117 **"If the euro as a whole is in danger"**: Brian Parkin and Rainer Buergin, "Merkel Faces Dissent on Greece as Schaeuble Stokes ECB Clash," Bloomberg News, June 8, 2011.

118 **"very intellectually honest"**: Mary Pilon and Matt Phillips, "Pimco's Gross Has 'Lost Sleep' over Bad Bets," *The Wall Street Journal*, August 30, 2011.

118 **"Let me begin by stating this"**: Bill Gross, "Mea Culpa," *Investment Outlook*, Pimco .com, October 2011.

118 **"anchor of stability"**: Joe Weisenthal, "The Costliest Mistake in All of Economics," *Business Insider*, October 16, 2011.

118 **"big mistake"**: Rob Copeland, "Bill Gross Built Pimco Empire on Prescience, Flair," *The Wall Street Journal*, September 26, 2014.

8. Edge

122 **"small investors don't always have access"**: Sree Vidya Bhaktavatsalam and Alexis Leondis, "Gross Says Pimco's Active ETF a Call to 'Mom-and-Pop' Investors," Bloomberg News, March 1, 2012.

123 **"charge exorbitant fees for very little"**: Bill Gross, *Everything You've Heard About Investing Is Wrong! How to Profit in the Coming Post-Bull Markets* (New York: Crown Publishing, 1997).

123 **"The challenge is obvious"**: Bhaktavatsalam and Leondis, "Gross Says Pimco's Active ETF a Call to 'Mom-and-Pop' Investors."

124 **"This is a watershed event"**: Joyce Hanson, "All Eyes on PIMCO ETF Launch," *Investment Advisor*, March 26, 2012.

125 **"Compliance [is] especially sensitive"**: U.S. Securities and Exchange Commission, "PIMCO Settles Charges of Misleading Investors About ETF Performance," December 1, 2016, Washington, D.C.

130 **"A once-in-a-lifetime situation"**: Richard T. Pratt et al., *New Developments in Mortgage-Backed Securities* (Washington, D.C.: CFA Institute, 1984).

138 **"We can find you"**: SEC, "PIMCO Settles Charges of Misleading Investors About ETF Performance."

141 **"pulled off an unusual feat"**: Kirsten Grind, "Bill Gross's Shiny New Toy," *The Wall Street Journal*, April 13, 2012.

141 **"has benefited from the overweight"**: SEC, "PIMCO Settles Charges of Misleading Investors About ETF Performance."

142 **"very good"**: Jackie Noblett, "Pimco's Total Return ETF Makes Strong Start," *Financial Times*, May 4, 2012.

9. Grow or Die

144 **"Like the casino's edge"**: Bill Gross, "Shaq Attack," *Investment Outlook*, Pimco.com, April 1, 2003.

149 **"I'm not a stockpicker"**: Karl Taro Greenfeld, "Neel Kashkari Wants to Be a New Kind of Republican," *Bloomberg Businessweek*, May 29, 2014.

150 **"the cult of equity is dying"**: Bill Gross, "Cult Figures," Pimco.com, July 2012.

151 **"We believe returns across"**: Steven Russolillo, "Bill Gross Is Wrong About Stocks: GMO," *The Wall Street Journal*, August 10, 2012.

151 **"No one should be surprised"**: Jason Kephart, "The 'Cult of Equity' Isn't Dying, It's Going Passive," Bloomberg News, August 6, 2012.

151 **"terrific"**: Roben Farzad, "Can Pimco Break Free of Its Bonds?" Bloomberg News, February 1, 2013.

152 **"the all-too-close relationships"**: Sewell Chan, "In Marketing of a New Mortgage Fund, Pimco Lists Former Bush Officials," *The New York Times*, December 16, 2010.

154 **"We didn't die on the way in"**: Charles Stein and John Gittelsohn, "Pimco Beats 99% of Peers with Ivascyn as Market Beast: Mortgages," Bloomberg News, January 27, 2014.

154 GROSS DETHRONED AS PIMCO BOND KING: Christopher Condon and Alexis Leondis, "Gross Dethroned as Pimco Bond King," Bloomberg News, August 29, 2012.

155 **"my life and my wife"**: Jody Shenn, "Pimco Mortgage Head Scott Simon to Retire from Bond-Fund Manager," Bloomberg News, January 25, 2013.

10. Ratfucked

159 **"raise eyebrows"**: Ryan Leggio, "PIMCO High Yield Skipper Jumping Ship; Gross Taking Helm," Morningstar, May 15, 2009.

162 **"subjected him to verbal abuse"**: Jennifer Ablan and Jonathan Stempel, "Ex-PIMCO Exec Sues Firm, Says Was Fired for Reporting Misdeeds," Reuters, March 13, 2013.

162 **"as a matter of policy"**: Ibid.

168 **"commitment to protecting the integrity"**: Gretchen Morgenson, "Was Someone Squeezing Treasuries?," *The New York Times*, August 7, 2005.

168 **"We established position limits"**: Seth Lubove and Elizabeth Stanton, "Pimco Power in Treasuries Prompts Suit Gross Says Is Nonsense," Bloomberg News, February 20, 2007.

169 **"was the original problem"**: Mark Whitehouse, Aaron Lucchetti, and Peter A. McKay, "Short-Bond Shortage Isn't Over," *The Wall Street Journal*, August 11, 2005.

169 **"The plaintiffs are a purported class"**: Lubove and Stanton, "Pimco Power."

170 **"all such trades were properly designed"**: Erin Coe, "Pimco Settles Short-Seller Action for $92M," Law360, January 3, 2011.

11. Taper Tantrum

172 **"Am I a great investor?"**: Bill Gross, "A Man in the Mirror," *Investment Outlook*, Pimco.com, April 3, 2013.

173 **"a chicken-shit way out"**: David Rynecki, "The Bond King," *Fortune*, March 4, 2002.

174 **"all bull market children"**: Bill Gross, "So CQ-ish," Pimco.com, October 29, 2008.

174 **"Perhaps, however, it was the epoch"**: Gross, "A Man in the Mirror."

175 **"reach escape velocity"**: Mohamed El-Erian, "8 Themes for Long-Term Investors in the 'New Normal' Markets," Nasdaq.com, May 13, 2013.

177 **"One to two month performance"**: Sam Forgione and Jennifer Ablan, "UPDATE 2-Pimco Total Return Fund Adds Treasuries in Tumultuous June," Reuters, July 15, 2013.

177 **"nonessential"**: Gregory Zuckerman and Kirsten Grind, "Inside the Showdown Atop Pimco, the World's Biggest Bond Firm," *The Wall Street Journal*, February 24, 2014.

183 **"moving the goalposts"**: Steven Goldberg, "What 'New Normal'? El-Erian's Pimco Fund Falls Flat," Kiplinger, November 20, 2013.

186 **"Why spend $20 million?"**: Bill Gross, "Mr. Bleu," Pimco.com, June 2015.

186 **"Icahn should leave #Apple alone"**: Jennifer Ablan and Katya Wachtel, "Pimco's Gross Tells Icahn to Leave Apple Alone," Reuters, October 24, 2013.

186 **"Sue and I are well on our way"**: Sam Forgione and Jennifer Ablan, "Pimco's Gross Urges 'Privileged 1 Percent' to Pay More Tax," Reuters, October 31, 2013.

188 **"participat[ing] in the implicit bilking"**: Bill Gross, "Kennethed," *Investment Outlook*, Pimco.com, February 2002.

190 **"Thank you for your comment"**: "BlackRock's Larry Fink and PIMCO's Bill Gross Discuss the U.S. Economy," UCLA Anderson YouTube, October 11, 2013.

191 PIMCO STOP BLOCKING THE HOUSING RECOVERY: "Protest at Pimco over Troubled Home Loans," *The Orange County Register*, October 31, 2013.

191 **"The era of taxing 'capital'"**: Bill Gross, "Scrooge McDucks," *Investment Outlook*, Pimco.com, November 1, 2013.

192 **"We're very satisfied with what we've done"**: "Bill and Sue Gross Take Unorthodox Approach to Giving," *Philanthropy News Digest*, December 22, 2013.

12. Secretariat

193 **"Wait a minute"**: Mohamed El-Erian, "Father and Daughter Reunion," *Worth*, June 7, 2014.

194 **"Before then, life had been predictable"**: Deepak Gopinath, "Pimco's El-Erian Shuns Banks That Break His Rules," Bloomberg News, September 23, 2005.

197 **"I have a forty-one-year track record"**: Gregory Zuckerman and Kirsten Grind, "Inside the Showdown Atop Pimco, the World's Biggest Bond Firm," *The Wall Street Journal*, February 24, 2014."

199 **"I could run all the two trillion myself"**: Bill Gross, "The Tipping Point," *Investment Outlook*, Pimco.com, July 1, 2013.

199 **"anyone other than Secretariat?"**: Zuckerman and Grind, "Inside the Showdown."

203 **"investment philosophy, process or approach"**: Miles Weiss, "Gross Overhauls Dialynas's Unconstrained Fund," Bloomberg News, March 5, 2014.

206 **"We don't have to talk in code"**: Laura Smith, Affidavit in Support of Criminal Complaint, March 11, 2019, Department of Justice, Federal Bureau of Investigation, Washington, D.C.

206 **"easy mark"**: Doug Hodge, "I Wish I'd Never Met Rick Singer," *The Wall Street Journal*, February 9, 2020.

206 **"as firms and individuals"**: Doug Hodge, "Restoring Trust in the New Normal: Remarks to SIFMA Annual Meeting," Pimco.com, October 23, 2012.

206 **"steady stream of news"**: Doug Hodge, "Restoring Trust in Our Financial System: It's All About Culture," *Pensions & Investments*, July 25, 2012.

207 **"stretched the truth"**: Laura Smith, Affadavit, DOJ, FBI.

207 **"The decision to step down"**: Nathaniel Popper and Matthew Goldstein, "Heir Apparent at Pimco to Step Down," *The New York Times*, January 21, 2014.

208 **"long hours and a frequently fractious relationship"**: Tom Braithwaite, "Hours and Friction Prompted El-Erian Exit," *Financial Times*, January 22, 2014.

208 **"His talents are truly exceptional"**: "PIMCO Appoints Leadership Team," *Investment Outlook*, Pimco.com, January 21, 2014.

208 **"had nothing to do with friction"**: Zuckerman and Grind, "Inside the Showdown."

208 **"a number of heirs apparent"**: Sree Vidya Bhaktavatsalam and Alexis Leondis, "Gross Says Pimco to Name More Deputies as El-Erian Quits," Bloomberg News, January 22, 2014.

210 **"Pimco's fully engaged"**: Alexis Leondis and Charles Stein, "Pimco's El-Erian Resigns as Hodge Named Chief Executive," Bloomberg News, January 22, 2014.

210 **"It was a surprise to us, too"**: Bill Gross, "Bill Gross: El-Erian's Exit a 'Surprise to Us,'" CNBC, January 29, 2014.

210 **"Believe me when I say"**: Sam Forgione and Jennifer Ablan, "Pimco's Gross Tells Clients 'We Are a Better Team at This Moment,'" Reuters, February 5, 2014.

13. Inside the Showdown

212 **INSIDE THE SHOWDOWN**: Gregory Zuckerman and Kirsten Grind, "Inside the Showdown Atop Pimco, the World's Biggest Bond Firm," *The Wall Street Journal*, February 24, 2014.

214 **"There is no way for Gross to recover"**: Felix Salmon, "It's Time for Bill Gross to Retire," Reuters, February 25, 2014.

214 a **"crusher"**: Sheelah Kolhatkar, "Bill Gross Picks Up the Pieces," *Bloomberg Business-week*, April 14, 2014.

215 **"The behavior described"**: Marc Andreessen, Twitter, February 25, 2014.

215 **"Bill, thank you very much"**: Brian Sullivan, "Bill Gross Responds to WSJ Portrayal," CNBC, February 25, 2014.

216 **"Now I feel like a jerk"**: Julia La Roche, "Bill Gross Calls into CNBC to Respond to the Scathing WSJ Article," *Business Insider*, February 25, 2014.

216 **"it's like dealing with family"**: Gregory Zuckerman and Kirsten Grind, "Pimco's Gross Defends Competitive Culture," *The Wall Street Journal*, February 28, 2014.

218 **"was so outrageous"**: Greg Saitz, "Pimco Fee Plaintiffs May Have Powerful Ally—a Former Director," BoardIQ, June 13, 2016.

218 **"I don't know if Secretariat made $200 million"**: Scott Reckard, "Pimco Trustee Assails Exec's Salary," *Los Angeles Times*, March 11, 2014.

218 **"I'm not suggesting he be replaced"**: Jeff Cox, "'Mediocre' Gross overpaid at $200 million: Trustee," CNBC, March 11, 2014.

220 **"I'm so sick of Mohamed"**: Jennifer Ablan, "Exclusive: Pimco's Gross Declares El-Erian Is 'Trying to Undermine Me,'" Reuters, March 6, 2014.

221 **"fractious interactions"**: Eric Jacobson and Michael Herbst, "Morningstar's Current View on PIMCO," Morningstar, March 18, 2014.

223 **"dominated by bond people"**: Mary Childs, "Pimco Dissidents Challenge Bill Gross in 'Happy Kingdom,'" Bloomberg News, July 8, 2014.

14. Stealing the Firm

229 **"two shots of whatever they shoot it with"**: Sheelah Kolhatkar, "Bill Gross Picks Up the Pieces," *Bloomberg Businessweek*, April 14, 2014.

231 **"been sorta silly"**: Trish Regan, "Bill Gross: I Thought I Knew El-Erian Better," Bloomberg TV, April 10, 2014.

234 **"We always had different styles"**: Gregory Zuckerman, "At Gross's Pimco, El-Erian Says 'Different Styles' Stopped Working Well Together," *The Wall Street Journal*, April 11, 2014.

234 **"in the singsong voice"**: Kolhatkar, "Bill Gross Picks Up the Pieces."

235 **"going to head back to a new destination"**: Mary Childs, "Pimco's Mather Sees Clear Departure from 'New Normal,'" Bloomberg News, April 25, 2014.

235 **"a little out over his skis"**: Mary Childs, "Pimco's 'New Normal' Thesis Morphs into 'New Neutral,'" Bloomberg News, May 13, 2014.

238 **"We've got a thesis here"**: Mary Childs, "Gross Says Pimco Funds Headed Back to the Top," Bloomberg News, May 14, 2014.

241 **"Pimco will always be Camelot to me"**: "PIMCO Hires Paul McCulley as Chief Economist," Pimco.com, May 27, 2014.

241 **"There is zero, absolutely zero daylight"**: Mary Childs, "McCulley Returns to Pimco as Gross Seeks to Restore Shine," Bloomberg News, May 28, 2014.

241 **"Gross is one of the most talented"**: "PIMCO Hires Paul McCulley as Chief Economist."

241 **"Forty-three years ago"**: Gregory Zuckerman and Kirsten Grind, "Bond Giant Pimco and Founder Bill Gross Struggle to Heal Strains," *The Wall Street Journal*, July 14, 2014.

243 **"when you're seventy years old"**: Bill Gross, "Bill Gross: Economy Can't Survive Much Higher Rates," keynote address, Morningstar 2014 Investment Conference, Chicago, Ill., June 27, 2014.

245 **"I wish I could"**: Zuckerman and Grind, "Bond Giant Pimco and Founder Bill Gross Struggle."

246 **"I'm not a particularly shy guy"**: Bill Gross, "Bob," *Investment Outlook*, Pimco.com, April 2014.

246 **"to be candid, sort of half erotic"**: Bill Gross, "Achoo!" *Investment Outlook*, Pimco.com, May 2014.

246 **"I'm sticking with live chirping"**: Bill Gross, "Time (and Money) in a Cellphone," *Investment Outlook*, Pimco.com, June 5, 2014.

247 **"far from uncommon in New York City"**: Jennifer Ablan, "Pimco NYC Office Tackles Bed Bug Infestation, Fumigates," Reuters, August 20, 2014.

247 **"'Bohamed Bel-Ferrian'"**: Kevin Roose, "Financial Firm PIMCO's New York Office Is Reportedly Besieged by Bedbugs (Updated)," *New York*, August 20, 2014.

15. Minutes

253 **"maximize wallet share"**: Landon Thomas, Jr., "Pimco Suit Sheds Light on Murky Investor Fees," *The New York Times*, November 9, 2015

263 **"bearing evidence of recent use"**: Bess Levin, "Jeffrey Gundlach NOT Set Up by TCW, Big Fan of 'Dr. Fellatio' Series," Dealbreaker, January 11, 2010.

263 **"I had every expectation of privacy"**: Mina Kimes, "Firing the $70 Billion Man," *Fortune*, March 10, 2010.

263 **"It's sixty-seven to zero"**: Tom Petruno and Tiffany Hsu, "TCW-Gundlach Trial Ends in Split Verdicts," *Los Angeles Times*, September 17, 2011.

264 **"Pimco doesn't want me anymore"**: Jennifer Ablan, "Bill Gross Told Rival Gundlach: 'I Am Kobe, You Are LeBron,'" Reuters, October 5, 2014.

270 **"huge early gains"**: Kirsten Grind, Gregory Zuckerman, and Jean Eaglesham, "Pimco ETF Draws Probe by SEC," *The Wall Street Journal*, September 23, 2014.

16. Bye-Bye to Those Days

274 **"will leave the firm, effective immediately"**: "PIMCO CIO William H. Gross to Leave the Firm," Pimco.com, September 26, 2014.

275 **"Pimco is at battle station alert"**: Erik Schatzker, "Pimco Is 'Rich in Talent,' Bill Powers Says," Bloomberg TV, October 7, 2014.

276 **"increasingly erratic behavior"**: Jonathan Berr, "Departure of Pimco's Gross Stuns Investing World," CBS News, September 26, 2014.

276 **"sense of optimism and enthusiasm"**: Kirsten Grind, "CEO Douglas Hodge Cites 'Overwhelming' Relief at Pimco," *The Wall Street Journal*, September 27, 2014.

277 **"Bill was going to leave eventually"**: Brian Sullivan, "Pimco Executives: 'The Firm Is Moving Forward,'" CNBC, September 30, 2014.

277 **"If you saw him on a Saturday"**: Mary Childs, "Ivascyn Survives Allianz Firing to Guide Pimco Post-Gross," Bloomberg News, October 1, 2014.

277 **"pretty peninsula near the ocean"**: Stephen Foley, "Daniel Ivascyn: The Straight Talking Portfolio Manager," *Financial Times*, October 1, 2014.

281 **"Being asked to dance"**: Myles Udland, "Here's Bill Gross' First Letter as a Fund Manager at Janus," *Business Insider*, October 9, 2014.

281 **"stayed to my last breath"**: Jennifer Ablan and Sam Forgione, "UPDATE 2-Bill Gross, in His 'Second Life,' Says Janus Role Is Simpler," Reuters, October 9, 2014.

281 **"My 30-year marriage"**: Udland, "Here's Bill Gross' First Letter as a Fund Manager at Janus."

282 **"Times have changed"**: Dean Starkman and E. Scott Reckard, "Bill Gross Gives Somber Outlook for Financial Markets," *Los Angeles Times*, October 9, 2014.

283 **"tens of billions"**: Kirsten Grind, Gregory Zuckerman, and Min Zeng, "Billions Fly Out the Door at Pimco," *The Wall Street Journal*, September 28, 2014.

283 **"An honor to be chosen"**: Jennifer Ablan, "Bill Gross of Janus to Manage $500 Mln for Soros Fund," Reuters, November 21, 2014.

284 **"Bill Gross is our Peyton Manning"**: Mary Childs, "Weil Counts on Gross as Peyton Manning in Janus Rebound," Bloomberg News, December 19, 2014.

285 **"Thanks @KirstenGrind @WSJ"**: Gerard Baker, "The 10-Point," *The Wall Street Journal*, January 8, 2015.

288 **"a very sad day for the money management industry"**: Miles Weiss, "Brynjolfsson: 'This Is a Sad Day' for Both Pimco and Gross," Bloomberg News, October 8, 2015.

289 **"a legally groundless and sad postscript"**: Dean Starkman, "Pimco Moves to Dismiss Bill Gross' Employment Suit," *Los Angeles Times*, November 9, 2015.

289 **"I have a happy night"**: Mary Childs, "Gross Gets Personal: 'I Just Wanted to Run Money and Be Famous,'" *Bloomberg Markets*, June 29, 2015.

290 **"you can sit on the couch"**: Claire Suddath, "This Lawyer Is Hollywood's Complete Divorce Solution," *Bloomberg Businessweek*, March 2, 2016.

292 **"Pimco has always been family to me"**: Mary Childs, "Bill Gross and Pimco Settle Suit over His Ouster," *The New York Times*, March 27, 2017.

294 **"Guess there is always one tattooed (black) sheep"**: Bill Gross, "Tattooed," PRNewswire, September 14, 2020.

About the Author

Mary Childs (she/her) is a cohost of NPR's *Planet Money* podcast. Previously she was a reporter at *Barron's* magazine, the *Financial Times*, and Bloomberg News. She lives in Richmond, Virginia, with her family and dog.

294 **"Peace on all fronts"**: Patricia Hurtado, "Bill Gross Says He Sought Peace in Text to 'Peeping Mark,'" Bloomberg News, December 14, 2020.

295 **"We've learned lyrics"**: Patricia Hurtado, "Bill Gross's Playing of 'Gilligan's Island' Muted by Judge," Bloomberg News, December 23, 2020.

295 **"We're gonna subpoena that, boy"**: Meghann Cuniff, Twitter, December 7, 2020.

295 **"Those who know me"**: Bill Gross, "An Open Letter from Bill Gross," PRNewswire, December 7, 2020.

295 **"just billionaire Bill Gross"**: Laurence Darmien, "Bill Gross Seeks to End Dispute over Lawn Sculpture: His Neighbor Is Having None of It," *Los Angeles Times*, December 7, 2020.

296 **"disappointed in the outcome"**: Laurence Darmiento, "Bill Gross Harassed Neighbor with 'Gilligan's Island' Song, Judge Rules," *Los Angeles Times*, December 23, 2020.

296 **"self-contained, inward-looking"**: Bill Gross, "OC LEADER BOARD: Why I Give What I Give, and Why You Should Too," *Orange County Business Journal*, May 24, 2021.